Laurie D. Finucane has always fe ...... on her soul. As a young person she received awards for stories and essays.

In 1985, she earned a Bachelor of Arts degree in Liberal Studies with a minor in English and became an elementary school teacher. She became involved in teacher training, completed a Master of Arts Degree in Educational Administration in 1999, and became the Director of Early Education for Fontana Unified School District, where she wrote grants, articles, and training guides.

Laurie retired from education in 2015 after thirty-four years of service and now writes for herself. She currently lives in Southern California with her husband Ken in a ranch-style home on two acres. Her hobbies and interests are writing, traveling with her husband in their RV, camping, gardening, baking, and enjoying her family, especially the grandchildren.

Shadow Street

a memoir of escaping a psychopath

AIA PUBLISHING

Laurie D. Finucane

Shadow Street
Laurie D. Finucane
Copyright © 2022
Published by AIA Publishing, Australia
ABN: 32736122056
http://www.aiapublishing.com

ISBN: 978-1-922329-34-9

For my knight in shining armor, Ken Finucane.
You are always in my corner. I love you.

Introduction

Writing this book was a truly therapeutic journey for me. I was able to work through years of excess emotional baggage I was carrying around. If I can assist just one person with this story, besides myself, then I will feel extremely successful in this endeavor.

Contents

Chapter 1:

The Room

I raised my head and realized I was sitting on the kitchen floor. A shooting pain starting in my ribs traveled up to my throat.

I could hear James yelling, "Git ta your room, boys! Mommy is fine."

The numbness in my brain was starting to escape, and my thoughts began to paint the scene preceding the actions resulting in my position on the floor. The angry, stark raving mad face of James flashed at me like a bullet. I could still feel his long skinny fingers around my throat as he screamed at me: "You're my wife, and you'll do exactly what I tell ya ta do, you fuckin' bitch!"

My arms and legs dangled like those of a rag doll while he shook me. His strength horrified my small body. "How many times are you going to let this man do this to you, Laurie?" I asked myself.

"Mommy!" I could hear Michael screaming. I began to try to pull myself up to get to my children. Suddenly, I heard footsteps. James was walking back into the kitchen.

"Git up and go take care of those boys, now!" James yelled. He left the kitchen, and I heard the front door slam.

"Maybe he'll leave for a few hours," I thought as I tried to push myself up. As I pushed up, excruciating pain came from my chest. I supported my rib cage with my hand, and the pain subsided slightly. I stood still for a second and then walked out of the kitchen, into the living room, down the hallway toward the boys' bedroom. Before I got to the bedroom, my two boys ran toward me and grabbed me.

This kind of episode was quickly becoming a normal part of my week, especially on the weekend, when James was home. Darkness surrounded me, and I feared I would never find my way out. I did have two little lanterns to light my way named John and Michael. They gave me hope and a reason to survive if James would allow it.

It didn't matter what room I was in when he caught me. Every room in our house potentially was a place for me to be trapped. My sense of hearing was enhanced and became my way of predicting if I was in danger or not. If his footsteps were heavy and loud, I was in danger. If they were light and shuffling, I was not.

An hour later he returned. His footsteps were light, but steady. "I don't think he's mad at me anymore. I think I'm safe . . . for now," I thought.

"Woman! Where's my supper?" he called out.

"I'm working on it," I said. I hurried to place the potatoes in the frying pan and knocked the salt and pepper off onto the floor.

"God dammit!" What'd you drop? Ya clumsy bitch!" he hollered.

"It's just the salt and pepper. I'm cleaning it up."

"Ya better. Ya have enough trouble keep'n this house clean as it is."

I scrambled to finish cleaning up and continued cooking the

evening meal. When dinner was ready, I called out "Dinner's ready." Before I finished putting everything on the table, my two sweet boys were in their seats anxious to eat. James took his time and watched as we all sat there. No one dared to begin eating the meal without him. The smell of the hamburger was tantalizing, but no one made a move. As he sat down, I forced a smile.

"Looks good, but let's see how it tastes," he said as he spooned the fried potatoes onto his plate. When he began to eat, I served the boys and myself.

"This is delicious, hon," he said. His face had completely changed from earlier. He donned a sweet smile. His voice was calm and higher pitched. I took a deep breath and began to eat.

I learned to keep my mouth shut and not express conflicting opinions. This was often a trigger. How did I ever end up in such a situation? Why did I have children with a man with such an explosive temper? These questions haunted me then, and haunt me now, more than thirty years later.

Chapter 2:

The Letter

Dust came billowing up underneath the truck. A large black bird with its wings spread flew in front of us, signaling our return. A gray squirrel popped up, peeping a warning sound. I rolled my window down to take in all the sounds and smells as we traveled down the dirt road to the place I called home. "I'm so blessed to have you in my life, Liam," I said.

"You're the best!" he replied. Peace and tranquility filled my heart as we stepped through our threshold.

I busied myself with the mundane task of unloading our truck and camper, while Liam attended to the huge pile of mail sitting on the dining room table.

"Laurie . . ." Liam said while opening our mail. His concerned tone of voice prompted an immediate response from me.

"Yes, my love. What is it? What's wrong?" I said.

"Uh . . . James . . . has . . . died."

After years of living in fear, I replied, "Are you sure?"

He answered, "It says so in this letter. It's an official letter from Social Security, so yes, I am sure."

I let out a huge sigh of relief and said, "Wow! John, Michael, and I are free from torment. Finally, the monster is gone from our lives."

My kind husband embraced me in his warm, loving way I had grown accustomed to, but my thoughts left the present and I was thrust back in time, not to grieve, but rather to reflect on the tumultuous journey I survived.

Chapter 3:

The Prequel

"Why did you name me Laurie?" I asked my mother frequently when I was young.

"Well, your grandmother thinks we named you after her grandmother. But the real story is, your dad and I were searching for a name fitting for the era you were born in. The 1950s was the first decade after our country was victorious in World War II, so we looked for a name with a meaning related to winning a war. Laurie means symbol of victory, and it goes great with our last name of Kelly."

"I was born on May 23, 1953, right, Momma?" I asked every time she told me the story.

"Yes, you were, my dear," Mom answered every time. She was a petite woman, but bigger than life when it came to dedication to her family. I can remember taking walks with her. She sang and told me stories all along the way, her dress and light-brown hair waving at the sun, fueled by the breeze.

"You're the oldest child, and I expect you to always look after and protect your sister, Amanda, and your brother, Tommy," was Dad's mantra. He was a gentle soul whose way of approaching people was conducive to comfort. Family was everything to my parents. I remember their kind eyes and perpetual smiles. They loved each other deeply and shared their love with the three of us. It was as if God's light was shining on their faces.

It was this strong beginning I drew my strength from to support me through the challenges I would face in young adulthood. Even now I can smell the fresh-cut grass, the donuts in the Helm's bakery truck, and my mother's pork chops cooking on the stove. I can still hear my mother's voice calling me home for dinner and my friends laughing. I can see our neighbor Joe working on cars in his driveway across the street, and old man Patton training his German Shepherd to perform tricks. I remember being loved and cared for by my family and neighborhood. "I'm sure everyone grew up this way," I often thought to myself.

My nightmare started three months before my eighteenth birthday. I was a senior in high school and extremely busy and happy. I ranked twelfth in a class of over seven hundred and easily qualified for a California State Scholarship and admission to the University of California at Riverside (UCR). I was involved in many activities and had many friends, but I was missing one thing—a boyfriend. The year was 1971, the Vietnam War was still in progress, and women were meant to have a husband to be valued. Our parents were a product of the 1950s, and those traditional values had taken a strong hold into the lives of their children, despite the turmoil of the 1960s. Watching the Civil Rights Movement, and the Kennedy and Martin Luther King assassinations unfold on television right before our eyes had influenced our outer views on life, but the core deep traditional values regarding love and marriage had sunk to the depths of our being like a block of cement.

"I want you to go to college," my mother often said. Openly, my parents supported my plans, unaware they were creating a woman who needed to be married and have children to feel complete.

By January 1971, I had meticulously prepared a plan for my life after graduation. I had just a little over half of the school year left and each day I grew more and more excited to begin my adult life. I was going to be an independent woman with a career and have total control of my destiny . . . so I thought.

Chapter 4:

The Detour

February 12, 1971, started out like any other day in school. I got up, got dressed, walked to school, visited with my girlfriends before classes began, and attended my first four classes. At lunchtime I bought my food and headed to the same table I sat at every day to eat my lunch. Little did I know I was about to meet the man who would derail my plans for the future.

Just as I was about to sit down, a handsome guy approached me and introduced himself. His name was James Hawkins, and he immediately told me he was drawn to me because of my beautiful singing voice.

I was in awe such a handsome guy was so interested in me. As he sat next to me, I had to crane my neck a little to gaze into his deep blue eyes. His voice was softer than that of most men I knew, but enchanting. We talked until the lunch bell rang. He told me he had noticed me months ago, when the school choir sang at an assembly, but he needed to build up the courage to approach me. We exchanged home phone numbers with the promise to eat lunch together every day.

After school, James called me on the phone and asked me

if I wanted to go on a date with him on Saturday night. I, of course, said, "Yes!" I was so relieved when he called. Now I had no reason to worry all weekend about whether I had said or done something to chase him away. When it came to boys, I tended to be overzealous, which most did not seem to appreciate.

I was finished getting ready thirty minutes before James was scheduled to arrive. My whole family and I sat in the living room watching our color TV, anxiously waiting for his arrival. My dad always insisted the boys I dated come into our home for a formal introduction and questioning, of course.

Luckily, James arrived fifteen minutes early, so there was plenty of time for my dad to grill him and for us to still get to the drive-in movie on time.

Dad answered the door, James walked in and sat down next to me on our beige vinyl couch. My left leg was shaking from nervousness about my dad's questions for James.

Dad began his questioning. They were simple questions, but embarrassing for me. He asked him about his parents and how long they had lived in California. My dad found common ground because they were both born in eastern states. Then came the most humiliating part for a teenage girl like me.

"Okay, James, let me give you a few simple rules regarding your date with our daughter."

"Dad!" I blurted out.

"I don't think James minds if I spell out the rules, do you, James?" Dad said with a stern look toward me.

"Not 't all, sir. Please go on."

"Laurie is one of three of our most prized possessions, and I expect you to treat her as such. You're to drive safely, treat her with respect, and have her home thirty minutes after the drive-in movie show ends. If you follow these simple rules, then we'll approve of a second date."

James agreed to Dad's rules, and I breathed a sigh of relief the inquiry had ended. Dad got up from his recliner and they shook hands. He then gave me a tight hug, and whispered in my ear, "Have a good time, sweetheart."

As we headed out the door, James took me by the hand. The smell of Old Spice cologne filled my nostrils as we walked toward the bright-red 1970 Dodge Challenger.

"Wow! What a neato car you have, James."

"Thanks, but it isn't my car. It belongs to my older sister. She let me borrow it."

"Well, it's really cool, and I'm glad she let you borrow it for our date. I love sports cars."

He opened the passenger door, and I slid onto the cold black shiny seat. I felt like I was exploring new territory, and it was exhilarating.

James wore a black leather jacket, a white t-shirt, blue jeans, and black boots. To me he looked like James Dean in the movie, *Rebel Without a Cause*, only with jet-black hair. The rebellious side within me liked to walk on the wild side, and dating James gave me this feeling.

The first date went well. We talked, we kissed and embraced. I felt safe and secure in his arms. I loved hearing him say phrases such as "You're so beautiful. I can't believe you're finally in my arms. I'm the luckiest guy in the whole wide world."

On the drive home that night I believed I was the luckiest girl in the world to have found such a handsome guy who picked me out of all the girls at school. James told me he wanted to see me every day, and if he didn't his heart would burst. I told him I felt the same way. When we arrived at my home, he took his class ring off and handed it to me and said, "I know it is just our first date, but I feel so sure we are meant to be together, and that is why I want to ask you to go steady with me."

Without hesitation I said, "Yes," and we embraced and kissed. This kiss with him was different from the ones earlier. He held me tighter, and his hands went forcefully up and down my back as if to claim something he had wanted for a very long time.

I left the car that night feeling wanted and needed by a man I equally was attracted to. I was thrilled he wanted to secure our bond by asking me to go steady, but I wasn't sure my dad shared my same sentiment.

As I entered my house, my dad was sitting in his recliner waiting for my return. "Hi, sweetheart. How did it go? You know you're five minutes late coming in, right?"

"Yes, Dad. But James had me in front of our house right on time like he promised. And the date was wonderful."

I walked to my dad's recliner, bent down, gave him a kiss and a hug, and told him goodnight. The smell of his cherry-flavored pipe smoke was in stark contrast with the cologne smell on James. As I walked down the hallway to my bedroom, which I shared with my sister, I felt a little deceitful as I didn't tell him about the ring I was holding in my hand.

Valentine's Day came the day after our first date. James rode his motorcycle over to my house, and we stood in my front yard and talked. I was excited because he was holding something behind his back.

"Is that for me?" I asked.

"Yes. But ya might not like it very much."

"Oh, I'll like anything you give me."

He pulled a heart-shaped box from behind his back and handed it to me. "Oh, I simply love chocolate candy!" I squealed. There was no cellophane around the box, so the lid came off easily. As I peered into the box, I realized there was not one piece of candy inside. The little brown papers were there, but nothing else.

"Oh my."

"Yah, the box fell off the back of my motorcycle on the way here," he explained.

"Oh well, it's the thought that counts. Thank you."

He grabbed me and gave me a very passionate kiss. I pulled away after a few seconds.

"James, my family is sitting in the living room and if they look through the window, they can see us," I said as my cheeks turned very warm.

"Aww, you're blushing. It's okay, I won't do that again. Least not here," he said with a smile.

The next day at school, my friend from drama club, Gina, approached me.

"I'm so excited that you're dating my brother James."

Confused by her statement, I said, "He's your brother? I didn't even know you had a brother."

"I do, and he's so crazy about you."

I found it a little odd she had not mentioned him before in any of our conversations during our sophomore or junior years, especially as they were both in the same grade, but just dismissed it, thinking the subject never came up. As it turned out, James was two years older than Gina but was held back two grade levels in elementary school.

During my high school years, I didn't date much, as there wasn't a lot of time left over. I was in the choral groups, drama, and joined many clubs. I was selected to be in the musicals put on by the music and drama departments. I was a Red Cross candy striper, and a Girl Scout who worked on acquiring as many badges as possible through community service activities. I was also active in my church, working with my pastor on increasing the number of teenagers attending church activities.

James, in contrast, did not belong to any clubs, nor did he

plan on attending college. He loved riding his motorcycle and playing billiards on his family pool table. He was a C-average student, who often struggled with reading and writing. He was, however, able to draw good sketches. My parents began to formulate the opinion James was not the boyfriend they had hoped I would find.

As I look back, there were warning signs all around me regarding James. I don't believe he chose me out of a normal attraction, but rather like a predator. He watched me for several months, much like a predator watches his prey before he attacks, or in this case tries to gain control.

My parents tried to warn me this might not be the best match for me, especially when they found out we were going steady. The more they tried to warn me, the more it drove me into his arms. I was a teenager and thought I knew everything and could handle anything. Little did I know what a treacherous journey I had begun.

Our first dance was a Luau in mid-March. My mother sewed a muumuu for me and a matching shirt for James. I was so excited and proud about the way we looked together. Appearances weighed heavily on my mind, and I was very interested in seeing what everyone else was wearing that night. As we entered the school gymnasium, where the dance was being held, the aroma of tropical flowers surrounded my nostrils. "This is not the normal smell of our gym," I thought to myself and giggled.

"What're you laughin' at?" James barked.

"Oh, just that this gym has never smelled better."

We presented our tickets at the table stationed just past the entrance. As we walked further in, I recognized some of my friends and waved to them and said to James, "Jim looks really good in his Hawaiian shirt. I don't see his date with a matching dress. I will have to look around more. Maybe she went to the restroom."

"Well, why don't you just go be with him, since he looks so good," James said angrily as he stomped away.

I found him a few minutes later sitting in the corner of the gymnasium, behind some decorations, by himself, pouting.

"James, honey, what's wrong?"

"Ya know, maybe ya should go with him."

"You took my comment the wrong way."

"If ya hadn't said what you said, I wouldn't be sittin' here."

"I didn't mean I wanted to be with Jim instead of you. I just like his shirt. That is it! He's my friend, nothing more. I'm so sorry, honey. Please forgive me."

"I need to calm down. Ya made me so mad with your stupid comment."

I stood by him for the next thirty minutes while he sat in the corner. Finally, he got up and we got our pictures taken, and enjoyed some refreshments. All the while he continued to pout.

"I'm not really havin' a good time because of your mouth. I'd like to go now, okay?"

"I'm so sorry I ruined the evening for you, James. Sure, we can go."

He blamed me for his behavior, and for some reason I accepted the blame. He made his reaction to my remark seem like a normal one and acted as if he was the victim of my behavior.

Our next date was in his parents' car, a brown Datsun 510, at the drive-in movie theater. This date seemed to go smoothly because it was only him and I, by ourselves. There were no distractions, and our focus was on one another. We started by kissing and, before I knew it, his hands were underneath my clothing. I surprised myself as I didn't even resist. My heart began to race, and I was breathing hard. James made me feel like I was the center of his universe. He said everything I wanted to hear.

"You're the best thing that has ever happened to me. I want to spend the rest of my life with you. I don't think I can live without you."

He took his hands out from under my clothing and placed my hand on his pants where his stiff penis was lying in wait. "I love ya," he said.

I, of course, responded back with "I love you too!" I wriggled with nervousness after saying this phrase. It was a serious phrase and one I had previously only said to members of my family.

I asked myself, "Do I love him? What does it really mean to love a man? Is marriage next? Am I ready? What about my plans for the future?"

He must have noticed I was deep in thought because he asked, "Are ya okay, sweetheart?"

"Yes, sorry. I'm just a little nervous. I've not done this much with any other guy."

"Oh, my sweet girl. You're a virgin," he announced.

"Yes, of course. I'm saving myself for my wedding night."

"I can't wait until it's our weddin' night."

My emotional needs were being pumped full of air, fueled by his intentional use of manipulative language.

I was being thrust quickly into a direction not part of my plans for the future, and it made me feel afraid, but at the same time excited. The sexual excitement gave me a tingly feeling I had not experienced to this extent. My vagina and my face were both on fire.

My blatant rebellion against what my parents and I together had planned for my life was acting as an accelerant. To become a wife was something I had pushed far away into the distant future, but here it was right in front of me. Soon, my thoughts began to fade, and I thrust myself into this moment in time.

"Unzip my pants and pull my dick out," James commanded. I obeyed his command.

As I did my fingers ventured upon hair and I remarked, "I didn't realize that guys had hair like us girls do."

"Really?"

"I really hadn't thought about it much. My little brother doesn't have any and he is the only boy I've seen naked."

We both laughed and then he said, "Okay, put your hand around it and stroke it up and down." I did as he said. His right hand did not leave from my body but did travel up under my bra to grasp my breast. All my thoughts now became focused on this moment. Nothing else mattered. James began to moan the faster I stroked. My hands were strong, and I found myself able to stroke hard and fast. He began to ejaculate, and the semen spouted all over my hand. His hand quickly exited my breast, and he used it to zip his pants up.

"If you reach over to the back seat there should be a towel you can use to wipe your hand and my pants."

When I arrived home that night, my feelings were all over the place. I was excited, but afraid. I was happy, but sad. I loved being loved and needed, but at the same time hated the complications that seemed to be included in this package called a relationship. I wanted to tell someone. I thought that someone might be my sister, Amanda. She was still awake when I came to bed.

"How was your date?"

"It was great, but . . ."

"But? What does that mean?"

"Well, he touched my breast."

"What? How could you let him do that? I can't believe you let him do that." She put her pillow over her head and made a sound like she was crying.

"Amanda, it wasn't that big of a deal. We didn't do anything else," I said just to calm her down. I figured she was too young to understand and scolded myself for thinking I could talk to a fourteen-year-old about my first sexual experience. I dismissed her reaction and decided that discussions about sex between James and me should stay private.

Our dates continued and so did our experimentation with sex, with one stipulation from me. I told James I wanted to wait to go all the way until I was married. He assured me I would still be a virgin on our wedding night.

In early May James and I agreed it was time for me to meet his parents. It was a sunny, warm Sunday afternoon, and his mom and dad were sitting in lawn chairs in their yard as we drove by en route to their driveway in back. The freshly painted green-paneled house with white trim was in the center of a perfectly manicured lawn, and as I exited the car the smell of freshly cut grass was unmistakable.

"Your house and yard are beautiful!" I exclaimed.

"Yeah, my mom and dad work hard on it. Mom likes everything to look perfect. She even gets on her hands and knees to cut the grass with scissors where the edger can't reach."

The front and back yard were all fenced as one, so the yard seemed enormous. James led me around to where they were sitting and introduced me.

"I'm very happy to meet you, Mr. and Mrs. Hawkins," I said

"Junior, go get two more chairs, so ya two can sit here with us."

"Okay, Mom," he said. I stood there in front of these two strangers, wriggling from nervousness. There was a slight breeze, and it made their cigarette smoke circle around my head like a ribbon. The smoke didn't really bother me as my dad and his siblings all had the "nasty habit," as my Aunt Patty called it. My dad was trying to quit by switching to a pipe.

My thoughts were interrupted by Mrs. Hawkins's voice. "Please call me Anna." Her request made me very uncomfortable because my parents had taught me not to call adults by their first name, but I didn't want to offend her.

"Okay, Anna," I said.

A couple of minutes later, James arrived with the chairs, and we sat down.

"I hear you're an honor student, isn't that right?" Anna asked.

"Yes, I am," I replied.

"That's wonderful, dear," she said.

James grabbed my hand and squeezed it. Mr. Hawkins, or James Sr. as I began to call him, had not uttered a word up to this point when he said, "Anna, go fetch me a cup of coffee."

"Okay, old man. Laurie, do ya want to come with me ta the kitchen?"

I agreed and began to follow her. She moved quickly like a rabbit. I had to spark a fire under my legs to keep up with her. She glided across the grass in her bare feet. Her very tight denim shorts didn't impede her speed and her tan arms were in rhythm with the rest of her body, totally exposed, jutting out of her sleeveless cherry-red top. She stopped to open the screen door and held it for me as I walked through their door.

I stopped to wait for her direction. The smell of freshly baked biscuits abounded.

"Mm. Mrs., um, Anna, it smells so good in here," I said.

"That would be my biscuits! Smells good, huh? We have 'em for Sunday supper every week," she boasted. "I'll put supper on the table in a few minutes," she said as she walked in front of me into her kitchen.

From where I stood in the living room, I had a view of not only that room, but also the dining room and kitchen. The

19

cleanliness and neatness of those three rooms was impressive. My thoughts drifted to my home, where neatness wasn't always enforced, but it was always clean.

"Can ya please take James Sr. his coffee, so I can work on supper?"

As I walked out to the yard carrying the coffee cup, my mind continued comparing our two families. Anna dressed so differently than my mother, who never went barefoot except on her way to bed, nor wore shorts so tight or high up. My brain was full of curiosity regarding what made women have different tastes in clothing. As I approached James Sr., he reached out for the coffee cup and said, "Thank you."

He was dressed very much like my dad. He had on a plaid collared shirt and gray work pants. The difference between him and my dad was the language they used. I never heard my father tell my mother to fetch anything, and he always used the word "please" when asking my mother to do something for him.

As I started to head back to the kitchen, James shot a loving smile my way. I had entered his world and embraced it with my heart and soul. In the kitchen, without the presence of anyone but her and I, Anna became this bubbly, talkative, interesting person. She spoke about the foods she cooked that James loved, how he helped around the house, and stories about when he was a baby. We giggled about how James seemed embarrassed when she called him Junior in front of me.

When supper was ready, I volunteered to set the table. As I picked up the plates from the cupboard, I heard a voice say, "Well, who do we have here?" I turned around to see the oldest child in the Hawkins family, Fiona, standing behind me.

"I'm Laurie," I said as I walked toward her and gave her a hug.

"Well, aren't you a pretty little thing. No wonder my

brother's crazy about you," Fiona said.

As I stood there blushing, Anna asked me to go tell the men that supper was ready.

I left the house through the kitchen door instead of the front door and immediately got lost, so I stopped and called out for James.

James quickly appeared laughing with his dad and Dan, Fiona's husband, right behind him and said, "Did ya forget where I was at?" All three men laughed.

"I came out a different door is all," I said, feeling embarrassed.

The whole family was present for dinner except for Gina. I could tell Fiona and Gina were sisters. They both had long jet-black hair and their faces were similar, but Fiona's nose was more petite. In fact, Fiona overall was more petite than Gina.

Fiona inquired as to the whereabouts of Gina and was told she was with her boyfriend. I sat quietly and quickly ate my biscuit, mashed potatoes and gravy, and cubed steak, but pushed around the unidentifiable vegetable.

"What's the matter, girl? Ain't ever et fried okra before?" asked James Sr.

"Is that what it's called? No, sir, never had it before," I said. I picked up a small bite with my fork and tasted it. "Mm. It's good!" Everyone at the table laughed.

As James drove me home that evening, he said, "Boy, I can tell my family really loves ya, but not as much as I do," he said, laughing.

"They made me feel welcome, especially your mom," I said.

"Yeah, my mom is one special lady. She's been through a lot in her life and still smiles. When I was four years old, she was in the hospital for three months 'cause she had TB."

"That must've been so hard to leave her family for such a long time."

"Yeah, my mom's one tough gal."

I would discover later, having TB was only the tip of the iceberg of hardships in Anna's life.

Before I knew it, the week of graduation came. At this point in our relationship, James dominated all my free time. He insisted I do all the senior week activities with him. However, on graduation day, I had earned the honor of being twelfth in my class and was assigned the twelfth position in line to receive my diploma. James wanted me to give that position up and walk with him toward the very end of the line. I told him I loved him, but I had earned this honor and he should want me to enjoy the benefit of my hard work. I was pleasantly surprised when he agreed. Little did I realize there was a price for this disobedient behavior.

The graduation ceremony was glorious. I was pumped full of pride. I walked next to my girlfriend, Marilyn. I didn't even think about James during the ceremony. I was focused on myself and on singing the song "We've Only Just Begun" with the acapella choir and hearing my name called to receive my diploma. Then, as if my brain was popping corn, a kernel exploded with thoughts of James just in time to hear his name being called. I cheered quick and loud. It wasn't until that moment that my focus shifted to one of excitement to attend the graduation night celebration with James.

After the graduation ceremony, I didn't find James, but it was prearranged for my parents to drive me home so I could change out of my graduation gown and dress into appropriate clothing for the night ahead. James was to pick me up to take me to the place where we would board the bus to take us to the graduation night celebration.

My parents planned a party with friends and family to celebrate my graduation. James and I were only required to make a brief appearance. When we arrived home, I quickly ran into the house. My Aunt Patty and my sister Amanda had left the graduation as soon as my name was called so they could set the food out for the party. The aroma of my mom's potato salad hit my nostrils as I ran by. I thought to myself, "I need to make sure I get a bite or two of it before I leave." After I changed my clothes, my dad summoned me to the table and showed me the cake they had special-ordered from the local bakery. It was a sheet cake with white icing, and written in blue letters were the words *Congratulations Laurie*.

"We're so proud of you," Dad said.

My mom came up from behind me and wrapped her arms around in a tight grip as if she was never going to let me go, and told me she loved me.

Their love for me emanated like the light from a chandelier. I was totally engulfed in the warmth and light when suddenly the doorbell rang, and I thought it might be James. "Mom, please let go so I can answer the door."

I pulled the door open quickly to find our neighbors standing on the porch. Three doorbells later, finally James was standing there when I opened the door. He grabbed my hand and pulled me in for a short kiss on the porch. I held on to him and led him through the living room, dining room, and kitchen to each group of friends and family, making sure we greeted everyone. There were lots of congratulatory hugs for both of us. After almost an hour had passed, James signaled to me it was time to leave.

I announced to the group that we were leaving to catch our bus. Everyone gathered around us as if we were leaving on an extended journey. Suddenly, I heard a little voice yelling, "Wait! Don't leave yet!" It was my little brother Tommy pushing through the group waving his homemade card for me over his head. His little face was illuminated with love, and I carried this warm feeling with me as we left.

We held hands as we walked to the car. He told me he loved me as he opened the car door. I was very happy about this momentous day and excited to spend the night with James. We only lived one mile from the school, so the drive was short. James was smiling as I talked nonstop about the ceremony, the party, and my excitement about attending the graduation night celebration.

As we boarded the bus, James whispered in my ear," Go to the very back and sit in the last seat."

I was wearing a brand-new polyester burnt-orange pant suit that scooted easily onto the dark green vinyl seat. I turned to James and said, "This is going to be so much fun."

"Maybe for ya."

"You don't think you're going to have fun tonight?"

"If'n I can get over being mad at ya."

"Why are you mad?

"Well, I guess I'm not important enough for ya to choose me over your friends."

"What are you talking about?"

"Ya didn't give up your spot to walk with me. I guess I'm not that important to ya."

"What? You agreed I should walk twelfth in line because I earned it."

"Sure, but I didn't believe you'd really do it. I was thinkin' our love was stronger than that, ya selfish bitch."

This was the first time he called me such a name and it shocked me. I sat there silent, horrified our peers on the bus might have heard what he had called me. I could feel my face heating up. I didn't want to say anything for fear his anger would get worse. I felt ashamed and stupid that I did not see this coming. I asked myself, "Was I being selfish? Does he have a right to be mad about my choice?"

As I sat there pondering these questions, he leaned over and whispered in my ear, "I think I must fuckin' love you more than ya love me. You're such a bitch."

I turned and said in a low voice, "I do love you." If looks could kill, then the look he gave me at that moment was the one capable of doing the deed.

"Ya fuckin' bitch," he whispered in my ear. "How can ya say that after what ya did to me? Ya really hurt me. You've no idea how much it hurts." He turned away from me and covered his face with his hands.

I leaned toward him and put my hand on his back. He immediately pushed it away. "Please, honey, what can I do to convince you how much I love you?"

"God dammit, bitch. I hurt so bad right now I don't even know. Leave me be."

I sat there, feeling like I had betrayed him and waiting for him to decide my path back to his good side. He turned his whole body so that his back was facing me and didn't speak to me the rest of the way there. I was angry at myself for not recognizing he expected me to sacrifice for him. I so wanted to please him, no matter what.

When we arrived at the amusement park where the celebration was to take place, he turned toward me, smiled, and grabbed my hand.

"Oh honey!" I said. My excitement for this night had returned, and I followed happily as he led me off the bus, hoping he had thought long and hard and had decided to forgive me for being so selfish. As we walked toward the entrance gate, he leaned toward me and said, "Honey, I figured out a way for ya to prove to me how much ya love me."

"Oh okay. How? I'll do anything you ask," I said without realizing what the agreement entailed.

"You'll let me touch you anywhere I want, any time I want, and you'll do anything I ask ya to do, no matter what," he said.

"Uh . . . okay," I said, knowing full well this request was sexual in nature.

"I love ya so much, honey!" he said as he grabbed me and kissed me. His request made me very uncomfortable, but I knew I needed to comply with his wishes to prove my love for him. I wanted to please him at any cost.

The first ride we got onto was a flying ship ride. It was dark, and each ship seated two people. As soon as the ride started, his hand went down my into my pants and underneath my underwear. I wriggled a little as my body was thrust up against the safety bar.

"Stop squirming, dammit," he said.

"There isn't a lot of room, sorry," I said.

The dark musty smell inside the ride filled my nostrils and killed any sexual excitement I might have been able to experience. James seemed happy, which made me happy. Every ride we went on that night was a similar experience. The only differences were which part of my body he grabbed, or if he had me touch his penis and rub it until it became erect. My whole graduation night experience was filled with worry about getting caught or not pleasing James. By the time we exited the park, I was emotionally and physically exhausted.

"Well, honey, ya did it. Ya proved ya love me!" James exclaimed as we walked to the bus. He was pleased, and my innate need to please him was fulfilled.

A few weeks after graduation, James signed up for the Air Force. He was worried that he might be drafted. He turned eighteen in 1969 and draft birthdates were continuing to be pulled—the draft was abolished in 1973. The Vietnam War was nearing its end, but the fighting was still happening, and men were being drafted and killed. He was scheduled to enter basic training in September, so we had the summer together. He worked a summer job for money and took me to restaurants, on hikes, fishing, amusement parks, etc. We were in love and saw each other every day. During those summer months our relationship appeared to be normal; he did boast about other sexual encounters he had before me to pressure me into doing more and more sexually. I was technically a virgin and had made it clear to him I didn't want to "go all the way" until we were married. That fact, plus the possibility of him heading to war, prompted his proposal of marriage. Together we set our wedding date for March 25, 1972.

At the tender age of eighteen, I didn't realize that his intense need for me was not because of love, but because of the beginning of a mental illness. He fed my desire to "help" people, by "needing" me. He made statements like "I can't live without you. I would just die if'n you ever broke up with me." I developed a sense of guilty devotion that drove me deeper into an abnormal relationship.

Since I was already enrolled at UCR and it was being paid by scholarships, I began attending there in September of 1971. My major was biology, which was considered a pre-med major. My original plans were to attend UCR for four years and then go on to medical school. But, before I even began these plans, they were already being diverted by James, due to his loneliness and abnormal need to control me.

Chapter 5:

The Joining of Two Families

"You can no longer tell me what to do, and whether you support me or not, I'm going to marry James!" I screamed. Dad raised his hand and in one sweep, whoosh! It landed square on the right side of my face.

"Frank!" my mom yelled. Dad stared at his hand as if some other force had seized control of it. I screamed and ran to my room. My face stung, but my pride was on fire. This was the last-ditch effort by my father to stop me from marrying James. He had been laid off from Kaiser Steel in September, 1971, and was questioning the financial responsibility for the wedding, as well as the effect this marriage would have on my future career plans.

I sat in my room, furious at my father. My mind was full of angry questions. "Why doesn't he want me to marry James? He married my mom, and no one tried to stop him. Would he rather I have intercourse before marriage and get pregnant? Does he think because I started attending college, I would change my mind about James? How dare he think my love for James is superficial enough to just change my mind so easily?" I longed to be out of this house and living with James. After a few minutes of sulking, I threw myself back on my bed and started thumbing through one of my magazines. Amanda was gone visiting her girlfriend, so I had the bedroom all to myself and my thoughts. I was surrounded by pink walls, and clothes flung everywhere. "My home will be much neater than this room. My sister won't be around to mess things up." Suddenly, my thoughts shifted in an entirely different direction. I realized my environment would completely change. These thoughts began to deflate my anger and let reality into my brain. I was going to marry James, and I was going to leave the only home I had ever resided in, as well as the family inside. Excitement and fear were coexisting within me. I decided I needed to apologize to Dad for my behavior. It was the adult thing to do. As I opened my bedroom door, I found Dad standing there on the other side. "Dad, I'm so sorry!" I said.

"I'm the one who is sorry, sweetheart. I never should have slapped you," he said.

"It's okay. I kinda deserved it."

"No one ever deserves to be slapped." We grabbed each other in a spontaneous hug.

"Your mother and I will always support you, even when we don't agree. We love you."

From that moment on, he and my mother helped me with the wedding planning wholeheartedly.

Now that my family was on board, the wedding plans were moving ahead full steam. What I didn't realize at the time is our two families were as different as day and night. In the animal world most species separate from their families when they mature and find a mate on their own. Humans, on the other hand, combine two very complex systems.[1] In our case, these

---

1. Monica McGoldrick, "The Joining of Families Through Marriage: The New Couple," in *Changing Family Life Cycle*, ed. Betty Carter and Monica McGoldrick (New York: Gardner Press, 1988), 209–233.

two complex systems were completely opposite.

My parents were traditional, conservative Protestants. They had high morals and high expectations for their three children. Our whole family, on both sides, had never been in jail, attended church on a regular basis, and had no history of domestic violence. Family stories included ones surrounding survival and love. My grandmother often told me the story about my father's birth and how her milk was not sustaining him, and he almost died of starvation. My grandfather found extra work to make more money so they could buy cow's milk and oranges to feed him, thus saving his life.

When my father was sixteen, they moved to California to save my grandfather's life as the cold damp weather in Pennsylvania was causing him to be sick with pneumonia every winter, so his doctor suggested they move west and so they did.

My mother was a native Californian, born and raised in San Diego, California. My mother had a wonderful childhood, living within a short walk of Balboa Park, which was home to the famous San Diego Zoo. Her father had survived the San Francisco earthquake of 1906, and her mother had traveled from Illinois to California in a covered wagon. My grandfather told me the story of the earthquake from his point of view as a nine-year-old boy and how he was devastated by the fact that the horses at the firehouse by his home had been choked to death as they were tied to the fence when the earthquake occurred.

My father met my mother while he was in boot camp for the Navy in San Diego. They were at a picnic with mutual friends. My mother wanted to get my father's attention, so she stole his shoes. It was love at first sight and they married six months later. My parents were in love even after marriage, and I witnessed very few arguments and lots of hugs and kisses between them.

My in-laws to be, however, had a different past, different

expectations and definitely a different set of morals. The first family story told to me was that of my father-in-law's father, who was famous in his town in Kentucky for "Hitting mules with his fist between their eyes so hard that the blow killed them instantly." Fortunately for me this man was dead long before I came into the family. This was a red flag when it came to domestic violence in their family. I was too young and immature at the time and didn't see it.

As I got to know the family, Anna became more comfortable telling me about their family history. She told me how she and her sister were betrothed to the Hawkins brothers in Kentucky. Anna was fifteen and her sister June was sixteen. It was a tradition to give a dowry to the family of the girls and her family was desperate for money at the time because her father had not worked much that year.

The Hawkins brothers, Clem and James Hawkins Sr. were thirty and thirty-two years old respectively. I would later discover, through conversations with Pat, the widow of Anna's brother Claude, that the marriage between James Hawkins Sr. and his wife was riddled with episodes of domestic violence. Anna didn't really want to marry James but did so for the good of her family. The combination of her young age and loss of control in her life created a rebellious Anna. But it is my belief that no matter how rebellious an individual is, they should never be beaten for that behavior. Evidently the beatings were frequent in the beginning of the marriage, but abruptly stopped for a short time, one night in a very tragic manner.

Anna was pregnant with their first child, and they lived on the third floor of an apartment building in Cincinnati, Ohio. They had moved there so James Sr. could find work as a carpenter; however, this move had separated Anna from her whole family. Her mother, father, two sisters and brother still lived across the Ohio River in Kentucky. I believe this separation from her family was on purpose to isolate Anna to gain more control over her.

As Anna approached her ninth month of pregnancy, she was feeling tired and lonely. When James Sr. arrived home from work, Anna used her words to lash out at him. Little did she know how his reaction would affect her and her baby's life. He smacked her down so hard that she fell against the apartment door. She raised herself using the doorknob and opened the door. She ran away toward the stairs leading down from their third-floor apartment. As she ran James Sr. followed her, grabbing for her dress. He caught the dress with his hand. She pulled to get away, and the dress ripped, hurling her forward down the stairs. She fell down fifteen steps and stopped on the next landing. James Sr. quickly grabbed her and picked her up and took her back into the apartment. His episode of rage turned into fear as she lay lifeless in his arms. He called the doctor, explaining only that she had tripped and fallen down the stairs. The doctor asked him to bring her to the hospital. By the time James Sr. put Anna in the back of his 1936 Ford pickup and began to drive her to Cincinnati General Hospital, she had already gone into labor. Once there he carried her into the emergency room where two nurses took her from him and put her on a gurney. Henry James Hawkins was delivered at 5:14 the next morning. The infant had suffered from a broken neck and did not survive the delivery. In 1948, no one questioned his story.

Anna was released from the hospital two days later. James Sr. had convinced her that if she hadn't run from him, she would have never fallen down the stairs. The sound and fury of the silence during that ride in the pickup back to the apartment must have been deafening.

The story they told everyone was that the doctor broke the

baby's neck during delivery. That is how the story was first told to me.

Their daily life resumed back to its normal for them. James Sr. was remorseful regarding the loss of his child's life, and his outbursts focused on breaking items instead of hurting Anna. However, an occasional backhand was not out of the question. James Sr. became more absent at home, I assume to avoid further confrontations with Anna. He would stop at one of the local bars and would engage in bar fights. These kinds of events would end with Anna going down to the city jail to post bail for him.

A year after Anna lost her first child, a second child was born. This time it was a girl they named Fiona, and James Sr. did not strike her even once during the pregnancy. Two more children came along, James Jr. and Gina. Domestic violence became something that occurred on a regular basis, with reprieves only during pregnancy. The family became good at hiding their secrets; however, when the community became aware of this pattern, James Sr. and his family decided to move to California, where they could have a fresh start—a place where there were no friends and only one relative, Anna's brother Claude, with his wife Pat and their two children. This was a place where no one but Claude and his wife knew their family history, including law enforcement.

Why they selected Fontana is a mystery to me, as Claude lived in Highland, about twenty miles east of Fontana. Was it a deliberate choice not to live too close to anyone they knew from the past?

My parents, on the other hand, moved to Fontana necessitated by my dad's acceptance of employment at Kaiser Steel. The decision to move there was made easier since a large portion of my dad's family already resided in Fontana.

The contrast between the two families was striking. I was

too immature to see it. Even if I did notice the difference, I was young and in love and thought love was all that was needed for a successful marriage.

Chapter 6:

The Wedding: Before & After

My dad was a planner and, now with a solid date for the wedding, he focused on planning a budget within the family's means at the time. He searched for stores carrying wedding dresses at discounted prices and talked to our minister about the date and costs. He called a family meeting to announce his budget plans.

Dad and I sat at our dining room table, waiting, while mom rounded up Tommy and Amanda. Tommy was in his bedroom, and I could hear him asking Mom why he had to come to this stupid meeting. Amanda showed up with a scowl on her face and plopped herself into one of the orange high-back vinyl dining room chairs.

"Ladies don't plop into a seat, Amanda. They graciously and easily slide into it," said Dad.

"Yes sir," answered Amanda as she tapped her fingernails on the brown table. Dad's grease-stained hands were folded and rested firmly in front of him.

Mom came to the table with Tommy dragging his feet behind her. "Glad you could join us, son." Tommy emitted a smile which made his blue eyes shine. His tousled blond hair and little-boy jeans and striped t-shirt haphazardly placed on his body seared a loving image into my heart.

"Your mother and I have calculated the amount of money we comfortably can afford to spend on your wedding dress. You know I'm not working right now, even though I'm hopeful I will go back soon. So money's tight for us."

"Yes, Dad I know, and I feel really bad I'm burdening you."

"It's not a burden. Your happiness is important to us; however, I need to make sure the rest of the family does not financially suffer because of your decision to get married at this time. So your mother and I have decided we can afford one hundred dollars for a wedding dress. Also, can you please talk to James and his family about using our church as your place for the wedding? The reason being, since we are members there is no charge to use the church for the wedding and the hall for the reception. Our only cost would be the small fee for our minister."

"Yes. Thanks. You guys always come through for me."

"Yuck! You guys are mushy!" Tommy added.

"Are we done?" asked Amanda.

"Amanda, will you be my maid of honor?" I asked.

"Yes!" Amanda squealed.

"What do I get to do?" asked Tommy.

"Well, you can be an usher if you would like to, but James is going to ask you, so act surprised when he asks you, okay?"

"Uh, okay, but what does an usher do?"

"An usher is very important. He shows guests to their seats."

"Groovy. I can do that," said Tommy.

I was very happy. My whole family was getting as excited as I was about the wedding.

The next several weeks involved a lot of trips to different stores, with no luck in finding a dress I liked for one hundred dollars or less. Finally, we happened upon a dress store in the

Montclair Mall. The clerk working there showed me several dresses and one of them caught my eye. It was an all-lace dress in my size, and it was within the one-hundred-dollar budget. The elderly clerk saw how excited I was and heard my father say that the dress and veil had to be a total of one hundred dollars. She quickly responded by showing me an inexpensive Juliet cap and offered to sew the veil on it herself for a very small fee. My father placed a deposit on the dress and the clerk gave us a date when everything would be ready. Our family left the store happy and satisfied.

I was so excited about my dress that I immediately called my sister-in-law to be, Gina, who was to be the only bridesmaid in the wedding and told her about my dress selection.

"It's all white lace, with long sleeves and a scoop neck. The skirt slightly flares out from the bodice. I've a matching Juliette cap, and the lady at the store is sewing my veil to my cap. And . . . I was able to get it all within my dad's budget!" I said.

She appeared to be happy for me, but she began to ask questions, such as "Are you sure this is the dress you really want?" I assured her this was the dress I wanted. She also asked the name of the dress shop, and I told her it was *Jean's* in the Montclair Mall.

Her questions puzzled me at the time but would make sense later. Gina was attending Skadron College in San Bernardino to study Fashion Merchandising and considered herself an expert on fashions. After our phone conversation, Gina immediately phoned her sister Fiona. In my excitement, I had disclosed the dress was within my father's budget. Their family had a discussion regarding my dress and decided they needed to send the two sisters to view the dress to make sure it was appropriate. James Sr. was working as a carpenter and was willing to help buy a better dress if needed. They had no idea regarding my family and our pride. I was perfectly happy with my dress.

So, a few days after I selected my wedding dress, the two sisters paid a visit to *Jean's Bridal Shop*. They lied to the clerk and told her I sent them to give their opinion of the dress. She let them see it and they promptly returned home to their family carrying the opinion that I had settled for this dress because its price tag was in my dad's budget. They thought I would have chosen a different dress if money wasn't a factor, and relayed this idea to their parents and James. Gina was elected to make the phone call to inform me of their family discussion.

The phone rang and Mom called out to me that it was Gina. I was so excited, thinking she was calling me to tell me she had selected a bridesmaid dress.

"Did you find a bridesmaid dress you want me to look at?"

"No, not yet. I wanted to talk to you about your dress."

"My dress?"

Gina confessed to me their episode of deception and the results of their family meeting. I was speechless and wasn't sure if I should be offended or thankful. I took a deep breath and respectfully turned down their offer.

My family and I had picked the dress out together, and I was not about to reject a family decision, besides the fact that I loved the dress. It was the spirit of the selection that mattered to me, nothing else. It was the last major decision my family and I would make together, and it was very important to me.

The message to the Hawkins family was loud and clear: don't mess with the Kelly family. After the aforementioned incident, the Hawkinses mostly stayed out of the wedding decisions except for groom responsibilities and decisions.

There was limited interaction between the two families, but there was the first formal introduction after our engagement. My parents invited the Hawkinses over for an evening visit and dessert to meet them and celebrate our engagement. My mother baked her chocolate Bundt cake and we all helped to tidy up the house. The doorbell rang and I answered the door and hugged James and his parents as they entered our home. I introduced them to my family. James pulled out two of our dining room chairs for us to sit in. We all sat looking at each other as if we were all enclosed in some sort of awkward zone of silence. Then, suddenly my brother Tommy came running from his bedroom into the living room asking about when he could eat cake. This interruption prompted some natural conversation between the two mothers about their children, linking their similarities.

The conversation between the two fathers also began, but it accentuated the differences between the two families.

"Our daughter has expressed to us that she and James would like to be married in our church, The United Methodist Church," my dad said.

"Yeah, they told us. We're fine with that choice. But, what 'bout the reception?" asked James Sr.

"Well, the social hall is right next to the church, and we thought we could have the reception there."

"Well, Frank, can we provide some beer and cocktails to make it a real celebration, if'n ya know what I mean."

"I'm afraid only non-alcoholic drinks are allowed on the church premises."

James Sr.'s face clearly showed his disappointment. "Okay, I guess we'll have ta figure out where we can have the real party. No offense, Frank."

"None taken."

Clearly, the two dads did not see eye to eye regarding the philosophy behind a wedding reception. My family saw it as a social event where the bride and groom are presented as husband and wife in a formal reception line, cutting of the wedding cake, and guests enjoying a piece of wedding cake and fruit punch. The Hawkins family saw a wedding reception as a time to celebrate, dance, get intoxicated and let loose. James and I were sandwiched between two completely different philosophical points of view.

The rest of the evening there was cake and talk between the mothers about bridal showers. When the Hawkinses left, Dad said, "They seem to be nice people, Laurie, but they do think a little different than we do. You may face some challenges with James regarding some issues in life."

"Oh, Dad, they're not that different. I'll be just fine."

After the introductory evening, our two families did not arrange to visit with one another until the evening of the rehearsal. The only exception was when both mothers attended the two bridal showers held in my honor.

The rehearsal was held in the church, with the minister, Reverend Ridgeer, in charge. He was a very compassionate and understanding man, and my family and I had become personal friends with him and his wife. James attended Sunday services with me several times and had the opportunity to meet Reverend Ridgeer, but no one else in his family had met him.

The rehearsal was scheduled for seven o'clock in the evening. At five minutes after seven, the Hawkins family came walking in abruptly and loud.

"Let's get this thing started!" James yelled out as he entered the sanctuary.

His family followed behind him.

"Hey, Frank. How the hell are ya?" James Sr. said as he approached my dad, extending his hand.

"I'm . . . good, thank you," replied my dad as he shook hands with James Sr. Dad then turned to Reverend Ridgeer and introduced the Hawkins family.

The sanctuary was an A-frame design with very high ceilings. You knew you were in the house of God, as the first thing you saw as you walked through the door was the enormous pastel-green cross raised high in the air. The altar was raised up above the light-beige pews which could seat up to five hundred worshippers. It was a humbling experience to enter this sanctuary, and it precipitated reverent behavior. This house of worship did not appear to affect the Hawkins family as it did my family. Not only did they make a loud entrance, they continued to be loud, except during prayer. Reverend Ridgeer kept clearing his throat, hoping they would get his message to be quieter. His white collar looked whiter than ever as his face became redder and redder. He was a small-built man, but when it came to his belief in God and his respect for his religion, he was ten feet tall. In all my experience with Reverend Ridgeer, I had never seen him move and talk so fast. Finally, he got through it, and I saw him take a deep breath as if to indicate to himself he had made it to the end with no disasters, when suddenly James ran up to the altar and sat on the sacred table. The minister, me and my whole family made an involuntary verbal sound of horror. James looked at me and then got down. Reverend Ridgeer sat down in one of the pews and looked like he was going to faint.

It was at that moment James Sr. announced the rehearsal dinner would be at their home. He invited Reverend Ridgeer, but he graciously declined. We all got in our cars and drove to their house. Our family was silent on the short drive there. We were all in shock.

The Hawkins house was a modest one, but very nicely decorated country-style and, as usual, spotless. My parents were impressed with the beautiful, completely fenced-in yard with the porch swing by the front door. As we entered, we saw that rectangle tables with chairs were set up in the living room and dining room with beautiful flowered yellow and orange tablecloths. Once everyone was seated, James's sisters and Millie, a neighbor, served us. The menu was fried pork chops, boiled potatoes, green beans, and dinner rolls. The food was very tasty, but my parents were horrified that the Hawkinses ate their pork chops with their hands instead of cutting them up. Also, later my mother would reveal to me, boiled potatoes are not something you serve at a formal dinner affair.

"Hey, Frank, that minister of yours doesn't seem to smile much. He looked a little tired when we left. I hope he'll be okay for the ceremony tomorrow," said James Sr.

"Yes, I think he was a little tired. He has a lot going on since Easter is next week. But he will be fine for tomorrow," said my dad.

"Frank, ya're from Pennsylvania, right?" James Sr. asked.

"Yes," said my dad.

"Did ya ever run across a ghost in one of the covered bridges back there?" James Sr. asked.

"Can't say that I did."

"Well, let me tell you my brother and I did on many occasions and every time we did, we pissed our pants. Right, Clem?"

"Yessiree! We sure did. Every single time," said Clem. Clem was visiting from Ohio to attend the wedding and was staying at his brother's home, so he was invited to eat with us that evening.

"Clem, tell them 'bout the time you saw a ghost in your house at night and it made ya run outside butt naked!" said James Sr.

"Well, I was sleeping like a baby, when all of a sudden somethin' tapped me on the head, I opened my eyes and there's a man floatin' in the air 'bove my bed. Well, howdy, I jumped right up outta that bed and ran outside. When I got outside, I realized I didn't have one damn stitch of clothes on!"

Everyone laughed, but I could tell my parents didn't approve of such a conversation at a rehearsal dinner. On the way home my suspicions became reality.

"I couldn't believe that two grown men were talking about ghosts! And on top of it, they were using foul language in front of women and children," my dad said.

"I'm sorry you're upset, Dad," I said.

"I'm not upset, just disappointed. I don't mean to criticize them, but I thought, well, it doesn't matter what I thought. My thoughts need to be on our family event tomorrow. Your wedding!" Dad said.

"I thought they were funny!" Tommy added. Everyone laughed.

As I walked into my home, I was overcome by anxiety about marrying James and leaving my family. My mom sensed my anxiety and said as she hugged me, "The wedding will be wonderful. It's normal to feel nervous and anxious. We love you and support you in all of your ventures in life." Her arms instilled such a sense of security and love.

The next morning was very busy, with visits to the beauty parlor for my sister, mother, and me. I woke up to a large pimple in the middle of my forehead, which my sister Amanda and I worked hard to cover up with makeup, giggling the whole time. Then, a short lunch and off to the church, arriving at about one o'clock to get dressed for the two o'clock wedding. As I was getting dressed in the church's first-grade Sunday school classroom, my dad allotted time for my two grandmothers to come in and privately wish me well. It was extremely emotional for my dad's mother because my grandfather had just died in December, and he had wanted me to finish college before getting married.

The last people to come in were my mother, father, brother,

and sister. Each of them hugged me and told me they loved me.

Amanda had helped me get dressed, but still said, "I can't believe what a beautiful bride you are!"

"Thanks Sis!" I replied.

An aura of love surrounded me. "I'm ready," I thought to myself.

James arrived at the church with his parents, sisters, and best man at approximately three minutes to two o'clock. I was getting a little nervous but managed to be emotionally strong.

My father knocked on the door. "He's here," he said.

"Well, it's about time."

"Sweetheart . . ." he said as he walked into the room.

"Yes, Dad. What's wrong?" I knew from his tone of voice something was wrong.

"Well, James Sr. is a little intoxicated. I can smell the whiskey on him."

"Has James been drinking too?"

"Not that I can tell," he answered.

"Good. Are they ready to start?" I asked.

"I believe so, sweetheart. He ran into the church just as I came to tell you he was here. No rush, honey. We are only about five minutes behind schedule."

"Okay, Dad. Let's walk over to the sanctuary."

"Oh, there's one more thing."

"What is it?"

"I wanted to let you know that the ushers asked me if they could sit some of the bridal guests on the groom's side of the sanctuary, because there was no room. I told them it was okay to do so because when I looked, only three rows of pews were filled on the groom's side. I hope you're okay with that approval."

"That's fine. I knew they didn't send out a lot of invitations compared to us, so it doesn't surprise me."

"Okay, let's get this party started!" We both giggled.

My dad and I stood in the breezeway between the sanctuary and the social hall waiting for my sister and mother to be seated and for the organist to start playing "Here Comes the Bride."

Dad whispered his thoughts of love and affection in my ear and then gave me a kiss on the cheek. The organist began to play the first several chords loud with a pounding motion so there was no mistake it was time to start walking. Our focus now was to move forward and for me not to trip on my dress. As we entered the sanctuary, I looked up and saw James smiling right at me. The beautiful, illuminated cross lit up his face. I was sure at that very moment this union was blessed by God.

As we repeated our vows and exchanged rings, happiness abounded. He truly loves me, I thought to myself. As Reverend Ridgeer introduced us as Mr. and Mrs. Hawkins for the first time, our faces beamed with excitement.

The wedding reception was held right next door to the church in the social hall. James and I walked out of the sanctuary, through the breezeway into the social hall, holding hands, with the members of the wedding party following close behind. The social director of the church lined us up in a receiving line and we waited for the guests to exit the sanctuary and enter the social hall. Our parents entered right after the wedding party and the social director motioned them to join the receiving line.

I could hear James Sr. say, "I'm not standing in that line. I didn't get married." He then proceeded to pull a small flask from his pocket, turned his back to the receiving line and when he turned back around it was no longer visible.

"James, please tell me he doesn't have alcohol in that flask," I whispered.

"Don't worry 'bout it."

After all the guests had greeted us in the receiving line,

we were ushered over to cut the wedding cake. We cut a piece together while my mom took a picture. Then we both grabbed forks to feed one another a bite as tradition called for.

"Smash it in her face!" yelled out Dan and James Sr. in unison.

My mom reacted immediately by saying, "Oh no! We don't need to do that." Just as she spoke, James smashed the cake in my face. Fortunately, only one piece stuck on my face, and everyone laughed. As soon as the Hawkins family was served cake, they quickly wolfed it down and announced their intent to leave the reception.

"Hey everybody, we're headed out to our house for the real party! All you are invited to come if'n you want to," James Sr. said. He then approached James and me, and said, "James, I do expect you to stop by our house before you head out on your honeymoon."

"Sure thing, Dad," James replied.

"Let's get this show on the road, honey. I want to get to my parents' house and then get rolling to The Coronado Del Mar Hotel!" James said as we viewed the table filled with wedding gifts.

"It was really generous of Fiona and Dan to give us such a special room for our honeymoon!" I said.

By seven in the evening, we were on the road after stopping at the Hawkins residence where we had a very loud and boisterous send-off, as most of the people there had been drinking heavily. Meanwhile, at my parents' home there was a small group of close family and friends who gathered there to unwind—without the help of alcohol. There was no obligation created for us to stop by there before our trip to San Diego, just a request from my mother to call to let her know we arrived safely to our destination.

Chapter 7:

The First Year and the Fight for Independence

It was dark when we arrived at the Hotel Del Coronado in San Diego. We both were very happy as we approached the front desk to check in to the hotel. James told the clerk we were on our honeymoon, and he was informed our reservation was for a standard room, not the honeymoon suite. Fiona had led us to believe otherwise.

We headed up to the hotel room with very different expectations as it turned out. He picked me up and carried me through the door and set me down on the bed and said, "I can't believe it. You're finally my wife."

He began kissing me when I said, "Wait! Please let me go to the bathroom and get ready for our first time. I want to look sexy for you."

"Okay, honey. But hurry up!" he said. As I entered the bathroom, I stared at myself in the big mirror above the marble sink and countertop, thinking about how I was finally going to go all the way for the very first time. The thought excited me. As

I exited the bathroom, James was lying on the bed naked with his body up against the beautiful white bedspread swirling with red roses. I sat next to him, and he said, "You look so beautiful, honey." He kissed me as he pulled my scarlet nightgown over my head and pulled down the matching panties. He rolled on top of me and slid his penis into me.

"Ouch!" I yelled out.

"Sorry, hon, but I've gotta push it in," he said as he thrust over and over until finally it popped into me. I didn't realize it was going to be so painful, but I just bit my lip and let him continue. As soon as he ejaculated, he rolled off me and lay beside me.

"Are we done?"

"Yeah."

"I thought there was a whole lot more. That's what you said. And I didn't know it was going to hurt so bad," I said as I grabbed my panties.

He rose up and looked at me. The light in the hotel room was on, so I could see his face quite clearly. He looked like a child who had been caught telling a lie but didn't want to admit it. Without saying a word, he got out of bed and went into the bathroom and closed the door. I put my nightgown on and sat on the bed for a few minutes.

When he didn't come out, I got up and knocked on the door and said, "Are you okay?"

"I'm fine. Go away."

I lay back down in the bed dozing off and on for about an hour. He was still in the bathroom. Finally, I got up and knocked on the door again, "James, honey. I really need to use the bathroom."

About ten minutes passed when he opened the door and came out. As he exited, I entered and neither of us looked at one another. When I came out of the bathroom, he was in bed, underneath the covers. The light was off, and he appeared to be sleeping. I lay down quietly asking myself, "Is this really how the wedding night is supposed to be? Will our sex life get better?"

The next morning, he seemed to be back to normal. He acted as if nothing had happened, but he was not affectionate toward me at all. There weren't even any kisses. At breakfast I decided I wanted to talk about it. "Honey, I didn't mean to upset you last night. I'm so sorry," I said.

"I don't want to talk 'bout it. All I can say is ya hurt my feelings really bad."

"I'm so sorry."

The rest of the day went okay, except for our affection toward one another. We did hold hands but there was nothing else. We shopped in Tijuana and walked on the beach. When evening came, I got nervous. I hoped this night was going to be more like a real honeymoon. This time we both jumped on the bed in our clothes and started kissing. "Oh honey, I love you so much!" I yelled out.

We both seemed to be more relaxed as we helped each other get undressed. This experience was much less painful and more exciting than the night before. With each thrust I called out, "Oh sweetheart! This is great!" Each time I repeated this phrase the more passionate he became.

"Honey, I love ya so, so much!" he repeated over and over. This time when we finished, he held onto me and kissed me until we both fell asleep.

After the honeymoon, we returned to his parents' house, packed up our belongings and set out for his new duty post at Williams Airfield, Chandler, Arizona. Prior to our wedding, his parents had purchased a twenty-nine-foot travel trailer on credit, so we had a place to live. James had made it very clear he didn't want to live in an apartment, so his parents offered the trailer as a solution. It was our responsibility to pay the payment for the trailer and pay the mobile home park space rent. We found a mobile home park right on Williams Field Road, only about five miles from the base. For the first couple of months we lived there, I stayed home. I tried to follow the pattern set by my parents. While he was at work, I went grocery shopping, cleaned, and cooked. James expected everything to be perfect. He developed a controlling ritual he followed every day as he arrived home from work. As he entered our trailer home, he would kiss me and then proceed to wipe his fingers in places to see if I had missed spots when cleaning.

"Ah, here is some dirt ya missed," was his standard phrase.

"I'm sorry, honey. I didn't see it," was my standard reply.

Our conversation would end with him saying, "Ya need to get better at this. I shouldn't be able to find any dirt at all. What am I going to do with you, honey?" At this time in our marriage, we both laughed at these statements.

In June, my parents and two siblings stopped at our trailer for one night on their way traveling across the United States in their camper van. My sister, Amanda, who was three years younger than I, stayed the night inside our trailer on the couch. After I fell asleep, James approached her and tried to kiss her. She fought back and started to make noise, so he stopped. In the morning, Amanda approached me and said, "Laurie, James bothered me last night."

"What do you mean, he bothered you?" I asked.

"He tried to kiss me on the lips while I was sleeping," she said.

My heart stopped for a moment. I couldn't believe what I was hearing. I believed my sister but wanted James to explain what happened. "I'm so sorry, Amanda. I will talk to him. Please don't tell Mom and Dad. I'll handle it," I said.

"Okay Sis, I won't say anything."

My parents came in a few minutes later and we all had breakfast together before they left. As soon as they drove off, I turned to James and said, "Amanda says you tried to kiss her?"

"Oh, she told ya."

"Yes, she told me. She was really upset. What happened?"

"Well, ya know I had a couple of beers last night. Right?"

"Ye-es."

"Well, I must've been a little drunk because I remember nothin'. I'm so sorry, hon. It won't happen again."

"Well, okay. I guess it could've been the alcohol. But I'm not going to tell my parents. Amanda agreed not to either."

"Good. I think it's better that way," he said as he kissed me.

After approximately four months of living the traditional married life, we both grew tired of having no money, so I convinced James I should get a job. We only had one vehicle, so it needed to be close to our home. It took me no time to find employment as a waitress at a café only about a mile away. I had a bicycle, so I put on jeans underneath my waitress dress uniform and rode to work.

I worked the early shift at the Western Café so I would be off work and home by the time James came home when he worked the day shift. When he worked the graveyard shift, I was gone while he slept.

This café was owned by a couple, but was run by the German-born wife, Helga. She had a very thick German accent, and I had to listen to her very carefully to understand what she was saying. Helga was approximately five feet, eight inches tall, with dark short straight hair and olive-colored skin. In addition, she had a severe limp on her left side. Her size was intimidating to me since I was only five feet, three inches tall and weighed ninety-seven pounds soaking wet. When I think back, I realize she would have been old enough to have been a child during World War II. She often gave small clues regarding this fact when we talked.

One day when she was eating a Hershey chocolate bar she said, "I love these so much. When I was a little girl, we could not get any of these. One time a soldier came to our town and gave us Hershey chocolate bars. It made me so happy. Now, uh, I can buy all the chocolate bars I want, and I'm so happy to eat them."

She also indicated she had a tough life before marrying an American and coming to America. She was very proud to own her own business and was very serious-minded about it. I found her to be strict but fair. She took a chance hiring a young woman who had never been employed before, and I was proud to have my first job. I was given one free meal a day at the end of my shift, but early in the morning, the cook, whose name was Rags, made me breakfast and told me not to tell the owner. So I didn't.

Rags was an older man who was an alcoholic and drank in front of me when no one else was in the place early in the morning, which was our alone time to share stories. It was a time where I could be myself with no worries about upsetting James with my words. The name Rags suited him as he looked like life had reduced him to rags. He had chin-length gray hair he slicked back and a rugged, sad face with a scrub-brush gray mustache. When it was just he and I, our conversations were often filled with stories about his life.

"You know, sweet girl; I been married three times and none of them have worked out for me. All of them were so nice at first, but not long after we got married, they all changed. It was like a spell came over 'em. I hope that don't happen with you and your husband," he said.

He went on to say, "Now, I did drink a little of the whiskey sauce, and I might 'a got just a bit nasty at times, but I don't see why you'd leave a man and take all his money. My first wife, Betty, now she might 'a had a reason as I kinda got in a little trouble with the law. I needed some money to buy my whiskey and Betty, she wouldn't give me back any of the money I gave her for rent. So I was at my friend's house and asked him to play a little poker. I have to say I did cheat him out of quite a bit of cash, and I might have stolen his car keys so I could drive down to the store to buy my whiskey. And dammit his car went too fast and crashed."

Rags shot me a look with a huge grin on his face, which was a reaction to the look on my face while he was telling me this story.

"Wow, Rags. I bet your wife was pretty mad."

"Yeah. For sure when I was arrested and then sent to prison for the first time. Hey, kid, you know while I was in prison is when Betty divorced me," he said as he took a swig of whiskey from his flask he hid underneath the sink. He didn't explicitly tell me why he went to prison the second time, but I know it had something to do with his last wife, maybe domestic violence. He referred to her as a religious nut who poisoned the mind of their son.

At the Western Café, I also befriended a regular customer. He was an older man named Carl. Carl was a short, round, and balding man who wore a brown suit he bought at the local thrift store. He changed his shirt every day, but he only owned the one suit and one light-blue tie. He came into the restaurant every morning and we bonded, as not too many people spoke to him for any amount of time for several reasons, one of them being that his suit was rarely sent to the dry cleaners. The second reason was that he had a severe speech impediment, and it took a lot of concentration to understand him. He lived alone in a one-room apartment and came to the café for companionship. He always had black composition books with him and was constantly writing in them when he wasn't talking. He often asked me to read his manuscript, which was mostly unreadable, and asked me to help him by editing it. I tried my best, but his scribbles were hard to understand. However, the conversations he and I had about writing were priceless. "I have stories to tell. In my brain. They are right there, and I write them down. They are about a man who loves life even though every man talks mean to him. I write much better than I talk. You are sweet to help me," he said on one occasion. Carl fed my need to be needed.

It didn't take long for James to begin to complain that this job was interfering with my wifely duties. "Suspicious Minds" by Elvis Presley played as I walked through the trailer door each day if James was home. I noticed, as time went on, the song would be played louder and louder each time. I made it a habit of handing him the cash I received in tips each time which usually totaled twelve dollars. He would take the money, smile, and turn down the music. I eventually became tired of his disapproval and resigned.

The job as a waitress was my official first job and it gave me the confidence I needed to reenroll into college. I enrolled at Mesa Community College and began taking pre-nursing courses. Attending these courses was also a respite from my life with James. He was almost always at home in the evening when I attended college. I believe he allowed me to attend because the result was for me to acquire more lucrative employment. Evidently, money was the key to gaining some independence.

However, this independence came with a price. I, for whatever reason, ignored the idea our marriage was in real trouble when James began his pursuit of couples willing to participate in swapping. His reason for starting this escapade? I am not sure if it was because I was becoming more independent and he wanted to have some dirt on me, or if it was part of his sociopathic behavior to push the rules to the limit.

He found a couple who lived on the base and planned to swap partners. I, the naive nineteen-year-old I was, had no idea this was a plan. A couple of weeks before the first encounter, James's attitude toward me spiraled down.

He came home from work one day during this time period and said as he walked through the door, "What the hell have you done all day today? Look at this place! It is a mess! You are such a lazy, stupid bitch! No man in his right mind would want you to be his wife. Look at you! Your hair is messy, and you are way too skinny."

The comments about the cleanliness of the place were not unusual, but comments about my appearance were new. He also began to frequently tell me no other man would possibly be interested in me sexually and avoided having sex with me. Therefore, by the time that we accepted a dinner invitation at the Dabble household, I had been primed for attention from another man.

Don and Denise Dabble had been married for seven years and had two children. Don was a short, stout man with dark hair, rosy cheeks, and a gentle voice. Denise was taller than Don, with a strong build, dark hair, and a worn, manly face.

"Please come on into our humble abode," said Don. His friendly smile made me feel welcome. As we sat around their dining room table, Don told us their story.

"Denise and I are first cousins, so we have known each other our whole lives," he said.

"You're legally allowed to get married?" I asked.

"Yeah, we got hitched in Georgia. It's legal there. Denise had already given birth to Amy Jean. She was kinda free giving of herself . . . if you know what I mean, and wasn't sure who the daddy was."

Denise tapped Don's arm and said, "Don!"

"Well, it's true, honey."

"Yeah . . . but you could've left that part out," she said.

Don continued, "I was in the Air Force and my Aunt Charlotte came to see me. She asked me if Denise and Amy could shack up with me since I was workin'. Aunt Charlotte was barely gettin' by at the time and her house was really small. I was lucky and had found me a three-bedroom house to rent for really cheap. One thing led to another, and I asked her to marry me, and then we found out we were pregnant with Cindy."

"That's an interesting story, Don," I said.

"Yeah, a lot of people think it's weird we're first cousins and got married," he said.

"If you love each other, that is all that matters," I said.

"Yes, we know we both love each other and will never get divorced. That's why I tell Denise if she gets the urge to screw another man, she should just do it," he said.

I wasn't sure how to reply to this statement, so I just giggled.

After dinner, I helped Denise do the dishes, while Don and James put the two children to bed. Don served us all his special rum punch and kept refilling my drink every time I drank about half of the glass. We started playing poker, and after two or three games, we all moved to the living room and talked. It wasn't long until I noticed Denise and James disappeared, but I was too intoxicated to care. Don and I sat alone in the living room, talking.

"You're so cute! I haven't been with a woman your age for a long time. You are so adorable!" Don said.

I was so flattered, and my response again was just to giggle. Don was approximately twenty-eight years old, and this wasn't his first rodeo, so to speak. He wasted no time in his push to the bedroom, including filling my glass with alcohol every time it was emptied. This behavior, combined with the last few weeks of degrading talk and inattention by my husband led to me allowing Don to seduce me. All along the way Don reassured me that James and he had prearranged this encounter, and that he was cool with him and me hooking up. I let my guard down and in fact due to my young age of nineteen, I believe a part of me was rebelling against my domineering spouse.

The next morning, the conversation on the drive home was strange.

"Wasn't it a great night! Don is such a great guy! Don't ya think?" James said in a happy tone of voice. He didn't appear to harbor any feelings of remorse, concern or jealousy at all.

"Yeah, it was a fun night," I said.

"I was surprised he was able to persuade you so easily. I thought you would need more convincing, but Don is quite the charmer when it comes to women."

"Yeah, I guess."

"I think Denise is a little older than I like, but I did enjoy being with her." At the time, I had no idea what this statement indicated. I would find out in later years what this statement really meant.

Our encounters with the Dabbles continued for about six months. At this juncture, they began to seek out another couple. Our relationship was becoming strained. He appeared to be growing jealous.

"You appear to be having more fun with this situation than I am," he said one day after we spent time with the Dabbles.

As the months went on, we saw them less and less, as we traveled home to Fontana more often. During one of the visits, I decided I would like to take my Siamese cat home with me. My family had kept him and loved him, but they understood he was my cat. Fiona had given him to me as a gift shortly after my engagement with James. But I quickly discovered this decision was not in the best interest of the cat or me.

From the moment we arrived back in Arizona, James seemed to be angry at the poor cat. The more he became angered, the more Simba seemed to do things James didn't like. Finally, I was so worried about the safety of my cat, I decided to ask my mother if she would like to have him. I told her our trailer was just too small to have a pet and we could bring him with us on our next visit. She agreed.

I put Simba in the back of the car on the floor. As we began to drive, Simba got wild and clearly did not like being in a car. We stopped several times as he was making a very loud Siamese cat cry and trying to jump on our heads. James resorted to restraining Simba by tying his leash to the door handle. The poor cat still howled, and James stopped the car several times just to hit him. Every time he did this, I screamed, "No! Please stop!" At one point he hit him with a wrench on the foot and it cut him. Blood was everywhere.

"Please, James, let me sit in the back seat so I can keep him quiet and calm until we get to my parents' house," I pleaded.

"Okay, I guess," he said.

I believe James agreed only because he didn't want to be bothered anymore, not because he felt bad for the cat. We finally arrived at my parents' home, and I delivered the cat to my mom, explained the cut as an accident, not revealing James's cruel behavior. Needless to say, I never owned another cat during the rest of our marriage, and I refrained from telling my parents any of these stories for several reasons, one of them being my young adult stubbornness to admit I had made such a drastic, horrible mistake.

I do believe in karma. Was it merely a coincidence this breed of cat's origin is from Thailand? Did this fact play a part in where the Air Force sent James next for his overseas assignment? The memory of his expression of hate directed at Simba would surface a year later when he was stationed in Thailand and writing to tell me how much he hated being there.

The human spirit is something often no one can explain, and which defies all logic. How I survived the first year is a matter of spirit and survival. One would usually believe the first year was the best for a couple and, compared to the other twelve years, it may have been the best year in this marriage.

Chapter 8:

My Husband, My Master:
How Did This Happen?

"**Y**ou're my wife, and you'll do as I tell ya," James began to say just a few weeks after we were married.

In my mind, once you were married, you stayed married. There were very few divorces in my family, so when I married James, I tried to follow the model set for me. I was only eighteen and didn't have any experience with someone suffering from mental illness. My subservient behavior fed his warped perception of what a relationship between a man and a woman should be. His ideas ran along the lines of him being the master, and I the servant. My parents had modeled that the man was the head of the household, so I conformed and resigned myself to the fact that I should always do what my husband told me to do.

My strong desire to help others was detoured by a mentally ill individual who capitalized on this weakness of mine. I unintentionally supported his poor mental health. I constantly sought his approval for everything I did, and it got to the point where my own identity began to blur. The only piece of me remaining was my desire to do something useful for others beyond my family.

My family became concerned when they witnessed the change in my behavior. James, at times, exhibited his power over me in front of them. However, when I was around them without James, my behavior went back to normal, for the most part.

"Mom, we need to leave the store and get back," I said one day while my parents were visiting, and we were out shopping together.

"I'm almost done, sweetheart. I'm sure James won't mind if you get home a little later," Mom said.

"I don't like to be late making dinner. He's always hungry when he gets home from work," I said nervously.

In the back of my mind, I was fearful of breaking any of the rules he had set forth. The rule in force on this day was: I was allowed to do any activity I wanted to if I was home by the time he arrived. The few times I didn't make it home on time led to threatening language and, later in the marriage, resulted in abusive physical contact.

When James was at work, I had a feeling of freedom, but that feeling would disappear the closer the time came to his arrival home.

As the marriage went forward, some of the tight restrictions imposed by James were lifted when I returned to taking college classes. He became tolerant of me being gone when he was home, as the ultimate goal was for me to make more money by getting a better job, paying higher wages. However, there was often a price to pay for any freedoms I was afforded.

"Woman!" James yelled from our bedroom as I walked through our front door from a long day of work and night classes at college.

"Yes, James, I'm here. What do you want?"

"I pulled out all of the crap you had in the cupboards. When I wake up in the morning, I want to see them all clean and neat."

"Ugh, but James, I'm really tired, and I won't have time in the morning to do it."

"Well, I guess you'll have to do it tonight. Just don't you be noisy. I'm tryin' to sleep."

"All right."

His tone of voice relayed the message I would suffer retaliation if I didn't complete the task assigned. I was willing to do whatever it was to keep him pleased with me.

I did have a passive aggressive side to me and used this skill whenever it was possible. If class got out early, I utilized the time to work on homework in the library or have a drink with a girlfriend. I never lied to James, but just didn't disclose the fact class got out early.

I believe it was through these types of activities I found a way to keep my identity from disappearing completely. I even took an elective course at college titled *Self-Awareness*. This course gave me a little insight into codependency and gave me some strategies that assisted me in coping with my dominant husband. But obviously, nothing totally solved the problem until I left him and began a new life for myself.

I was determined to make him believe he was totally dominant over me, as a strategy for survival. Later, when I was separated from James and was seeing a psychologist, he helped me understand that my determination to fool James and acquire a college degree were all a part of my subconscious plan to prepare myself for some daybreak away from him and the hold he had on me. This preparation enabled me to break away both physically and emotionally and not succumb to my codependency.

Wikipedia explains codependency:

Laurie D. Finucane

In sociology, codependency is a theory that attempts to explain imbalanced relationships where one person enables another person's self-destructive tendencies (such as addiction, poor mental health , immaturity, irresponsibility, or under-achievement) and /or undermines the other person's relationship. (1) Definitions of codependency vary, but typically include high self-sacrifice, a focus on ones's own emotions, and attempts to control or fix other people's problems.(2)

Chapter 9:

Year 2:
The State of Emotional Crisis

"Let's move! Push her into the delivery room, kid. I'll get the doc," said Sully.

Sully was the short, stout, white-haired head nurse on the labor and delivery floor of the Desert Samaritan Hospital in Mesa, Arizona. This was where I was able to acquire employment as a unit aide. Sully, whose real name was Margaret O'Sullivan, had served in the Korean War in the combat zone. She was gruff, but she took a liking to me and taught me many things about the job and life. She made me feel smart and competent, pushing me back on track with my career goals. I followed her around every night I worked, listening to MASH unit war stories.

"You know, Laurie, the docs during wartime were focused on saving soldiers' lives in those tents in the field. When I assisted a surgeon, they would call out for one instrument and throw the bloody one away into the air. I got hit with them a few times. But believe me, it was all worth it to see some of those young soldiers recover. Of course, some of them didn't. I saw a lot of death, and that is why I am here in Labor and Delivery. I love to witness new life."

This is how the second year of marriage began. James remained stationed at Williams Airfield, and I continued to attend Mesa Community College. It was through the college I was able to find the job at the hospital. It was a new, modern hospital, and I was assigned to the graveyard shift and loved it! When I was working, all my worries regarding James disappeared. Sully was eager and willing to teach me about life.

"Get ready, young lady. In three nights, we will have a full moon. You haven't worked on a night like that yet," she warned.

"Why, Sully? What will happen?" I asked.

"Well, some of the mommas-to-be will be affected and go into labor before they normally would. So we might see a spike in deliveries on a full moon night."

"Thanks for the warning, Sully."

"I just want to make sure you're ready. You never know what you might have to do if we have multiple deliveries in a short time. Just remember everything I have taught you and you will be fine. I've total confidence in you, girl," she said as she pinned up her long white hair into her scrub cap.

Sure enough, when the night arrived, there was an onslaught of women in labor. All our labor rooms were filled by the beginning of the shift and stayed that way throughout the whole night. At one point, all the staff were busy with the deliveries. Sully left me alone with all the women in labor and gave me explicit instructions and reminders of how to handle it.

She told me, "You got this!" I took a deep breath and proceeded to set up the only empty delivery room all by myself. Next, I went to check on the three women in labor. As I entered the first room, the patient, who was pregnant with baby number six, looked at me and said, "Missy, this baby is coming!"

I immediately ran to alert the doctor assigned to that delivery and found him fast asleep in an office. I had moved the patient into the delivery room and had her all set up. All we needed was the doctor.

From my observations of Sully, I knew exactly what to do. I positioned the patient in the stirrups and draped her appropriately. I could see the baby's head crowning. The patient pushed once and out came the infant into my arms. It was a little boy! I stood there holding this brand-new beautiful little boy when the doctor came running in. He took the infant from my arms and cut the umbilical cord. I assisted him just like a nurse would have and he commended me.

When Sully finally came back to the labor room area, she heard what I had done and patted me on the back and stated, "That a girl! I knew you could do it."

As a result of this job, my confidence grew, but with a price. James began to disappear on his nights off. "Sorry, sweetheart, I didn't know I was going to be gone all night. I was driving around and got lost," he said on one of the nights he didn't come home.

Other times his excuses were just as ridiculous. "Honey, my car broke down and it took all night to fix it," or "Honey, Fred and I were playing cards, and I lost track of time."

He was also working the graveyard shift at this time and our nights off didn't always correspond, so I just brushed these occasions off as not important.

I often spouted off to friends, saying the phrase "I trust him." I cannot explain now why I was okay with this, but I can only guess I just didn't want to fight with him. When we did fight, I was the one who received "the raw end of the stick," so to speak.

Another plus to having the job at Good Samaritan Hospital was I also became personal friends with the LVN I worked with named Alice. Alice was a single mom of two teenage daughters and took me under her wing. While stationed at Williams Airfield, James was given several TDYs, or temporary duty assignments, which took him away for one to two weeks at a time to work temporarily at another base. Several times Alice and I would have the same nights off while James was absent on his TDY assignments, and she invited me over to spend the night with her and her daughters. Alice had experienced a lot of hardships in her life but had managed to get her nursing license and provide for her daughters. She ran a tight but loving ship. Alice was short and a little overweight, but by no means unattractive. Whatever experiences she had with men didn't seem to have been good as she would often state that dating wasn't something she had any desire to do at that time in her life. I felt accepted and safe in their home as there were no males at all. I didn't talk a lot about my troubles with James, but somehow, I believe she sensed my emotional struggle. The two or three times the four of us spent together made me forget the oppression I felt when I was with James. One of the nights we decided to attend a drive-in movie. Alice, her oldest daughter, and I drank wine coolers and sat on the hood of her car to watch the movie. I felt young and free just as a twenty-year-old should feel.

During this second year, my emotions were in a state of chaos regarding James. My thoughts were constantly focused on how I could please him. I would cook his favorite meals, dress in clothes he liked to see me in, and say things to him he liked to hear, like "You're a wonderful husband, and I'm so happy we got married." Sometimes these tactics worked, and sometimes they didn't. He would lash out by destroying items or throwing things at me with extreme force. At this point in the marriage, he had not struck me, but often threatened bodily harm.

One example of his inconsistent behavior was the

incident I termed as the "cornbread incident." I knew James loved homemade cornbread, so I made it often for him. On one occasion when we were having dinner together, I made cornbread. I made it the same way each time, with no change in the ingredients or time I baked it. He sat at our tiny table in the trailer we lived in, eagerly serving himself a large helping of the stew I had prepared. Last, he cut a piece of cornbread and took a bite. Immediately, he spat it out all over his plate, picked up the entire pan and threw it against the wall.

Then, he looked at me angrily and shouted, "You didn't put any salt in this shitty cornbread!"

Next, he got up from the table, knocking all the food off onto the floor, and stormed out of the trailer, got in his car, and drove off. He didn't return for hours. Of course, I blamed myself for the incident and when he returned later, I apologized.

"Honey, I'm so sorry about the cornbread. I'll make sure it has salt next time," I said.

"It's okay, sweetie, I forgive you. But if it hadn't had tasted bad, I wouldn't have reacted that way. Sorry," he said.

I often wondered what James told the men he worked with about me. Later, I would realize his conversations with some of them, and one man specifically, might have spawned behavior precarious for me.

On one night when James was working and I was off from work, a visitor showed up. It was one of the airmen that he worked with at the airfield. I had met him once, and knew him by his first name, David. He was a good-looking young man— tall, dark, and handsome. He was dressed in nice civilian clothes as if he was going out on a date.

If ever I believed in guardian angels, this was one of those times. A voice inside me said, "Do not open the door." He knocked; I opened the window next to the door of the trailer.

"David?"

"Yes."

"How can I help you?"

"Let me in."

"Why are you here?"

"I am here to see you."

"Why?"

"You know why."

"Honestly, I don't."

"Just let me in and I will show you."

"It's late and I am tired. Please come back another time when my husband is here."

It was at this point that the encounter took a dark turn.

"Your husband knows I'm here."

"You're lying!"

Next, David banged hard on the door and shouted, "Let me in!"

His voice echoed throughout the darkness. I was praying someone would hear him and call the police. I knew our closest neighbors were gone on vacation. I had no phone. All I could think to do was to turn off the lights and sit in the middle of the trailer hoping that there was no way he could get in. I sat alone and afraid of what would happen if he was able to break in. My ears were focused on listening to his movements. I could hear footsteps. Three or four in a row and then a pause. During the pause I heard a different noise. My mind put these sounds together and concluded he was pulling off a screen and pushing on the window to see if he could pry it open. I sat there, frightened, listening for any sound indicating he had invaded my small abode. I kept listening intently. The footsteps continued with sounds of deep breathing and sighs. Finally, the steps sounded like they were going away from the trailer. Then, a car engine sound.

"Has he given up?" I thought to myself. Then, the sound of a car pulling away. The sound became quieter and quieter. I pulled the blind back to make sure he was gone and took a deep breath of relief. I went to bed but didn't sleep. My mind kept active with questions. Did James know David was coming to visit me? If so, then why wouldn't he warn me or stop David? Why did David think James knew? Did they have conversations about me?

When James arrived home in the morning, I ran out to his car crying, "James! David came over last night and demanded I let him in. I didn't let him in, so he tried to break in! I was so scared!" I said.

He got out of his car and embraced me. "Oh, honey, I'm so sorry. Are ya okay?" he asked.

"Yes. I'm fine. He didn't get in. He said you knew he was coming," I said as we walked into our trailer.

He had his arm around me. "Laurie, I knew nothin' 'bout him comin' over here last night," he said.

"Well, I was pretty sure you didn't. I knew he was lying," I said.

He kissed me and said," You need to calm down. I'm sure it'll never happen again."

"I hope not! Are ya going to talk to him?"

"Sure. Don't worry, honey."

David never returned during the remainder of the time we lived in Arizona. At the time, I was convinced James had nothing to do with the incident, but I remained uneasy for quite a while.

Shortly thereafter, I became good friends with a woman named Claudia, who I met at college, whose husband was the sheriff on the nearby Indian reservation. James was never interested in socializing with Claudia and her husband, but he didn't stop me from developing a relationship with them. They became my supporters and my connection to normalcy. Claudia and Walt Otto were older than me by about fifteen years and treated me like I was their little sister. When James was working, they invited me over for dinner and company. They had one child—a boy who was nine years old at the time. I found solace in having this couple as an emotional anchor. I never revealed any of the abnormal behavior of James and me. I had a place where I could feel and act normal in Arizona.

James and I acquired other friends together who were not what I would classify as normal. Beyond our friendship with the Dabbles, there was a group of friends that we would "party" with a couple of weekends a month. All the people in this group were in the Air Force or dating or married to someone in the Air Force stationed at Williams Airfield. In Arizona, in 1972–73, the drinking age was nineteen. I was legally able to drink alcohol and so was everyone in our group. We would camp in tents at the river and drink all weekend. Some of the people also smoked marijuana, including James. However, I abstained as the smoke caused me to cough violently.

James would frequently flirt with any of the single women who would attend these parties. I, on the other hand, would sit around and visit with anyone who was willing to engage in conversation. There was one man with whom I would talk during these parties. His name was Ski. Ski was his nickname as he had a long Polish name that was hard to pronounce. Ski and I could talk about anything. He didn't ever have a date, or a girlfriend, so he was available to talk to when James and I attended these parties. The last party we attended, James took off on his motorcycle with a woman who wandered into our encampment, and didn't return for a few hours. I was extremely distraught over his disappearance and expressed my feelings while sitting by the campfire with Ski.

"Ski, where did that woman come from? Who is she?" I asked.

"I've never seen her before, Laurie. She's not part of our group," he said.

He was leaning forward toward the campfire with his hands on his face and his elbows resting on his knees. His face was pitted with acne scars, but the campfire light seemed to hide their existence.

"Let me go ask some of our friends if they know who she is or where she came from. Just sit here and try not to think about it. I am sure he will be back soon," Ski said. He was only gone for a few minutes. "I'm afraid I have some news you aren't going to like," Ski said when he returned.

"What?" I asked.

"Some of the guys are saying that James invited the woman to meet him here," Ski said.

"Oh, that's just what I wanted to hear," I said.

I was shivering, so Ski took off the brown plaid shirt he was wearing over a white t-shirt and placed it on my shoulders.

"I don't understand why you stay with him, Laurie. He shouldn't have invited that woman here," Ski said. His stature was small, but his heart was big. He grabbed my hand and patted it.

"It's partly my fault, Ski."

"What in the world . . .?"

"We have swapped with Don and Denise. And . . . I sort of agreed we could have an open marriage," I confessed.

"Oh, my lord! Really? Everyone knows about Don and Denise. I can't believe you fell into their trap. And let me guess. It was James's idea to have an open marriage. Right?"

"Well, we never really talked about it."

"But we all know he does what he wants. Right?"

"Ye-es. But we really do love each other."

"Sure, sweetie. You keep telling yourself that. Just know I'm on your side, no matter what. I wish I could do more for you."

"Just sitting with me and talking helps me a lot."

When James returned, Ski took James aside and spoke to him. I am not sure exactly what Ski said to James, but I am sure it was in defense of me. While they chatted, I confronted the strange woman.

"I want you to leave! How dare you crash our party and fool around with my husband! You whore!" I yelled.

Surprisingly, she didn't yell back. Her young painted face and shoulder-length red hair almost glowed in the campfire light as she stared at me with a look of confusion. She shrugged her shoulders and turned away from me. I watched her tight corduroy pants and the back of her flowing white silky blouse fade away into the pitch-black darkness. She left as quickly as she came. I do believe James invited her and she had no idea his wife was present. James and I passed out in our tent that night and left the next morning early. We had a brief discussion about the events of the night before.

"Ya know I was upset about that woman you were with last night. Who was she?" I asked.

"No one important. Just forget about her. I heard all about your feelings from Ski. He needs to mind his own business," James replied.

"He was just being kind to me when I needed it."

"There's a rumor I'll be gettin' orders to a different base soon. So good riddance to this place."

I sat silent the rest of the way home. This was the last river party we attended. In fact, I never saw Ski again after that night.

Chapter 10:

1973–74
War at Home and Overseas

"Honey, I got new orders today," James said as he got out of his car.

"What? Where are we going next?" I asked.

"I'm goin' overseas to Thailand."

"Can I go with you?"

"No, silly. We're at war still. They won't let ya go."

"Oh, no! How long will you be gone?"

"It's a one-year tour startin' this November."

We went into our trailer and just sat for a few minutes. I think both of us were in shock. We always knew it was a possibility, but we were hoping the war would end before he had to go. He was an airplane mechanic, so he was to be stationed at Udorn Air Force Base. Udorn was one of the frontline air bases in the Vietnam War. His orders were for twelve months, starting in November 1973 to November 1974. Even though the war was winding down, I was horrified at the idea, because American casualties were still occurring. Both of us feared this assignment, but we had no choice. Our country was at war, and everyone needed to sacrifice.

I had considered the idea of staying in Arizona while James was overseas, but my family convinced me to move back home. James and his family moved our small trailer back to California. We found a trailer park close to his parents and mine.

On the day he left, I had very mixed emotions. We had been separated before, but not for an entire year. Questions filled my mind. Will he treat me better after having been gone for a year? Or will he treat me worse after a year in a war zone? I had heard stories about soldiers who had been traumatized by an experience they had during a war. Many of them came back and abused their wives. What about the ones who were already abusing their wives? Did they get worse?

We walked with our arms around one another with tears coming down our faces as we approached his departure gate at LAX. When we got to the gate, Anna grabbed James and hugged him. Her woeful sobbing was muffled by his uniform jacket.

"Well, I gotta go now. They're boardin' my flight. I love you so much, honey! I'll write ya every day," he said as he kissed me goodbye.

Anna, James Sr., and I watched him walk through the gate until he was out of sight. We waited a few minutes until we saw the plane taxi out onto the runway.

"We gotta go now," said Anna.

"Can't we wait and see his plane take off?" I asked.

"No. It's bad luck to watch it disappear into the sky," said Anna as she ushered me away.

Once James had been at Udorn for a couple of months, he began a campaign to the Air Force chaplain at his base to try to be sent home on a hardship request. In his mind, his family needed him to be home and that was reason enough for him to be sent home. The paperwork needed for such a request was extensive, and his mom or I would have to have been terminally ill or totally without any means of support. Neither was the case. Neither his mom nor I were willing to lie to the United States federal government. To keep James calm, we treated the situation with kid gloves.

~

Quote from a letter dated 4 Dec. '73:

> *I am not too bad today, but I am really depressed a lot. I want to come home to you so very bad! . . . honey have you thought of away or found a way to get me home to you? I want out of here honey so bad that I can't see straight. I hate it over here! I hate this damn hell hole! I want to come home to you! Honey have you got our wedding pictures yet? I hope so! I Love you my darling! I sure hope that my mom has got that paperwork almost done! I've got to get out of this place! Honey, I am sure that you will like the suits I bought.*

In retrospect, I definitely see a quick change in mood while he wrote the letters. He went from sad to happy in two sentences. I believe one of the reasons he was so unhappy was the Air Force was controlling his life and he had no one there to control.

After he left, I enrolled at Chaffey College to continue classes required to be admitted to the nursing program, and applied for a nursing attendant position at San Bernardino County Hospital. I kept myself very busy on purpose to take my mind off him and the stress he imposed on me through his letters.

He wrote letters incessantly and expected the same amount in return from me. Unfortunately, I was not as fixated on his absence from my life the way he was about my absence from his. Besides trying to get his tour of duty shortened, he was also trying to make arrangements for me to visit him when he went TDY to Clark Air Base in the Philippines. He tried to arrange for me to travel there to meet him; however, he found it to be an impossible task at a time of war.

~

Quote from letter dated 16 Jan. '74:

> *Oh Laurie, honey, why am I so depressed? I should be very, very glad to leave here [Thailand]. I am glad but I'm depressed so much. Maybe it's 'cause I am worried that the AF will screw me over and not let you come to me in the P.I. or send me back home! I am so very worried.*

He was totally lost not being able to know exactly what I was doing or where I was going every day. I, on the other hand, was focused on getting a job. I wanted to have some cash on hand for my needs and not be dependent upon my parents, as he wasn't consistently sending home any money. The dependent checks to me from the military were delayed somehow, as he was getting the full amount in his checks.

As I look back, there may not have been a bureaucratic error, but purposeful paperwork completion delays on his part in an effort to restrict my activities. I would discover later he was frequently going to bars and paying for sex with young women and girls, utilizing the funds that were supposed to have been sent to me for support during his absence. The painful reality was he was taking advantage of the situation there in Thailand. He even went so far as to pretend to account for the money in his letters to me.

Quote from letter dated 15 Jan. '74:

> *I sure do hope that everything works out for us, so we can be together in the P.I. I really do need you honey!!! I miss you so very much!!! Plus today I got you a money order for $145, plus I bought me a bag to carry stuff I have left to carry. I bought me some bic pens too. So it all costed me $4.23 The bag was $3.75 and it's a good one too. Now, I owe $4.50 for my house girl, and $17.50 to some guy. So by the time I pay everyone off I'll have $7.00. In this letter is a list of everything I have spent money on and owe and what I have left for myself. As you can tell I don't have very much left for myself. But that's all right I don't need very much for me. I only want you to have everything you need and want!*

Most of the time when he said he was sending money orders, they didn't show up. Some would arrive and his explanation for the ones I didn't receive was it was wartime, and the mail wasn't very reliable. He would convince me he was able to get his money back on the money order, because he saved the receipts.

Meanwhile, in the States, I quickly landed a job at a local truck stop, working in their travel center. My duties included running the scales to weigh the trucks, as well as manage the store, the showers, and the motel rooms. I was not thrilled with the low wages or the hours, but it was a job while I waited for the county to finish the hiring process.

Being a young, small, and somewhat attractive woman put me in a position to be well liked by the truckers who utilized this facility. An added plus was I learned quickly and was honest. Once the regular truck drivers learned I was not available romantically, they relied on my skills to assist them in completing their job. I did get some satisfaction in helping them, but I quickly grew bored. However, on occasion something would happen that would bring a small amount of excitement.

One of the older truck drivers befriended me. His name was Jake, and every time he came in, we would have conversations.

"I love coming in here to talk to you. You remind me of my daughter, Carissa. She is nineteen years old. How old are you?" he asked.

"I'm twenty," I replied.

"I've a favor to ask of you."

"Okay, Jake, ask away."

"I've trouble seeing small print. Can you please read some stuff out loud to me before I sign it?" asked Jake as his big eyes peered at me through his thick eyeglass lenses.

As soon as I agreed, he showed me a folder and with his grease-stained hands pulled four pages from it and handed them to me to read to him out loud. After a few weeks we became so comfortable with one another we began to tease each other by assigning one another nicknames. He began to call me Tiny, and I called him Mr. Peepers.

One evening when I was working, Mr. Peepers came in and asked me to read out loud to him. While I was reading it to him, another driver came into the center. He waited less than a minute but grew impatient very quickly.

"Hey, lady, can you stop reading to the retard and help me?"

I grew very angry quickly but kept my cool. "I'll be with you in just a moment, sir," I replied.

Mr. Peepers also stayed calm with his back turned to the man. I need to add that Mr. Peepers was not a small man. He was somewhat lean, but very tall, probably around six feet, four inches. The man standing behind him only came up to his shoulders. However, he was hunched over the counter listening to me, and I was not sure the man knew how tall he was. I did finish reading to Mr. Peepers quite quickly and scooted down the counter, so Mr. Peepers could work on signing his paperwork.

I asked the man, "How can I help you?"

"First off by not being a stupid bitch!"

Mr. Peepers rose up and stood over the man. His overalls stretched tight against his huge chest as he pushed the man up against the wall by grabbing his shirt collar. "You can call me names all you want, but do not call her names," he said.

"Sorry, man, I didn't know you had a thing for her," the man said as he released his grip on him.

Mr. Peepers just growled a little and walked away. I then got the man what he needed, and he left. Mr. Peepers came back to the counter a few minutes later.

"Are you okay, Tiny? I'm so sorry the driver treated you so poorly."

"It wasn't your fault. I'm fine. I appreciate your help, Mr. Peepers. You sure scared that guy."

"Yeah well, he needed to be scared."

That was the only difficult incident I experienced during my short employment at the truck stop. It was nothing compared to what James was experiencing.

⁓

Quote from letter dated 4 Feb. '74:

Anything to get me home. Oh, Laurie honey I want to come home so bad. I hope that I can take it for eight more months. I've got to get to come home. Oh, I was just talking to a guy that just left Korat and he said that two more guys were killed there. One was a captain and he was shot in his bungalow downtown and the other guy was stabbed to death at the bus stop. It's starting to get bad in Thailand now. Duron is a lot worse than Korat ever was, it's only forty miles from Viet Nam and I talked to these guys going back to the States that just came from there and they said that there was shooting thirteen miles from Udorn. They better give me an M-16 when I get there if they are doing any shooting. Don't worry honest, I'm too crazy to have anything happen to me. Besides, I just too downright mean too.

Two months after I had applied for the San Bernardino County Nursing Attendant Program, I received notification I had been accepted. I quickly gave my notice to the truck stop owner and sadly said goodbye to Mr. Peepers. I decided not to write about the experience in my letters to James.

Chapter 11:

Safe Harbor and Freedom

"**I** can't believe they are allowing abortions. I know they passed a law, but I'm not happy about it," said one of the nurses.

I just listened to the conversation around *Roe v. Wade* as I sat in the nurses' lounge. I had already revealed to the head nurse my willingness to care for female patients who were having abortions. She was pleased, as she told me some staff had refused to have these women as patients. I told her that if they were humans who needed care, I was there to give it.

It was now 1974, and James had been gone almost three months, and I was beginning to find my adult self. I was nearly twenty-one years old and wanted to explore my interests. Working at San Bernardino County Hospital helped me to do just that.

I received training through a six-week course on site at the County Hospital. It was nine hours a day, five days a week for the six weeks and was totally a hands-on course. Once I received my certificate, I worked as a floater, working in all departments whenever there was a need. I was able to give my full dedication to my job since my husband was overseas. It was a year in which

I was able to mature and find myself. I had a front row seat witnessing life and death. I was given the chance to work at least a few days in every department before being offered a permanent position on the medical/surgical floor. Even then, I had an opportunity to work in other departments as I was always available to work double shifts.

Weekly, approximately six women were admitted to our floor who were scheduled for what the nurses called saline infusion abortions. The procedure for this type of abortion is to inject saline into the abdomen of the woman after her cervix is dilated to induce the expulsion of the fetus.

The first patient I cared for was a fourteen-year-old girl, Melanie, who had gotten pregnant by a seventeen-year-old boy. This girl, or woman, finally realized she was pregnant after her third month of pregnancy. A few weeks later she finally got the courage to tell her mother. At that point, her mother took charge by taking her to a doctor and inquiring about an abortion. By the time this occurred, the pregnancy had progressed to the point where a saline infusion abortion was the only choice and thus, she was admitted to San Bernardino County Hospital to have this procedure. Horrified and fearful at the thought that Melanie's father would find out about the pregnancy, the mother only stayed with her daughter for the first couple of hours after the procedure was performed. As her mother was leaving, I came on shift. I came upon a frightened child who wasn't sure what all of this meant. Through her tears she begged me to explain what exactly was going to happen to her.

I approached with caution and asked her, "What did your doctor tell you?"

"He said the pregnancy would end," she said.

"He's right."

"But what happens?"

I tried to explain as well as I could to prepare her for what was about to happen without scaring her to death.

"You are going to give birth to a fetus or baby that isn't alive. You will have labor pains like you would in a live delivery and the baby will be born traveling through the birth canal and out through your cervix."

"What? I am going to deliver a dead baby! Oh no! I thought it would just go away. Dissolve or something," she said, crying.

I held her hand and supported her through the entire process. I didn't agree with the fact she was having an abortion, but she was a human being and needed emotional support. The nurse on duty that evening who was responsible for Melanie's care expressed to me she didn't agree with abortion, so therefore she would only perform the absolute minimum care for any patient who was having one. Within me emerged a conflict, because my philosophical view was that it was not my role to judge a person, and, in this case, I wasn't sure this fourteen-year-old girl was totally in charge of this decision. I also knew this day would probably haunt her for the rest of her life, and if I could ease just a small part of her pain, then that is what I was here to do. I believe this was God's way of preparing my path for the arrival of my son John.

I stood by Melanie's side and held her hand as she went into labor. She yelled for her mom on several occasions.

"Do you want me to call your mom?" I asked her.

"No, she can't come. My dad is home, and he doesn't know about this," she said through her tears.

I continued to hold her hand and tried to comfort her the best I could. Finally, the ordeal was over. I cleaned her up, removed the fetus and prepared it for the morgue. When I returned to her bedside, she had fallen asleep. The next day when I came on shift, she had already been discharged.

In addition to caring for female patients having abortions, our unit was also given the pleasure of treating patients from the Glen Helen Rehabilitation Center, which at the time only housed men. Whenever a prisoner was brought to the unit, it seemed the room selected was always in my group. I didn't mind as the sheriff assigned to monitor them was very nice and, if there was time, we had some interesting conversations. Diego was in his 40s and was studying to become a doctor. He was working on his bachelor's degree in biology at the California State College at San Bernardino. When he finished, he was planning to go to medical school in Mexico. Since I had majored in biology for a short time at UCR and aspired to be a doctor, we found things to talk about. It gave me pleasure to have a male friend to talk to who wasn't my husband.

Besides friendly conversations about medicine, Diego schooled me regarding some of the prisoners. Many of those I cared for were quite chatty and told me things about their lives. For example, one good-looking young man told me a very believable story about how he had been charged and convicted of stealing funds from his work at a bank, but it was just a paperwork error, and his lawyer was going to get the conviction overturned. He also had me convinced he was single and wealthy. During a conversation with Diego one evening, I revealed what this charming young man had told me. Diego burst into laughter.

"You believe that pile of garbage?"

"It sounded like the truth."

Diego went onto to tell me the real story, which was that this young man was a con artist who had swindled good people out of tons of money and finally got caught. He also added that he was married.

"These prisoners are the best liars you will ever meet," Diego told me.

I appreciated Diego's lessons on life and especially appreciated his professional skills.

One evening I was delivering a meal to a prisoner. The procedure was for me to knock, look in the window in the door to view the prisoner, and then Diego would unlock the door and stand in the doorway while I delivered the meal. On this occasion, before Diego unlocked the door, I looked through the little square window and noticed something was strange. As I peered through this window in the heavy wooden door, all I could see was the beige exam privacy curtain.

I turned around and looked at Diego and said, "Diego, is this prisoner here? All I can see is the curtain. I can't see . . ."

He interrupted my sentence by placing his finger to his face indicating for me to be quiet. He ushered me to the side and unlocked the door, walking in first, with his gun out of his holster. As he crept in, the prisoner jumped from behind the curtain in an attempt to overtake whoever was entering the room.

"Stand back or I'll shoot!" yelled Diego.

The prisoner wasn't able to jump far enough to reach Diego and was shocked to see a gun pointing at his face, so he stood still and raised his hands. Diego immediately secured the prisoner to the top of the bed and called his supervisor.

I stood there like a statue, too scared to move. As soon as the prisoner was secured, Diego said, "Wow! That was a close call. I am glad you alerted me. You can go on with your duties. I'll catch up with you later."

I left and went back to completing my duties. Later I saw the same prisoner being escorted out by two other sheriff's deputies. Diego found me shortly after, and we talked about the incident.

"This prisoner had nothing to lose and was going to use you

as a ticket to escape, Laurie. He was a clever one. He must have worked for at least a couple of hours to slide his handcuffs all the way down to the end of the bed," Diego said.

"Boy, I'm glad he couldn't pull it off. I'm very thankful you were there, Diego," I said.

"I was just doing my job. That guy won't be a threat here anymore. They took him back to prison. Our theory is he faked being ill, so he could be sent here. Most of these guys think the hospital setting affords them easier escape opportunities," Diego explained.

I was very thankful the situation went down the way it did. My faith in men to protect me was restored, briefly.

Chapter 12:

The Return

I stood as close as I could to the exit door of the aircraft. As passengers began to walk out, I anxiously awaited the moment I would be able to embrace my husband. It was December 3, 1974, and James's parents and I were at LAX waiting for him to disembark the commercial airplane on his final leg of his trip home. I stood there with anticipation and some fear. I had uncertainty regarding our relationship, and so longed for him to really appreciate our love in person as he seemed to, at times, in his letters. As he walked off the airplane, my jaw dropped when I realized the man in the bright turquoise tuxedo with shoulder-length hair was my husband! I totally expected him to be in uniform, with a military-style haircut. Somehow, he had been able to grow his hair long and go unnoticed. Once we recognized James, his mom and I ran to him screaming and embraced him. Then, of course, he grabbed me separately and gave me a dramatic big kiss.

"I missed you so much, honey!" James said.

"I'm so happy you are finally home! I can't believe it," I replied.

"Hey, Mom, you look great! Hi, Dad, it's so good to see ya!" James said.

"Thanks, sweetheart. It's so good to have you home, Junior," his mom replied.

"Welcome home, son. I'm happy to see ya, but why in the hell are ya dressed like that?" his dad asked.

"I was so tired of wearing my uniform every day for the last year, Dad. Also, I wanted ta surprise ya all," he said.

"Well, ya sure did that!" his dad replied.

His mom and I laughed. As we walked through LAX and out to the parking lot, James and I did not let go of one another. He opened the car door for me and slid right behind me, tapping me on the behind as I got into the car.

"James!" I said.

"I sure've missed that little butt."

"James, your parents are here."

"Oh well, they'll get over it. They know how I am."

His mom and dad were quiet on the drive home. James and I talked to each other incessantly. We had a lot of things to say to each other. A few of his questions made me feel uncomfortable.

"How often did ya go out with your girlfriends?"

"Not very often. Maybe three times. I mostly worked and went to college."

"Were there any guys in your colleges classes you talked ta?"

"There were some, but I didn't talk to them."

"Are ya sure?"

"Yes, I'm very sure."

"Well, I figured there might be someone, because you didn't write every day like I did."

"There was no one else. I just got busy. I love you so much, and I'm so happy you're back with me."

The fact I had been away from him for a year had brought

me to the realization that life with James was stressful. Writing letters to him created stress for me because I wanted to make sure I was being supportive while he was facing the horrors of war. These were some of the thoughts in my mind as he caressed me in the back seat. Also, my thoughts went back to the time before he left for Thailand and his treatment of me. His unpredictable behavior and my inability to read the signals of when he "changed."

James had six weeks off, thirty days of leave, and two weeks to move from California to his next base in New Mexico. We stayed at his parents' house, taking over his sister Gina's bedroom for the month we stayed in California. He appeared to be so happy to be home that his treatment of me was subdued. He displayed a lot of affection in front of his family, and some of it felt fake to me at the time. We did visit my family, but they appeared to be disappointed that we didn't stay with them for at least a day or two, especially since we celebrated Christmas and New Year's while we were visiting. I did not want to push the issue as I was enjoying the peaceful time, hoping this was not temporary.

The only awkward moments during our visit came when James wanted to make love in such a crowded environment. There were only two bedrooms, and both were occupied. His parents were in one bedroom and his sister, Gina was in the second one. Her room had two beds in it, so Anna decided we should sleep on one of the beds. For the first two nights, Gina slept on the sofa in the living room.

By the third night, as we were getting ready for bed, Gina asked, "Hey, do you two mind if I sleep in my own bed? The sofa is not comfortable, and I have to go to work tomorrow." Gina was working at the Sears store in San Bernardino and still attending Skadron College.

"Sure, we don't mind, Sissy," James replied.

This is when it became awkward. While Gina was sleeping, James would not stop trying to do sexual activities. He would whisper in my ear, "Honey, touch my dick."

We had been separated for a year and nothing was going to stop the urge. At times, we engaged in sexual intercourse, all while Gina slept. These sexual encounters were not enjoyable for me as I was constantly worried Gina would know what we were doing. The bed was a twin size and the spring mattress we slept on was old and squeaky. After about two weeks, my fears became a reality. James woke up early one morning and decided we should engage in intercourse.

Suddenly, we stopped when out of the darkness we heard Gina's voice shouting, "I can't believe you guys are doing things while I am in here!" She then stormed out of the room and finished the rest of the nights on the sofa.

James's military orders after returning from Thailand stationed him at White Sands, New Mexico, at Holloman Air Force Base. When it got closer to the time for James to report to his new assignment, we made plans for the move. We went car-shopping for a larger car, as our little Toyota Corolla wouldn't have accommodated quite everything we planned to take with us. We traded it in and purchased a 1971 blue Oldsmobile Cutlass and packed it as full as possible and hitched a small U-Haul trailer to pull behind and headed for New Mexico. We had calculated it was a twelve-hour drive, but I had acquired a small chihuahua while James was gone, so we added time for dog breaks. My parents gave us some money to pay for a night in a motel along the way. James reluctantly agreed to stop for one night.

We didn't end up getting on the road until the early afternoon. The first few hours of the drive were great! James was in a good mood and Poppy, my chihuahua, appeared to be enjoying the ride.

Two to three hours into the ride we were in the middle of the desert and James got bored. He turned the vehicle off the road, trailer and all into the desert, and headed for a small group of trees. I was upset but stayed quiet to avoid any conflict or confrontation with James. When he stopped, he started laughing and said to me, "This looks like a great place to do it," I knew immediately he meant it was a great place to have sex. He got out of the car, grabbed a blanket and extended his hand to me. He led me to a place in the center of the trees where we couldn't be seen from the road. He shook out the blanket and laid it on the rocky desert ground.

"Here ya go, my sweetheart," he said as he motioned his hand for me to sit down.

"You didn't see any scorpions or spiders, did you?"

"Nah, I didn't see any," he said as he laughed.

As I sat there, he joined me on the blanket. Before I knew it, he was on top of me, pulling my pants down. His cold hands went underneath my panties and pulled them down so his erect penis could enter inside of me. My teeth were chattering, and goosebumps were forming on my legs and hips. He still had his pants on with only his zipper open. As he pumped against me, my buttocks were being pounded by the rocks beneath the blanket. "Ouch!" I called out. He didn't stop. His heavy breathing was blasting a rhythm in my ear.

He grabbed my long hair and pulled on it, moaning "Oh, honey! I love ya!" The pumping stopped and he rolled off me, got up, zipped his pants, and said, "Okay, let's get back on the road."

As I rose from the blanket, I realized I had sore spots all over my body from the rocks underneath me. "James, honey. Those rocks really hurt me," I said.

"Oh well, you'll live. Hurry up and get in the car."

"I need to walk Poppy."

"Okay but do it fast. I want to get goin'."

As the night approached, I began to complain about being tired and hungry.

"Honey, can we please stop to get something to eat? Or maybe even stop for the night at a motel? I'm getting tired. Dad did give us the money for a motel."

"You're such a baby! I know your daddy wanted you to get your beauty rest. Well, Daddy isn't here now. I am, and I'm not ready to stop," he proclaimed.

Our dog was so good and hadn't barked to ask to go to the bathroom at all, but I thought he might feel sorry for her. "James, honey. I think Poppy needs to pee," I said.

"She can wait 'til I stop," he said.

Finally, we needed gasoline, so he stopped. It was about eight o'clock in the evening. I went into the convenience store and purchased some snacks and walked the dog. James commented that I should be satisfied for a while longer and continued to drive. By the time eleven o'clock arrived, I was dozing off and on. I caught James nodding off several times. It was at that time we arrived in Tucson, Arizona, and James decided that we should stop, so he pulled into the parking lot of a Motel 6.

"Okay we can stay here. Go check us in."

I got out of the car and walked around the corner of the building to find the office. As I walked in, I saw signs that stated no pets allowed, so I kept quiet about Poppy. My dad had given me twenty-five dollars for a motel room, so I was so relieved when the sleepy-eyed young male clerk announced, "That will be nineteen dollars and ninety cents." I quickly handed him the twenty-dollar bill my dad had given me when he hugged me goodbye. A feeling of sadness came over me for a moment.

I had grown accustomed to living near my parents and apart from James.

When I went back to the car, I told James, "They don't allow dogs here."

"Who cares, they won't know she is here. But it is up to you to keep her quiet."

We grabbed our overnight bags and the dog and went up the outdoor concrete stairs to the room the clerk had assigned us. James unlocked the door and headed straight for the bathroom. When he came out, he was in his underwear and ready for bed. He walked toward me, kissed me good night and landed on the bed. I put Poppy down on the floor and went into the bathroom to get ready for bed. When I came out, James was sound asleep. I checked on Poppy who was also asleep. I crawled into bed but had trouble sleeping. I tossed and turned all night with worry about the dog, and our marriage. Morning came and we were back on the road.

"Do you want to drive first, honey?" James asked.

"I didn't sleep very well last night. I was worried Poppy would bark."

"That's stupid. She did fine. But it's okay. I'll drive."

As the morning went on, he continued to be very nice, but not without cause.

Just before noon he asked, "Honey, will ya give me a blow job while I'm driving?"

"I don't know. I'm nervous people will know what we're doing," I replied.

"Well, I didn't want to stop at a motel, but I did. So you owe me a favor," he said as he gave me a stern look.

So, against my own feelings, I complied. The sound of a diesel engine would prompt me to rise up and look to see if a truck driver was peering down at us and as I did, James would forcefully shove my head back down into his lap. As he did this, my mind became full of thoughts as to what would happen if we stopped suddenly. "Would my teeth accidentally bite down, and if this happened how would he react? What if the force was so great that I bit his dick off? Could he bleed to death before help arrived?"

Once I was finished, I breathed a sigh of relief it was over. As the day went on, I held my breath hoping there were no more sexual requests. On the evening of the second day, we arrived at Holloman Air Force Base.

Chapter 13:

The Pregnancy Journey

I was awakened by the sound of a roaring lion. I had never lived so close to a zoo. The air smelled fresh and clean. Alamogordo was a unique town and, compared to Fontana, it was as different as day and night. But this place would forever hold a special spot in my heart. It was the birthplace of my first child.

We rented a duplex which was half of a home built in the early 1900s. An elderly woman lived in the other half. We had the original bathroom, which included an old-time bathtub with no shower. Our kitchen had been added to our half and was poorly done, with virtually no cabinets to store dishes.

We arrived in October, and it was beginning to get cold, unlike the weather in Southern California. I missed living near my family and the loneliness was almost unbearable. My thoughts drifted to solutions to my loneliness. "If I was busy with a baby, I wouldn't be as lonely, and our families would visit more often. James might treat me better if I am the mother of his child." These thoughts prompted me to push James to start our family.

The road to conception was a tough one, as James was

diagnosed with gonorrhea shortly after we arrived in New Mexico. We both went to the clinic for examinations and the prescribed treatment was a penicillin shot. During my exam, the female Air Force captain gave me a sermon about how our boys suffered overseas during wartime.

"As women, it is our duty to always support our men. It is not unusual for an airman to stray and have sex with women other than their wife when they are overseas fighting a war. Unfortunately, it is one of the consequences of wartime. You need to be brave and not judge your husband. Hopefully, in the end you will look back and note how this strengthened your marriage," she said.

I left thinking his behavior overseas was normal. Little did I, nor anyone, know or even suspect my husband had had sex with young girls while he was there in Thailand. Years later I would discover revealing pictures of young Thai girls carefully hidden in a briefcase.

As I look back, some of his stories about his time in Thailand make sense now. He told me about being robbed multiple times on the streets of Bangkok. They took his watch one time, his jacket another time. He would describe the people of Bangkok as extremely sophisticated thieves. However, he left out one key fact: he was paying for sex with young girls and could have lost those items when he disrobed.

After the treatment for gonorrhea, there was a change in his behavior. He made attempts to be romantic while we were trying to get pregnant. This treatment lasted a few months into the pregnancy and was a welcome respite.

While James was in Thailand, I had saved about $2,000 from my wages at the hospital. Just after we moved to New Mexico, James Sr. and Anna experienced a financial crisis. James Sr. was a carpenter by trade and there was an unexpected slowdown in the home building business. Since he wasn't working, they came to visit us. We were so excited to see them and thought they were visiting because of our news about being pregnant. Instead, a few hours after they arrived, James Sr. said, "I need to ask ya two a question."

"Okay, Dad. Ask away," James replied.

"Well, ya know I am out of work, and it may be a few more weeks before I get any work."

"Yes, sir. How can we help?"

"Son, before you left you told me you had some money in your savings account."

"Yes, we have $2,020 in our savings."

"We saved it so we can buy stuff for the baby," I interjected.

"I know, sweetheart, and if you can find it in your hearts to loan us $2,000, I'll get it back to you as soon as I get back to work. Hopefully, it'll be way 'fore our grandchild is born," James Sr. said.

"Sure, Dad. I'll go today and withdraw the money. Right, honey?" James said.

"Sure. We're glad to be able to help," I replied.

As I sat at our old, used Formica dining table, sadness began to well up inside of me. I didn't want to reveal my feelings to my in-laws, so I managed to put a smile on my face. I was glad to help but was nervous, because our savings was our financial cushion. They stayed for two days and then left.

"I hope they can pay us back before the baby comes," I said.

"I'm sure they will, honey. I just feel so great we had the money to help them."

So, during my pregnancy to build our savings back up, I acquired a weekly free advertising newspaper delivery route. I walked my route with my chihuahua in the bag. Once again, my codependency was in full force, now allowing his parents to take advantage of me. They never paid the money back, but instead would later give us their used stove as payment for the loan, after they bought a new one.

I was approximately five months pregnant when we embarked on a trip to Kansas to see his cousin, Richard. James called him his cousin even though he wasn't related to him by blood. Richard was the brother of his Uncle Claude's wife, Aunt Pat. Richard and James had bonded when Richard came to California for a visit. Richard, I would discover later, had some questionable behavior when it came to younger women. However, at this moment in time, I was not aware of any of this and thought Richard to be a wonderful person.

It was in late April when we left for Kansas. My pregnant belly poked out slightly. I was excited to finally be large enough to justify wearing maternity clothes. I was nervous about traveling with James, especially while pregnant. I kept waiting for sexual requests, but none came. We only stopped for gas, food, and to go to the restroom. There was no motel stop on this 800-mile trip and no dog this time. Our Cutlass had comfortable seats, so I napped off and on. James drove the entire way. As we pulled onto their property, I was awestruck by the huge oak trees that lined their dirt driveway. As I opened the car door to get out, I could feel the breeze on my face. This road trip was tiring, but much less stressful than the trip from California to New Mexico.

Kate and Richard greeted us with open arms and made us feel very comfortable. Their home was farm-style with very large bedrooms. Kate was a very down-to-earth woman. She had shoulder-length curly brown hair, wore no makeup, and dressed in jeans, a t-shirt, and sneakers. Richard was tall, with black hair he slicked back. He looked like he was living in the '50s as he wore only white t-shirts and jeans. Their home was very cozy and clean.

The closest town to where they lived was Perry, Kansas. Kate's whole family lived in the area, and they all treated us like family. The population of Perry at the time was only around seven hundred, which even in comparison to Alamogordo was very small. Richard and James chose to work on motorcycles and cars which left me free to follow Kate around on her daily errands.

Kate parked her pickup truck and asked, "Are ya okay to do some walking today?"

Kate had been diagnosed with cervical cancer the year before and had undergone a hysterectomy and in this small town there was not a soul who didn't know. Everyone we passed asked her the same question. "How are you feeling, Kate?" She answered with the same answer, "Feelin' great! Thanks for askin'!" Every time someone passed us you could feel the warmth of this small, kind town. I embraced it and digested it into my soul. For just a few days I became part of this place. The tall brick buildings and old-style storefronts gave me the feeling I had traveled back in time. After we finished the errands in town, we stopped by Kate's aunt's house for lunch. We sat in the dining room where the smell of biscuits baking and vegetable soup on the stove dominated my sense of smell. This was a home where meals were sacred, and cooking was not only necessary but considered an art. Kate's Aunt June spoke to me like I was one of her children.

"My dear, you look like you could use some home cookin' to add more meat to those bones. You eat up now. You're eating for two," she said. Her words cradled me with love, even though this was the first time we met.

When we returned to Kate and Richard's house it was time to begin preparation for dinner. Kate insisted I take a nap while she made a pie for dessert. As I lay down, our baby reminded me he was there. I found myself wishing life with James was always this happy and comfortable. When he and Richard came in for dinner, James spoke to me like I was his queen.

"How'd your day go, sweetheart? I missed ya."

"I had a glorious day! Kate and I went into town, saw many of her friends and had a delicious lunch prepared by her aunt. How was your day?"

"Richard and I had a great day workin' on the cars and motorcycles in his shop. And we had time to catch up on what we both have been doing since we saw each other last," he said.

The four of us sat around the table that night and all four nights we stayed there, conversing like we had known each other all our lives. This vacation was very good for me, and I began to feel more secure in my relationship with James. His kind, loving behavior was what I craved. Then it was time to leave to return to New Mexico.

I was enjoying my life in this bubble of happiness and didn't anticipate the drive home would be different from the drive there. I was wrong and was jerked back into my reality when about two hours into the drive home James made a request.

"Honey, give me a blow job, will ya?" I must have had a look of shock on my face as I stared at him without answering.

"Well, what are you waiting for? DO IT NOW!" he shouted.

"Okay, okay. You know it's hard for me to bend down like that with my belly in the way," I replied.

"Oh, my. You're not that big yet. Get busy."

Once again, if I rose up, he forced my head down. I was short of breath after a couple of minutes, but kept on going, praying it would be over quickly. Then there was an added request on this trip.

"Hey, honey. I think you should raise up your shirt and bra and flash your boobs at that truck driver."

"What? I can't do that."

"Uh, yes, you can, and you will."

"Honey, that is too embarrassing. I can't," I pleaded.

"You will do it! If'n you don't, you'll go topless all the way back."

Going topless for the rest of the trip horrified me more than just flashing truck drivers, so I complied. I am not sure why I let him bully me without putting up more of a fight, but a voice deep inside of me signaled fear of what he could do. I was screaming inside, but no one could hear me. My pregnancy bound me to this man forever.

Chapter 14:

Advent

As I lay there feeling sorry for myself, I heard the helicopter land. Its engines hummed for approximately ten to fifteen minutes. My sweet baby had been born, but he was struggling to survive. I was sure he was being loaded on board. Then I heard the engines rev up and the sound gently disappear in the distance. I will never forget the empty, lonely feeling. My heart ached.

This was my introduction to motherhood. It began in the early morning of August 28, 1975. I got up early because I was having labor pains. I wasn't alarmed due to the fact I had been having them on and off for a few weeks. But on this morning, as I walked into the kitchen, a gush of liquid burst from between my legs. I walked back to the bedroom where James was asleep.

"Honey, I think my water broke," I said as I tapped him.

"What? Are ya okay?" he asked as he sat up.

"Yes, but I think we should probably head for the hospital. I'll go wake Mom," I said.

My mom, dad and brother came to visit in late July. The men left in August, but my mom stayed to be with me when

I delivered.

I walked out of the bedroom and knocked on my mom's door and announced to her my water had broken. She responded immediately.

As we drove the fifteen-mile drive to the base hospital, I remember watching the sun rise. Its warm bright rays gave me the feeling this was a new day—the day I was to become a mother. I had no fear of the birthing process and was excited that the day had finally come. I also had hope James would behave differently after becoming a father. A sensation of peace surrounded me. Later, I would discover this feeling was the calm before the storm.

When we arrived at the Holloman AFB hospital, I was admitted and put in a bed in the labor and delivery section of the small hospital. I was checked by the attending doctor and was told I was only dilated two centimeters. By noon, my labor pains were hard and steady. By three, my labor pains were so intense the fetal monitor was registering high stress levels. The head nurse, who was a captain in the Air Force, came in to check on me. She told me she was going to consult with the doctor since my labor was so intense with no progress in dilation. She was gone for about half an hour and came back and sat with me for a few minutes.

"The doctor has decided to wait a few more hours before deciding whether or not to do a Cesarean section. I am not sure I agree, but he is the one who is in charge. I can get you something for pain if you want it," she said.

James came in just as she was giving me this information. His response to my pain was, "Be tough, be strong! She doesn't need anything for pain."

The captain seemed to be irritated with his response but didn't say anything. As she got up to leave, she reassured me she would keep a watchful eye on me. James stayed with me for about an hour, continuing to spew out his supportive statements.

"Ya can do this. You're a Hawkins. Tough as nails."

He then left and my mother appeared at my side. She was sitting there for only a few minutes when I began to go in and out of consciousness, so she summoned the captain, who then asked the doctor to order pain medication.

After the pain medication was given, the pain was gone, but the contractions continued, and I began to hallucinate. Finally, after sixteen long hours of labor, my body began to respond and dilate. At that point the obstetrician, Dr. Browner, who had been seeing me throughout my pregnancy, came on duty. After checking me, he leaned down close to my ear and said, "Laurie, I am so sorry, but it is too late for a Cesarean section. You are going to have to deliver this baby, but I will be there," he said. The next thing I knew I was being rolled into the delivery room.

The delivery was a visual blur to me, but I could hear everything. I didn't hear a cry from my baby for what seemed like an eternity after I felt them pull him out of me. I heard the doctors and nurses discussing my vitals, "Doctor, her BP is two hundred twenty over one hundred twenty!" someone called out.

Another voice called out, "Quick, hand him to me so I can get him breathing!" My thoughts centered around my baby, and my ears were searching for the sound of a cry when I heard a different voice say, "We are losing the mother!"

I felt cold, and then hot, and the touch of many hands on my body. Then a calmness came over me when I heard John start to cry. It was a weak cry, but the most pleasant sound a mother who has just given birth can hear. It was at that time I heard another voice say, "The mother's vitals have stabilized."

No one showed me my baby, I could only hear him. A short time after his first cry, he was whisked away from the delivery room and me. After I spent some time in the recovery room, I was transferred to a hospital room. My mother and James both came in for a brief moment to express their love and reassure me that everything would be all right. My mother looked exhausted. James told me they were going home to get some rest but would be back in the morning.

"I'm just worried about our baby," I said.

"The doctor told me our baby is stable for now and that they're runnin' a lot of tests," James said.

"I peeked at him through a crack in the nursery curtains and boy, was he screaming," my mom said.

"That's a good thing, right, Mom?" I asked.

"Yes, I believe it is."

It was about three in the morning by the time I was left alone, and I was overwhelmed and exhausted, but also extremely worried about my sweet baby boy. As I lay there thinking about him, a doctor who was assigned to John's case came into my room.

"I am so sorry, Mrs. Hawkins, but your baby has been having seizures. We're not equipped here to handle his condition. Not only is he having seizures, but an X-ray revealed a large mass in his lungs. I've requested a helicopter to transport him to William Beaumont Army Medical Center in El Paso, Texas. They will be able to address his medical needs," he said.

"Uh, okay. When is he leaving?"

"Well, immediately, of course."

I began to sob and asked, "Can I please see him before you take him away?"

"You haven't seen your baby at all?"

"Not at all," I tearfully replied.

"Well, I can arrange a brief visit between the two of you."

I thanked him and he gave me a quick hug and left.

Approximately five minutes later, a nurse brought John to me. His little body was thrashing about, and I held him very tight and spoke to him, telling him I loved him through my tears.

The nurse remained at my bedside, tapping her foot, which to me indicated the helicopter was on its way. I continued to hug him tight, kissing his head over and over, until she reached down telling me time was up. I handed him to her reluctantly. Once she had him, she practically ran out of the room. I felt a sense of overwhelming grief and fear I would never see him again.

The next morning my father called me from California. My mother and James had not arrived yet. I thought I could be strong, as James had requested throughout this ordeal.

"How are you feeling?" my dad asked.

"I'm really sore. A nurse came in a little while ago and told me she was going to help me get out of bed and sit in a chair for a few minutes. I'm scared about how much it is going to hurt," I said.

Our conversation went well for the first few minutes. We continued to discuss my condition and then how we named the baby by using the middle names from the great-grandfathers on both sides. Then, he asked me how John was doing. As I began to try to form the words to tell my dad about John, my sadness and fear took over my body and all I could do was cry. Once I started to cry, I sobbed. My dad knew I had had a difficult delivery, but nothing else.

"Honey, what happened?" he said as he began to cry too.

I told him what the doctor had said to me about my baby, and there were moments when no words were spoken, we both just sobbed.

James also spoke to his mom and dad on that day regarding John's condition. They decided to take a road trip to Alamogordo. Their six-year-old niece was spending the weekend with them, and they decided she should come with them. I thought it was odd at the time, but my focus was on my child. I would later discover that her presence gave James an opportunity to molest her, as she reported to police years later.

Our little home was very crowded and busy, so my mother stayed most of the day with me at the hospital to avoid the chaos and to comfort me. James did not stay as long as my mother when he came to visit. He would drop her off and get back to our house to visit with his family.

The Hawkinses only stayed three days and then returned home, without coming to see me at the hospital. Nor did any of them travel to El Paso to check on John, which disappointed me. I was extremely anxious regarding John's condition and thought maybe someone might travel down to El Paso to check on him, but no one did. I was getting little information. The only message I received indicated he was in a stable condition, but his stay at William Beaumont Medical Center was likely to extend for at least two weeks. It didn't help my mental state when a hospital worker wheeled a baby in a bassinet into my room while I was in the restroom on the third day of my five-day stay in a private room. I could hear the baby crying, and for a moment thought John might have been brought back, but hope faded when I heard the worker come back and say "Sorry" as she quickly wheeled the bassinet away.

I was released from the hospital on the morning of the fifth day after giving birth. By 1:00 p.m. I was insisting James and my mother take me to El Paso to see John. My mother got two pillows for me to sit on and off we went on the drive to William Beaumont Medical Center. James was willing to go but seemed a little distant. I can't say I wasn't in pain because I was, but my determination to see my baby helped me to endure it.

Upon arrival we were directed to the Neonatal Intensive Care

(NICU), which was on the seventh floor of the main building. I was so nervous because I didn't really know what obstacles I was going to encounter regarding John's condition. This was the first time I was able to see John since the night he was born. As we entered the NICU, my eyes were immediately drawn to John. Somehow I knew where my baby was in the large room full of incubators. I was drawn to him like a moth is drawn to light. The attending nurse called out to me, and I quickly identified myself as John Hawkins's mother. She quickly let her guard down. "Okay, Momma, you can open the incubator and touch him, but do not pick him up."

As I walked toward him, I compared him to all the other infants there. He looked like a giant. Most of the infants there weighed between two to five pounds, whereas John weighed seven pounds, eight ounces.

I opened the incubator and began touching him and talking to him. "Hi there, John. It's me, your mommy. I'm sorry I haven't been here, but I was just released from the hospital today. I love you."

This was the first time I really set my eyes on him. His head was misshapen, and his eyes were a little puffy, but he opened them, and we stared at one another. I touched his hand, and gently rubbed his skin. I carefully stroked his head around the two intravenous tubes. His little head had been shaven where they were attached. He looked so frail. I began to sob. My mother and the NICU nurse caressed me. James just stood there emotionless.

At home before we left for El Paso, I used a breast pump and brought some of my milk for John. The NICU nurse allowed me to feed him some of my milk through a lavage tube. He wasn't strong enough to suck on a nipple yet. The birth trauma had taken a toll on my baby. My mother took pictures so she could show my dad. James touched John and spoke to him a couple of times. After about three hours, James and my mother left for a little while to go get something to eat. I refused to leave. I wanted to be with John as long as I could. Taking care of myself was the last thing on my mind.

While James and my mom were gone, an attending physician stopped by to check on John, so I questioned him about his condition.

"Is the mass on his lungs cancer?"

"No, Mrs. Hawkins. Once he was here, we did more X-rays and found no mass in his lungs. Our guess is his little body was so compressed from the delivery, somehow a shadow was created making it look like a mass, when in reality there wasn't one."

"Oh my God! Are ya sure?"

"Yes, we're absolutely positive there is no mass in his lungs. We are concerned about the seizures he is having, but we're working on getting those under control before we discharge him."

I was so relieved to know there was no mass in his lungs. I knew seizures can be serious but was confident this medical team would help John get better.

After four hours had passed, James whispered in my ear, "Hon, we have to leave. I've gotta work tomorrow."

"Okay, I understand," I responded. I bent down close to John and said, "John, my love, Mommy has to leave, but I'll be back soon. I love you so much."

I kissed him, closed the incubator, looked at the NICU nurse and began to cry again. She said, "Don't worry, we're taking good care of him."

I walked out of the NICU slowly. James walked on one side of me and my mom on the other. I turned one last time to see my sweet child before we got on the elevator. My mom put her arm around me and wiped my tears as they fell from my eyes. I was so glad she was with me.

That evening as we drove back to Alamogordo, I couldn't get my baby's image, alone in the incubator, out of my mind. My whole body ached to hold him against me. I longed for him to come home.

James went back to work the next day and my mother reserved her airline ticket to go home. She felt more secure about leaving since we had visited John and she witnessed the excellent care he was receiving. I wanted to go back to see John the next day, but my mom convinced me to rest at least one day. On my third day out of the hospital, I insisted again and again we drive down to see him while James worked. I was getting stronger every day and so was my desire to be with my baby. My mom didn't complain at all about the daily trips and kept commending me on my dedication to my child. James would ask questions regarding John's progress, but rarely offered any words of encouragement or support, nor did he travel down to see him again. John stayed in the hospital for a total of two weeks. My mom left four days before John came home.

I continued to drive down to El Paso to visit John by myself every day after my mom left. During one of those visits, I met with John's pediatrician at the William Beaumont Medical Center who cautioned me regarding John's development.

"Mrs. Hawkins, I need to let you know that John may experience some developmental delays because of the birth trauma he experienced," he warned.

"Okay, what do I do if I notice he's not developing normally?" I asked.

"Make sure you bring it to his pediatrician's attention when you notice any delays in his speech, motor development, or cognition. Be insistent that his needs be addressed."

I relayed the information to James; however, his response

was, "John'll be just fine."

The day John was released, James got permission to take the day off and went with me. We were both happy to be finally bringing John home.

When we arrived home, Donita and Lonnie were there waiting for us in front of our house as I had called them just before we left El Paso. They lived only a few blocks away and during my time in New Mexico, Donita was my best friend and my confidant.

Donita and I met through our husbands who worked in the same flight. We bonded immediately as if we had known each other our entire lives. We both tended to be tight-lipped about how our husbands treated us behind closed doors, but our lips loosened at times around one another. Donita and I shared the same maiden name, Kelly.

"I'm sure we are related in some way," she would often say to me, especially when I was depressed about my marriage. This statement conveyed to me the message we were sisters and not alone in our marital plights.

Donita and Lonnie were from Dayton, Ohio. Donita came from a loving, supportive family, while Lonnie came from one riddled with domestic abuse. Donita revealed his background to me one day while she and I were alone, visiting.

"Lonnie can have a real temper, you know. He screams at me about things, just like James screams at you."

"I hate it when he screams at me."

"Well, I try to be patient with Lonnie. Does James ever hit or break things?"

"Sometimes."

"Well, Lonnie does all the time."

"Has he ever hit you?"

"No, and he always feels bad when he breaks things. He says

he will never hit me. He doesn't want to be like his dad. His dad hit Lonnie's mom and him. When Lonnie was sixteen, he ran away from home after his dad punched him in the nose and broke it. He lived with his aunt until he joined the Air Force."

"Wow. Is that why his nose is crooked?"

"Yeah. I don't understand how his dad could do such a thing to his son. Lonnie doesn't want to have any kids. He is afraid of becoming like his dad."

"Are you okay with not having any children?"

"For now. I am hoping he changes his mind in a few years."

"Well, James's dad is a rough man too, but as far as I know he never hit his kids. His mom has hinted that when they were first married, James Sr. liked to push her around, but after she had kids, he stopped."

"I don't understand why any man would hit or push his wife around."

"Me either."

Donita and I spent a lot of time together, but often avoided discussing our painful encounters with our husbands. It was like we could read each other's thoughts and instead of reliving the anguish, we focused on talking about the fun things, like food or family experiences. However, the elephant was always in the room, we just chose to look around it. We were both strangers in a place that was very unlike the place we came from. Donita was the one touching my stomach and getting excited when the baby kicked. She was my light in this sea of darkness that I was navigating through.

Donita and I were so excited as we brought John into the house. James and Lonnie sat in the living room drinking beer, while Donita and I took him into his bedroom to change his diaper after the long ride home. Being two young women who were new at motherhood duties, we were talking as I pulled his diaper off. I heard a noise that sounded like a water hose spraying against something and commented to Donita about the noise. At the same time both of us realized that John had started to urinate and there was no diaper on him. We both began to giggle as I re-diapered him and cleaned the crib. Donita and I had a great afternoon that day, staying together, apart from the men.

John had arrived home, and I hoped my life with James would change for the better.

Chapter 15:

Life After Birth

"Where in the hell've ya been?" he yelled.

"I was at Donita's and lost track of the time," I said. Before I knew it, his fist landed just below my rib cage. I was so surprised I just looked at him in shock.

"Did ya like that? Try being late again and I'll hit ya harder next time," he said as he walked away from me.

I can't explain why I didn't do anything after the first hit. I ran to our bedroom and lay on the bed sobbing quietly. His anger was intense, and it scared me. I blamed myself for his action. I thought about telling someone, but I was embarrassed. My codependency was operating in full force and making me believe my actions were causing him to behave this way. I was constantly seeking his approval of me. My behavior fed him power to use and abuse me.

John's birth was a traumatic experience for both of us in different ways, and impacted our lives more than I could have ever imagined. When going through the experience of one's child suffering or being sick, I had always assumed a couple would have similar feelings regarding such a matter. In this case I was wrong. I would later find out that the birth of our child was one of the events that increased the severity of mental illness in James. Some experts later told me that when I became a mother, he had difficulty in grappling with the concept or idea I was no longer a young girl. James would later be diagnosed with paranoid schizophrenia, as well as exhibiting behaviors of a sociopath.

Nothing in my life had prepared me to grapple with mental illness on such a large scale. I was intelligent enough to know that some of his behaviors were not normal, but not everyone is normal every day. It was after John was born that the abnormal behaviors began to manifest on a more frequent basis. "Schizophrenia is a serious brain disorder that distorts the way a person thinks, acts, expresses emotions, perceives reality and relates to others."[2]

These behaviors were presented in such a way that I was treated like a piece of property and not like a human being. Before our child was born, there were a few instances of unusual behavior, such as insisting that we wife-swap, or throwing a tantrum when food was not prepared the way he liked it. These unusual behaviors became almost daily after our child was born. By using the word unusual, I am referring to behaviors that most normal people don't exhibit. One of the new behaviors was punching and hitting me when he became angry. John was three months old when this behavior began.

James never accepted the fact John could have any type of delay or problems at all.

"Look at him, hon. He's completely normal. There's nothin' wrong with my son," James would say often.

As I looked at those beautiful big blue eyes and dark straight

---

2. *St. Charles Psychiatric Associates*, s.v. "Schizophrenia Overview," accessed April 14, 2022, https://stcharlespsychiatricassociates.com/schizophrenia/.

hair, I could almost believe it myself, but then the memory of his birth would flood into my mind, hearing the doctor's words. "John may experience some developmental delays due to the birth trauma."

It was too much for James to accept that any child of his might not be perfect. I, on the other hand, was constantly observing John and looking for the warning signs. Therefore, the more I mentioned any concerns, the more James exhibited annoyance with me. So I began to keep some of my concerns to myself.

I was the main caretaker of John. I took him for his appointments with a pediatrician, I got up in the middle of the night with him, I changed the diapers, I fed him. James did sit with me when I fed him and watched me when I gave him the phenobarbital to control his seizures. We remained in New Mexico until James was honorably discharged from the US Air Force when John was four months old. Without hesitation we decided to move back to California near our families.

Transitioning back to California was relatively easy. I found a house to rent in Alta Loma. James found a job at General Dynamics, and I accepted a job at the local Carl's Jr. James refrained from hitting me for a brief time, I believe since our families were nearby, and we were both starting new employment. Life for all intents and purposes appeared to be back to normal. We lived near our families and John appeared to be developing at an almost normal rate. I was keeping a close eye on him. The pediatrician kept reassuring me that John was only slightly behind and was progressing as expected for a child who had experienced birth trauma.

Since I was back in California, friends and family came to visit quite often. Most of my female friends only came to the house when James was at work. At the time, I didn't think much about it, but in retrospect, I think they avoided coming over when he was at home as he often made them feel uncomfortable on many levels.

Our landlord was the grandmother of a friend of the family, and she lived next door. She watched the outside of the house like a hawk and did not observe anything unusual or destructive other than me taking the screens off the windows to wash them. In contrast, she never knew inside there was a different story unfolding. Though he refrained from hitting me, he did push me around and break items on a regular basis. One day he got angry at me for not cleaning the kitchen well enough.

"God dammit! When'll ya learn ta clean like I like it? Ya make me so angry! Ya stupid bitch!" he yelled. He walked out of the house to the garage and came back carrying a hammer. I had a collection of record albums I stored in a cabinet in the living room. He crouched down and reached for the cabinet handle and flung it open. As he did this, some of the albums fell out onto the carpeted floor. "See! This is what I'm talkin' 'bout. These should never fall out onto the floor just because I opened the door! Look at this mess!" he shouted.

I stood there frozen as he raised the hammer and brought it down on two of the albums. "No!!!" I screamed. He looked up at me, smiled, and brought the hammer down again on two more albums. I began to sob. He continued to smash away until he had struck every single album, breaking each one.

"There, let's see if'n that'll teach ya ta keep a neater house. Clean this mess up now!" he shouted. He stood up and headed for the front door. "Ya should be grateful it was the albums I smashed with the hammer and not ya," he said. I was grateful, but not because he didn't hit me, but because he got in the car and left for a few hours. Fury had built up inside of me, but I dared not release any of it in front of him.

We ended up living at this residence for about a year and a half. During this time, I worked even harder to avoid angering him. I fooled myself into thinking I was living a normal life.

Chapter 16:

The Neighbors: A Moral Dilemma

Encounters and friendships in high school can never prepare you for what happens when you engage with the same people later as adults. As teenagers, we believe we know everything about our friends. In my case, the reconnection with high school friends proved to be wonderful yet challenging. I did not have the emotional tools to handle surprises regarding their character while amid my relationship with James.

I reconnected with two high school classmates who had married one another. Carrie and Mitch were both friends of mine, as all three of us were members of a music club in high school. James had met them in high school through me.

Carrie heard through the grapevine that James and I had moved back to California and called me on the phone one day. We arranged to meet for lunch and had fun reminiscing about our days in high school. During our conversation, I mentioned we would love to find a home to purchase in Fontana, like her and Mitch had done. A few months later, Carrie contacted me again.

"Hi! Guess what? The house next door to me just went up

for sale."

She gave me the contact number for the real estate agent, and I called her immediately. The agent scheduled an appointment for us to meet her. When James came home that evening, I told him about the house.

"James, honey. The house next door to Mitch and Carrie's is up for sale . . . and I made an appointment to speak to the real estate agent about it for tomorrow evening," I said with slight hesitation as I was never sure about his reaction to things I said or did.

"Great!"

I breathed a sigh of relief. Before I knew it James and I had qualified for a Veteran's Assistance loan for $20,000 and purchased the home.

We were all excited when we moved into the home on Shadow Street in April 1977. There were only eight houses on this dead-end street. Mitch and Carrie, along with James and I, were the youngest owners on the block for the first three years we lived there. Everyone else was at least fifty years of age or older. The houses were built in the 1950s, and this neighborhood was located almost equal distance from both of our parents' homes. When we moved, I quit my job at Carl's Jr., so having a girlfriend with whom I could easily visit with daily was perfect. All I had to do was walk next door. My husband and I had a couple whom we could party with on the weekends without having to get a babysitter. During good weather evenings, which happened a lot in Southern California, we would put our children to bed and sit in the front yard between the two houses with our doors open to be able to hear our children if they awakened. Their two girls were slightly older than John, but they treated him like a little brother and played with him when other children wouldn't.

We had a lot in common as we had all attended the same

high school and grew up in the same town. Our two families became entwined as we went on trips together, picnics, and celebrated some of the holidays together as well. I thought I fit in with this group, but time would reveal something different.

In 1980, Carrie's father committed suicide. It was a devastating event and put a severe strain on Mitch and Carrie's marriage. This event would grow arms and reach beyond their marriage and into mine, handing me a moral dilemma.

One day a few months later, I went next door when Carrie and the girls were not home. Mitch invited me in, which wasn't unusual. I felt comfortable with him and didn't think anything about it, but I should have.

"Hey, Laurie. Carrie and the girls are gone shopping. Did you need something?" Mitch asked.

"I was just coming to see if Carrie had an onion. I'm making dinner and didn't realize I needed an onion for my casserole."

"Let me go look and see if she has one. Come on in." I walked in and waited in the living room while he searched for an onion. A minute later he came out carrying one and handed it to me.

"There ya go, sweetheart."

"Thanks, Mitch. I'll buy one to replace it next time I go to the store." Suddenly I felt awkward and said with a nervous laugh, "Okay. I . . . guess I'll get . . . back to my casserole."

"Hey, can you stay for just a minute? I'd like to talk to ya about something since we're alone."

"Okay, I guess."

"Ya know I really care about you, right?"

"Yeah, Mitch. I . . . care about you too."

"Well, lately I can't get you off my mind. I think some day you and I will be together. If you know what I mean."

All I could think of was my friend Carrie and how I was

sitting on her plaid loveseat listening to her husband suggest we have an affair.

"You're crazy, Mitch. I could never do that to Carrie."

He responded by just laughing out loud. I ignored his comment and walked out the front door. As I turned to close it, I looked up to see him shoot me a quirky smile.

A few weeks later, Carrie began confiding in me with stories of her infidelity.

"Hey, guess what?"

"Ya know I'm not good at guessing, Carrie. What?"

"Remember our friends Mary and Sam?"

"The ones who own the auto parts store in town?"

"Yes."

"What about 'em?"

"Well, I kept thinkin' to myself, I'd really like to know what Sam is like in bed."

"Carrie, what are you saying?"

"Well, when we were at their house the other night, while Mitch and Mary went to the store to buy more beer . . ."

"What? You didn't? Did you?"

"Well, yes we did. And he is such a good lover."

"Oh my, Carrie. Mitch didn't suspect anything?"

"Not that I could tell."

"I'm sure he would have said something to you later if he did."

"Please, ya can't tell a soul."

Unlike my experience with the Dabbles, this was a different situation. There was no open arrangement to swap. Instead, there was a lot of hiding and deception. I knew the man she was sleeping with and his wife, and this time I wasn't a participant, but a confidant. Every time I was aware of a visit with Mary and Sam, I would run over to her house and wait anxiously for her to tell me a story of her intimate encounters with Sam. I was fascinated by her stories; however, they all came with dire warnings if any woman slept with her husband that way.

"Ya know, friend, I'd kill any woman who slept with my husband," she said one day.

I had always viewed her as a very caring and compassionate woman, so hearing such a statement come from her mouth surprised me.

"Carrie, how can you say that while you're sleeping with another woman's husband?"

"Dunno. I just know that's how I feel."

Her stories were so intriguing to me that sometimes I would tell James. This was a huge mistake, because he would use this information against me later to destroy any friendship with Carrie I might have been able to salvage.

My true moral dilemma began when Mitch's prediction came true.

One evening James and Mitch were sitting in our living room drinking beer together when I arrived home after attending a college course.

"Hey, hon, I'm thinkin' ya should fuck Mitch," James announced as I walked through the door.

"What?" I asked. I was tired and my mind was not expecting James to make such a statement.

"Ya heard me. I want ya ta fuck Mitch."

Mitch's large body was strewn across our light-brown leather chair in a very relaxed position. His brown skin almost camouflaged in the chair made his white teeth appear like those of the Cheshire Cat from the story, Alice in Wonderland. His smile was the same as the day he predicted we would have sex. The tone of voice James used conveyed the message I was going to do what he said to do, or I would pay a price in the form of violence. I do not know if Mitch was aware of this fact, but I do know a discussion between the two men had occurred. Mitch got up from the chair and walked over to me and embraced me. I turned my head and saw James walk out of the front door. Mitch caressed me in a very caring way and whispered in my ear, "I told you we would be together some day."

Mitch was a better lover than James or Don. He made me feel loved and appreciated, something James didn't even appear to try to accomplish.

James disappeared for a few hours and returned in a good mood. He never seemed upset regarding my relationship with Mitch, which confused me at times. For the next five years, our relationship would continue off and on, until my marriage ended.

Chapter 17:

What'd Ya Say?

"John, stop makin' that noise!" James yelled.

The yelling startled John out of his self-imposed trance where he rubbed his hands together while imitating the sound of a motorcycle. I watched him stare at James for a few moments, then relocate himself somewhere farther away where he could make his sounds again.

John did not initiate any communication with James. Despite all the tension in our household, John always managed to keep smiling. His sweet disposition enabled me to foster the strength to keep going against all odds. John and I had our own way of communicating. I learned very quickly what his sounds and movements indicated. James was continually frustrated with John as he had no idea what John wanted or needed.

By the time John was two years old, it was apparent to me he was experiencing delays in development. His speech development stopped abruptly, and he did not return affection. Some of my course selections while working on my associate degree were purposefully picked as their content related to children. My interest in having a career in the medical field waned, and I decided upon a new career goal, one where my work schedule coincided with John's, and I had the opportunity to learn more about language development in children. I made the decision to work on becoming a teacher. I began to take courses supporting not only this new goal, but also my needs as a parent of a child suffering from autism.

Pediatricians were reluctant to give me a diagnosis of autism as his symptoms didn't match the definition of autism that was mainstream in the late 1970s. My voice now became an advocate for my son. He was born in 1975, the year that the United States Congress passed legislation concerning the rights of handicapped children.

Right after John's second birthday, my sister-in-law, Gina, began working as the secretary for the Special Education Department Director for the Fontana Unified School District. I expressed my concerns about John to her and she relayed the information to her boss. He arranged an appointment for John to be assessed. James wasn't happy about the idea of John being assessed. After all there was nothing wrong with his child, but since his sister was involved, he reluctantly agreed. The assessments revealed that John was delayed in expressive and receptive speech. I began reading every book I could get my hands on that gave me information regarding language delay in young children. John was provided speech therapy and at the age of three was placed in a special education program run by San Bernardino County for four hours a day. In addition, he also qualified for transportation to and from the program.

The more I became obsessed with finding out more information on how I could help my child, the more James denied that our child had a problem. He kept making statements such as "If John went to a regular preschool with normal kids, then he would act normal."

James and John's relationship became even more strained because he forced John to do physical activities that were challenging and scary for him. At James's request, Anna and James Sr. purchased a two-wheeled bicycle for John a few months before he was three years old. The next day James put John on the bicycle with no training wheels and expected him to ride it.

"C'mon, John, put your feet on the pedals and go!" James told John.

"James, he's never been on a two-wheeled bicycle before. Maybe you should get him some training wheels?" I said.

"He rode a tricycle. He's almost three. He should be able to ride this bike with no problems."

John's sweet little face looked at me as if to say, "Momma, I'm scared."

"John, get off for a minute. Let Daddy show ya how to ride this bike."

James got on the tiny bike with his legs up against his cheeks and tried to ride it. He soon realized he couldn't manage it.

"Okay, John. Daddy will get his big bike and show ya how to ride."

James got on his big red ten-speed bike and rode down the driveway and onto the street in front of our house.

"There, John. Were you watchin'?" James asked.

John smiled a big smile and shook his head up and down. His dark, straight hair bounced all around his head. I reached down and gave him a hug.

"Stop babying him, woman!" James yelled.

I stepped back and then watched James put John back on the bike. James held it and then pushed it down the driveway. "Pedal, John, pedal!" James yelled as he let go of the bike. John began to pedal, but the bike drifted to one side and John and the bike fell to the ground. John looked up at me but didn't cry.

"Get up, son," James called out.

John pushed the bike off himself and stood up.

"Okay, get on it and try again!" James said as he picked the red and blue bike up waiting for John to climb on.

My little brave John got on the bike again and again and again, traveling a little farther each time before falling.

After an hour of this I pleaded, "James, don't you think he has practiced enough for one day?"

"Don't ya see he's gettin' better each time? He's tough. He's my son."

"He is getting better, but both of you look tired."

After another half hour of practice, James applauded when John rode about six feet on his own.

"Okay, son. That's it for today," James said.

My sweet John looked up at me, and I saw relief in his little blue eyes. He never stopped smiling the entire time. I took him by the hand, and we went inside the house.

James had high expectations for John as most parents do, but James was so determined to prove to everyone that John was a normal boy. He often had no tolerance when John's delays were obvious and had absolutely no patience with John's inability to speak clearly. He would ask him repeatedly to repeat a word or phrase.

"John, ya need to tell Daddy what you want with words, not noises. I dunno what your noises mean. I won't let ya get away with noises like your mother does."

Some days James would just walk away and say, "You take care of him. I've no idea what he wants."

On the worst days, James would scream at John over and over, "What'd ya say? What'd ya say? John, what'd ya say?"

These episodes usually ended with James spanking John, while I screamed, "Stop, James. He can't talk."

James typically responded by pushing or hitting me and storming off, while John and I sat hugging one another and crying. The tension between the three of us over John's speech delay worsened over time. It would take several years of speech therapy before John's speech improved at all.

There was one person in the Hawkins family who supported John and me wholeheartedly, and that was my mother-in-law, Anna. When John was two years old, she was hired as a special education aide for Fontana Unified School District at Virginia Primrose Special School. She constantly tried to instill an understanding of John's problem into James, and sometimes it seemed like she influenced him. But when she was not present, the evidence of her influence quickly disappeared.

Chapter 18:

Added Complications

Crash! I ran from the kitchen into the living room not knowing what I was going to find. There he was, just standing there looking at me, smiling. Behind him I could clearly see broken glass all over the floor.

"John, please, honey, don't move. Mommy is going to come and pick you up," I said. I picked him up and moved him to the couch.

"Stay right there, baby, until I can clean the glass up." I picked up the tennis racket he had found and determined it was what he had used to break the front room window into pieces. He remained on the couch as I had asked, making his sweet noises the whole time. To me his little noises were not annoying, but music to my ears. I so loved this little gift from God. As soon as I finished, I called my dad.

"Dad, can you please come and fix my front window?"

"Uh, okay. But how did it get broken?"

"John got hold of a tennis racket and smashed it. I'm not sure when James will be home, and it is supposed to rain tonight."

My real reason for calling my dad to fix the window was

I knew James would be angry at John and at me. But if it was fixed, I might not even have to tell him.

John's behavior started to progressively worsen, especially when he would try to communicate and not be able to articulate his words. This fact, along with the tension in our home, caused John to act out his frustrations and emotional anxiety by exhibiting destructive behaviors. These destructive behaviors were often triggered by events or places such as transitioning from home to the bus, or sometimes for no apparent reason at all. Once he arrived at his program or a restaurant, or someone's house, he would calm down after a few minutes. If we went to a place with lots of noise, it often resulted in John attempting to run out or away, knocking things like chairs or lamps over.

Attending 4th of July celebrations was especially difficult. He was terrified of fireworks. When John was almost three years old, his behavior at our family gathering on July 4th was, for me, almost unbearable. He began to run wildly and scream when the first firework was ignited. James immediately gave me a stern look. My dad ran into his house and came out with a hat with ear flaps used for winter weather. He approached John by kneeling down to his height a few feet away from him.

John stopped screaming, and I heard my dad say, "John, Grandpa has a magic hat for you. When you put it on your head, the fireworks will not scare you anymore."

John moved closer to my dad and grabbed the hat out of his hands and put it on his head. As soon as the hat was on his head, he ran over to me and sat in my lap. I wrapped my arms around him and smiled at my dad. My sweet little boy with his cherub-looking face smiled too, and we all enjoyed looking at the lights in the sky that evening.

On our way home James said, "I don't know what ya do that makes our son react to things, but I wish you'd stop whatever it is."

"James, I don't do anything to cause him to react to things. He's special. He has delays caused from birth trauma."

"I don't believe that hogwash. You're smothering him and causin' him not to develop right. It's all your fault."

"I'd love for John to be normal!"

"I don't know what to think anymore. You and my mom have very different ideas about John than I do. Your dad got him to calm down right away."

"Yes. And we all had a great time."

"Your dad is better with John than you are."

"Dad is good with him, but he doesn't have to take care of him every day."

"Well, I wish you'd stop him from having those fits."

"Me too."

I always wanted to include John in all normal activities, but it was tough at times. It was even tougher when James was with us and grew impatient and at times angry. James continued to be in denial regarding John's disability and even more determined to prove he was normal. John continued to try to please James. One afternoon after he had learned how to ride the two-wheeled bicycle, John disappeared. He was nowhere to be found in our house or the neighborhood. James and I were about to call the police when our phone rang.

"It's Dad. John is here with us. He rode his bicycle here. Did you know about this?"

"No! We've been looking everywhere for John. Thank God he's there with you. We'll be right over to pick him up."

I hung up the phone and turned to James. "John is at my parents' house!"

"How'd he get there?"

"Dad says he rode his bike there."

"See, I told you that boy is normal. He's so smart. He knew how to git to Grandpa and Grandma's house without anyone helpin' him."

When we arrived at my parents' house, James acted like a very proud parent. My reaction was one of horror. I kept thinking of all the terrible things that could have happened to my little boy.

Any change was difficult for John. When he began the San Bernardino County Special Education Program, they sent a small bus. A few weeks into the program they switched to a regular school bus that parked at the end of our street, waiting for him to board. This seemed to be a wonderful idea, until I realized John was afraid of the bus. Each morning he threw a horrible tantrum when the bus arrived. I worked diligently at making him board the bus, but it was a struggle for both of us. I now realize that it was probably the sound of the bus, as it was the large, average, yellow school bus. His screams were so loud the whole neighborhood could hear him. The elderly woman across the street came over quite often and prayed over him as he screamed. After a few weeks, the program returned to providing the small bus again and John's tantrums ceased.

By the time John was approaching three years old, his difficult behavior was very evident to anyone who was around him for even a small amount of time. For many reasons, I felt nervous every time I took John out into public places. At this time in America, the public was just becoming more aware of special needs children thanks to the Kennedy family and the Special Olympics. This awareness was not widespread. People still made comments and pointed at John when we were in public. Once while I was waiting in line at the grocery store, John began to scream and flail around, throwing himself on the floor. He did this without warning or provocation. Everyone around me seemed to think he was throwing a tantrum regarding wanting me to buy something.

So much so, the clerk said to the couple in front of John and me, "Some people don't know how to handle their child correctly."

When the couple left and it was my turn to check out, I said to the clerk, "And some people do not understand children with special needs." His face turned red, but he did not apologize for his comment. He quickly checked me out.

To complicate our lives further, my mother-in-law suggested I take John to the dentist as she thought she had seen a cavity in one of his teeth. I decided to take her advice and scheduled John for a dentist appointment. I called several places but discovered there were no children's dentists in the area that accepted our dental insurance. The next step was to call my dentist office and explain that I had an almost three-year-old special needs child who needed dental care. I was afraid I wouldn't be able to find a dentist who would see John. Our dentist's name was Dr. Sawyer. When I called his office and explained the situation with John, he immediately agreed to see him. I was overjoyed and relieved that my search for a dentist was over.

John was in a very good mood the day of the dentist appointment, and I had hope it would go well. Dr. Sawyer was very patient with John; John was not happy about the dental exam. Dr. Sawyer was able to identify one cavity and scheduled a second appointment. As we were getting ready to leave, he came into the lobby to speak to me.

Dr. Sawyer motioned for me to sit down. As I sat down, I became very nervous as he approached me, thinking he was going to tell me that he could not treat John.

He sat down next to me and said, "I know you are aware of John's disability. What if I told you that I might be able to help him improve?"

"What do you mean? How can you help?"

"Well, I'm part of a group of healers, and we've had success in treating children with various ailments."

I was intrigued and curious. He went on to invite me to his home later that week. He gave me an address, a time, and a day for me to bring John to be "healed." I was so desperate in finding help for John, that I agreed.

On a Thursday evening, John and I got ready to go out.

"Where are you two going?" James asked.

"Oh, I'm going to the library to get a book for one of my college courses, and I thought I would take John so he can pick out a book."

"Oh, okay. Have fun."

I lied to him to forgo any possible negative reaction. If it were to turn out to be a cure for John's problems, then I would tell James the truth.

As I got closer to the address Dr. Sawyer had given me, I noticed I was in a neighborhood of what I classified as newly built mansions. I was nervous there would be items that John could break easily. When we arrived, it was indeed a mansion. I walked up the long cement sidewalk. The house was so new, the lawn had just been seeded. I knocked on the door and a tall, young man opened the door. I asked if this was Dr. Sawyer's home and the young man said, "Yes, please come in."

As we entered, we were ushered to the left of the large entry hall into a large library-type room. There were bookshelves all around the room, but some were empty and there was no furniture except twelve chairs arranged in a circle filled with people who looked to be in their twenties. Only one chair was occupied with an older familiar face—Dr. Sawyer. A table at one side of the room held refreshments.

"Hi, Laurie, come on in. Alex, please get her a chair so she can join us," said Dr. Sawyer. I sat down and held John in my lap.

The evening began with quick introductions by first names around the room. Next, Dr. Sawyer led us in a prayer, looked at me and then said, "Please tell our group about John."

As I began to speak in front of this room full of strangers, I kept fighting back tears. In my mind, I was upset at myself because I was so desperate that I put John and me in such a situation with unknown consequences. I proceeded to tell the group about John.

I began with "John was born on August 28, 1975, at the Holloman Air Force Hospital, where he suffered from a very long, intense labor and birth trauma . . ."

I ended with this desperate plea for help. "John's behavior is erratic and unpredictable at times, and as a mother, I don't know where to turn."

Immediately after I finished my little speech, a young woman, who introduced herself as Tina, got up from her chair and walked toward me and embraced me in a hug. Then they all got up from their seats and sat on the floor. I sat in my chair wondering what was going to happen next.

Tina patted the beige carpet with her hand and said, "Laurie, please bring John and sit here with us."

"Do you think John will let us put our hands on him?" Dr. Sawyer asked.

I looked at John. He smiled at me and seemed unafraid. "As far as I can tell, it would be okay. John seems to be comfortable at this moment."

"Okay then. John, would you like to lie down on the floor right here in the middle of all of us?" Dr. Sawyer asked.

John giggled a little and immediately went to the middle of the circle and lay down. I smiled at this happy little boy lying in the middle of a circle of strange adults.

"Now please put your hands on John's feet," Dr. Sawyer requested.

Just as I touched John's feet, about six members of the group came over and put their hands on John's arms and legs. Dr. Sawyer put his hands on John's forehead. Then he led the group in a chant, which, at first, I thought was a healing chant.

"In the name of Jesus Christ, by the power of his cross and blood, we bind the spirits, powers and forces of the earth, the underground, the air, the water, the fire, the netherworld and the satanic forces of nature."

The longer this healing session went on, the more I realized that they were assuming John's problems were being caused by demonic possession. Their voices got louder and louder as they repeated the prayer over and over. When the volume of their voices began to rise, John began to wriggle and get anxious. I believe they thought the evil spirit in him was getting nervous. John's behavior appeared to cause the group to change their chant. Now, they repeated the following statement faster and louder for what seemed like an eternity, but in fact was only about five minutes.

"Bind all unclean spirits from this child."

When the volume of their voices reached almost a shouting level, John tried to force his way up and away from them, but they held him down.

It was at that moment I yelled out, "Please stop!"

They immediately let go of John, and he jumped up and landed in my arms. Everyone rose from the floor and Tina reached out and took John by the hand and led him to the table where there were cookies and punch. She grabbed a cookie, bent down to John's level, and handed it to him.

"Was this his reward for withstanding their treatment of him?" I thought to myself.

I couldn't help myself and blurted out, "John and I need to leave. It is almost his bedtime."

They all nodded their heads in unison.

"We would love to have you and John join us again sometime soon," Dr. Sawyer said.

"Thank you. We might," I said knowing full well I had already decided never to come back and subject John to this again.

Tina walked me to the door and said, "I think we had some success tonight driving out the evil spirit causing John's problem. I hope you understand that to fully complete our mission to cure him he definitely needs more sessions."

"I do understand. I just need time to think about it," I said.

"I understand. Have a good evening."

"Thanks. You too," I said as I walked out the door vowing to myself to never subject my child to this kind of session ever again.

Chapter 19:

Playing the "Survivor" Game

The streetlight illuminated the end of our driveway, but I could hear his car coming about one minute before it reached that point. It was two in the morning and James had not come home. I couldn't sleep, so I got up, went to the front room window, and stood there . . . watching, listening. My mind played a game with me.

I asked myself, "Where's James? Why hasn't he come home?"

My mind would come up with different scenarios. Maybe he crashed into a ravine and is trapped in his car. Maybe he had sex with a strange woman and her husband came home and murdered him. Maybe he is just an asshole and doesn't care if I worry.

James had begun to disappear for whole nights and sometimes several days without contacting me at all. In the days with no cell phones, the only way a person knew if someone was still alive was, if there was no contact from authorities, then one could presume they were okay.

My mother always said, "No news is good news."

I would proceed with my daily activities, which involved

working, going to college, and taking care of our child. When he finally did arrive home, he often said, "It doesn't matter where I was, bitch. I'm home now."

I became skilled at hiding our secret that he had a mental problem. When conversing with family or friends, I would make excuses for why we couldn't attend functions if he happened to be gone. Sometimes, I even made up stories to hide the reality.

I soon gained the ability to artfully develop coping strategies to hide the truth about what was going on, even from myself. Most of the people I interacted with believed my husband was normal due to the fact I NEVER revealed the abnormal behaviors to the outside world. As far as anyone knew, there were very few problems in our marriage. Even the neighbors had no idea. James also hid his true self, as the image he portrayed outside of our home was very different. He was the kind, compassionate helpful neighbor. He mowed the grass for the elderly neighbor free of charge, played with all the kids in the neighborhood on the weekends. It was truly like he was two different people.

During this same time, he acquired new friends I became acquainted with, and it was these relationships as a collective that gave me the opportunity to peek into his world outside of our home and neighborhood.

Through his work as a technician for General Dynamics, he met Gregg and his girlfriend Cha Cha. Gregg was a short, thin, handsome man of Asian descent and Cha Cha was a petite, beautiful young woman of Hispanic descent. We started out having dinners together at restaurants and shopping afterward. After a few months, James suggested we invite them over to our house for dinner. You would think I would have recognized the pattern, but I didn't. After dinner that evening, we all consumed quite a bit of alcohol. Then without warning, James and Cha Cha disappeared, and I was left alone with Gregg.

"Hey, sweetie, come and sit close to me," he said.

"I'm good where I am."

He was sitting on our couch, while I sat across from him on our loveseat. He got up and sat as close as he could without sitting on top of me.

"There, it's okay. I moved."

He leaned in to kiss me and I turned my head. I had promised myself to never repeat the wife-swapping scenario again.

"Gregg, I don't want . . . to sleep with you," I managed to say, through my alcoholic stupor.

Once again, he leaned to kiss me and once again, I turned my head. Then, I stood up and walked into our dining room. Gregg followed me and grabbed my breast. I pushed his hand away.

"Well, this snot what I spected from you," he said in an angry tone.

Little did I know the consequences Cha Cha suffered because of my actions that night. As soon as he realized an encounter with me was not going to happen, he got up and immediately found James and Cha Cha. They were in another room out of my sight, but they obviously were engaged in some sort of sexual activity. I was intoxicated to a level where I saw flashes of events happening around me, and at one point I looked up and saw Gregg dragging Cha Cha into the living room by her long black hair and dropping her on the floor right in front of me.

"Stop, Gregg! You're hurting her!" I could hear James yelling. Snapshots of Cha Cha struggling with Gregg while she lay on the floor kept flashing in front of my eyes like a slideshow.

"No!!!" Cha Cha screamed. I saw Gregg's fist come down and land on her nose, and blood came spraying out. I sat frozen on the couch saying nothing and doing nothing. It was as if the alcohol had paralyzed me. I wanted to help her, but I couldn't move. Was it fear or the alcohol? I am not sure, but I did nothing.

The next scene I witnessed was James standing motionless and silent near Cha Cha and Gregg. Cha Cha lay unconscious with blood pouring from her nose, and Gregg was standing over her. I believe I blacked out for a moment and awakened to Gregg standing in our doorway with Cha Cha in his arms. Then he disappeared, and I awoke to harsh words from James.

"What the hell did you say or do to Gregg? What kind of fucking hostess are you?"

My brain registered the accusatory questions being thrown at me, but my voice was unable to respond. I woke up on the couch a few hours later, just as the sun was rising. I walked to the bedroom and found James sound asleep in the bed. Once again I thought there had been a pre-arrangement without my knowledge or consent, but somehow I was to blame for Cha Cha's broken nose.

When James awakened later in the morning, he acted as if nothing had occurred the night before, and I was in no mood to remind him. I called Cha Cha a few days later to check on her.

"Are you okay?"

"Yes, I'm fine. I have a broken nose, but I went to the doctor, and he says it should not change the shape of my nose much."

"I'm so sorry, Cha Cha. I feel like it was my fault."

"Your fault? Not at all. I tripped on my own feet."

"I'm not sure that's what happened."

"Well, I know that's what happened. I drank too much and tripped on my own feet."

"Uh . . . okay. Maybe I was too drunk too . . ."

"Well, I gotta go. Thanks for checking on me."

I hung up the phone and began to question my own memory of that night. I only saw Cha Cha in person one other time. James kept me informed about the couple through conversations with Gregg at work and revealed they were pregnant about three months after their visit to our house. When she gave birth to a baby girl, I visited her and delivered a present. The visit and conversation were short, and neither of us mentioned the night her nose was broken.

The agreements made with friends of James's were not always sexual. A different kind of pre-arrangement was made with another friend of his from work whom I called Tex. I gave him this nickname because he was from Texas originally. I would often go meet James for lunch and Tex joined us at times. In my opinion Tex was a schemer, and I didn't trust him.

"Hey, Laurie, have you seen those ads in magazines selling twenty acres of land for a really cheap price?" Tex asked me at lunch one day.

"Yes. Why?"

"Well, if you pay for my gas and food, I can drive and look at it and let you know if it's worth the investment."

"Tex, I don't have the money to buy the land, so why would I pay for you to go look at it?"

"Well, because I want you to pay for me to take a trip. That's why," he said as he burst into laughter.

Tex continually told James and me about how he searched for investments, and he just knew one would someday pay off big.

I never dreamed James would ever invest in something Tex had proposed, until he came home one day and said, "Hey, babe, Tex connected with this drug dealer who can cut him a deal on some pills at half price. Tex says he can resell the same pills and make over a hundred and fifty percent profit! He asked if'n I was interested in buyin' some and he would sell them for me."

"James, I don't trust Tex. How much money did he want you to give him?" I asked.

"Well, we've 'bout two thousand dollars in our savings, so I was thinkin' 'bout giving him sixteen hundred. He told me if'n I gave him sixteen hundred, he could turn it into almost five grand in just two months."

"James, I really don't want to give Tex any money at all for his crazy scheme."

"Ya know what? I'm going to do it anyways, and when I bring you almost five grand, you can thank me then. You'll see, this is a good thing."

"Well, I guess this is your decision, then, and I hope you are right."

I was never given all the details, but frankly, I didn't want to know. Whenever we saved any money, he always found a way to spend it, no matter what I said. My opinion never seemed to matter. James was in charge. The next day Tex showed up at our house.

"I hope you two are ready to make some money," Tex said as we all sat in our living room staring at one another.

I sat on the couch next to James and Tex sat across from us on the loveseat. His long legs stretched way beyond the seat, with his cowboy boots fully exposed.

"James told me how nervous you are about this investment, but I can assure you this will work out."

"Okay, Tex. I'm happy to hear those words."

James stood up and took the cash from his jeans pocket and handed it to Tex. James nodded and sat back down on the couch. Both men looked nervous to me, like they were hiding a secret.

"Well, I hate to cut this visit short, but I need to go meet with the drug dealer who is going to sell me those pills at a discount," he said as he smiled and winked.

Tex always looked a little grubby to me and his dishwater-blond, straggling hair helped cement my opinion. As I watched Tex walk out the door, a fear I would never see him, nor our money again consumed my thoughts. This fear turned into a reality as weeks, months and years went by and James never mentioned Tex nor the money. When I would ask James, his response was always the same.

"Tex did what he said he'd do, and it didn't work out. Get over it, bitch." I never saw Tex again or any of the money.

The collection of friends James acquired during this period weren't all men, but all of them were not what society would deem as "normal." Meg was a woman James met through some of the guys at work.

One Saturday morning James got out of bed earlier than normal and announced, "Meg's comin' to pick me up and we're goin' rabbit-hunting."

"Okay. But who's Meg?"

"I met her through Ron at work. She acts like a guy, hon. You ain't got nothin' to worry 'bout."

"Okay . . . How long will you be gone?"

"Dunno. Maybe all day."

"Okay, John and I will probably go hang out at my parents' house."

A few minutes later an older blue Chevy pickup truck pulled into our driveway and out stepped a woman wearing a white t-shirt, blue denim overalls and big black boots. Her long dark-brown hair flowed down her back.

I opened the door and introduced myself and invited her in. She used her hand to push her hair back behind her ears and looked at me with a nervous smile. Her face was plain, but not ugly.

As she took a seat on our couch she said, "Thanks for being cool with James goin' with me out to hunt rabbits. It's nice to have someone to go with who likes huntin' as much as I do."

"No problem, Meg. My son and I are going to visit my

parents for the day."

"They live far from here?"

"No, just a few miles. Are you married, Meg?"

"No, not too many men wanna marry me," she said as she laughed.

"Oh, Meg, that can't be true."

"Oh, believe me, it's true," she said with a deep one-breath laugh.

James came out of the bathroom and said, "Well, Meg, are ya ready to get this show on the road?"

I walked them out to her truck. She opened the door on her camper shell to load his gear. I noticed her truck was packed with all sorts of camping gear and rifles. James kissed me and said, "Dunno what time we'll be back, hon."

I watched and waved as they drove off, feeling relieved to have a Saturday without him and feeling a tad guilty about it.

His excursions with Meg became more frequent and later each time, and even extended overnight. When he wasn't with Meg, he began to disappear for long periods of time on weekends. When I asked about his whereabouts, I got one of two reactions. One reaction was for him to yell at me saying, "Git over it, bitch! I like to drive around without the noise of you and John so I can think."

His other response was to tell me a story such as follows: "Babe, I just kept driving and driving until I got so tired, I didn't even recognize where I was. Then I realized I was almost out of gas and started lookin' for a gas station. Well, then when I stopped for gas, I started talking to the guy who owned it, and he was so nice and invited me to spend the night at his house. His name was Kyle, and his house was small, but nice for a bachelor pad. He fed me a huge breakfast and gave me directions back to you, hon."

Unfortunately, I would believe these fairytales, as I wanted to think I could trust him. My parents had taught me trusting your spouse was the right thing to do. Some of the modeling of good marriage tactics worked for me in this relationship, but many of them allowed James to take advantage of me.

I continually kept fooling myself into thinking James's behavior was not unusual or strange. In my mind, I would justify or explain away the behaviors he was exhibiting and without any professional knowledge or guidance regarding mental illness, I was always questioning myself when I thought a behavior was strange or out of place. I believe my family did the same thing at times. For example, we were at my parents' house for dinner one evening when my grandmother was visiting. James began acting strange toward John. He laid him on the floor and tied him up with an electrical cord when he began misbehaving. My brother, Tommy, who was in school studying to be a psychiatric technician, recognized immediately James's behavior toward John was not normal.

He approached James and said, "James, untie John right now."

James looked up at him and said, "Mind your own business!"

"John's my nephew, so he's my business, and what you're doing is wrong."

Without any warning, James rose and punched my brother in the arm. Tommy's reaction was to punch James right back. Before I knew it, James was on the floor on top of Tommy, and both were hitting each other.

I screamed, "Stop!"

They both looked at me and Tommy pushed himself away from James.

"Both of you stop fighting right now!"

My brother gave me a confused look and said, "Sis, I was

just trying to protect John."

In my heart I knew he was right, but James was my husband and the person I would have to face at home later, and I was fearful of that encounter.

I looked at James and said, "We need to leave now."

My parents and my grandmother all appeared to be in shock regarding this quick conflict. I am not sure they saw what sparked the incident as they were engaged in conversation when it happened. They did see the physical fight and were yelling out also, but my voice rang louder than theirs. This was the first physical fight between two adults I had ever seen occur in our family and I was totally horrified. As we drove home that night, I waited for James's reaction. Shockingly, he didn't say a word about it. Even after we arrived home, he did not mention it at all, and I was literally afraid to bring it up for fear of retaliation. As I put John to bed that night, I said a little prayer for this nightmare to end. I just wanted John to be safe and for James to start acting normal. I prayed to bind all the unclean spirits from James, as I feared that the evil was not in my child, but in my husband.

Chapter 20:

My Rebellion

The bell hanging from the entry door rang every time someone entered the store. For me, it was a signal to look up and see if any young man worth looking at was in my realm.

In January 1977 my father left his job at Kaiser Steel when they began downsizing before their final closure in 1980. He and my mother purchased a franchise for a Circle K store in Bloomington, California. I was continuing to take courses toward my new goal of becoming a teacher, but I wasn't working at the time, so he asked me to go to work for him. I ran the swing shift from three in the afternoon to eleven at night.

This store became a family venture, as my mother, brother and sister also worked there, along with the daughter of my mother's best friend, Valerie.

Valerie and I were close friends like our mothers, so having the opportunity to work together twice a week seemed like a fun idea. Valerie was separated from her husband and was in the process of playing the field, as we called it then. Quite often she didn't hesitate to sleep with men who came into the store. Deputy sheriffs were her favorite ones to choose, as I believe she felt safe with them.

My rebellion wasn't planned but was made possible by the fact many men came into the store to talk to Valerie. I was attracted to some of them and began flirting, not realizing I was treading in dangerous territory. All I knew was that this activity filled an emotional cavern within me and young attractive men were interested in talking to me. One younger man who came in was quite taken with me. "Hey, sweetness. I'm Brad Covington. Who are you?" he asked one day.

He was very tall, so he leaned forward and put his elbows on the counter so he could stare at me with his beautiful blue eyes. His blond shoulder-length hair encircled his tan-skinned, kind-looking face. His smile was subtle, but there. If it weren't for his overalls, I would have thought he was a surfer.

"How did you get so tan?" I asked.

"I'm outside a lot tending to the worm farms."

"Worm farms?"

"Yes, my friend and I began this business together. He has the money and I have the knowledge and do the work. The worms help us produce a fertilizer that increases crop productivity. Right now we are selling our product to soybean growers."

"Very interesting. I had no idea worm farms existed."

"Well, don't feel bad. A lot of people don't know they exist, but it can be a profitable business. I am working hard to ensure my friend gets a profit on his investment."

"Your friend is lucky to have you helping him."

"I hope so. If you would like, I can take you out to one of our farms some time."

"I would love to see a worm farm. I majored in biology at UCR for a short time. Living things interest me."

"I'm a living thing. Are you interested in me?"

"Most certainly."

We both laughed and I made sure he knew my work schedule just in case he wanted to come and visit again. The next three times he came in, we just chatted. The fourth time he walked up to me and whispered in my ear, "Hey, when you get off work tonight, can I pick you up so we can visit in my car?"

It was a Saturday night and James had already informed me he wouldn't be home until Sunday morning. John was spending the night with my parents.

I agreed without hesitation, which surprised me. I was well aware this encounter was going to lead to sex. The possibility of having sex with a man of my choosing made me feel free.

My shift seemed to be going so slowly. I could hardly wait until it ended. At five minutes to eleven o'clock, I looked out the front window of the store and saw Brad's white truck parked right in front. As soon as I finished my work, I walked out to his truck. He rolled down his window.

"Hi, beautiful. Want to take a ride with me?"

"Sure!"

"I thought eleven o'clock would never come," he said as I climbed in.

He gently grabbed my neck and pulled me close to him and kissed me. Chills went up and down my spine.

"I thought we could go to my place so we could sit and talk. Are you okay with that?"

"That'd be groovy. Is it close ta here?"

"Yeah, it's a house up in the hills above here. Only about five miles away."

"Okay . . . But I need to let ya know I need to leave no later than one o'clock so I can get some sleep before I have to go pick up my son in the morning."

"Good to know, pretty lady," he said as he winked.

While he drove, I talked nonstop. I was excited but very

nervous. When we arrived, he came around and opened my door and gently kissed me again as he lifted me out of his truck. I wrapped my legs around him, and he walked with me to and through his front door, kissing me the entire time. He set me down only long enough to close the door. This tall, gorgeous man picked me up like I was a feather and walked a short way to the couch, where he laid me down and pulled my shirt off. It felt so natural. I wasn't shocked nor scared. His gentle kisses went from my mouth down to the top of my pants. He looked up briefly, saw the smile on my face and continued to disrobe me. Before I knew it, he was inside of me, stroking my hair and gently kissing my face while he pumped his penis. The feeling was wondrous and ended sooner than I wanted it to.

As we finished, he rose up and said, "That was great!"

"I agree," I said, and we both giggled.

After we both dressed, he sat next to me and caressed me, stroking my hair and saying phrases like "I can't believe how beautiful you are." After a few minutes he rose up and said, "I suppose I should put a light on." Once again, we both giggled.

As he turned the light on, I noticed the living room was pretty bare. There was the couch we were sitting on and one chair. There were no decorations on the wall. The light he turned on was an overhead light attached to the ceiling.

"Wow, you need a decorator," I said.

"Yeah, this isn't mine, I'm just staying here while I work on the farm nearby."

His answer made me nervous, wondering if this was just a one-night stand, but then he asked if he could see me again and that feeling faded.

We both continued to enjoy the intimate time we spent together, and there was a mutual agreement there were no strings. I believed we both thought this was a private, friendly relationship. I was soon to find out my belief was wrong.

As usual, he came and picked me up after I finished my shift at work at the store. He didn't mention anyone else would be there. When we arrived, a friend of his was there. I'd met this man before as he came into the store as a customer. I knew he was married and had a family, so I stupidly suspected nothing. The three of us sat and visited for a while, drinking. Brad ushered me into the bathroom where we proceeded to have sex. When we came out, Dean was just sitting there drinking his beer.

Next, the three of us sat on the floor and continued to drink quite heavily. The next thing I knew was Brad was on top of me on the floor pulling my pants down and calling Dean to come over. He quickly took Brad's place and I tried to push him off. Brad came over and whispered in my ear, "Don't fight it." I stopped fighting and let Dean finish. As soon as he was done, I pushed him off, got dressed and asked Brad to take me to my car. He did as I asked. As I drove home that evening, I remember feeling so ashamed, stupid, and betrayed.

I asked myself, "Why do men I'm attracted to think of me as someone to share with other men? What did I do that makes them think this way? Why did I believe Brad actually cared about me as a person?" I never went with Brad again. I saw him several times after that, but never asked him to pick me up again, nor did he offer.

After my relationship with Brad ended, my behavior became reckless. My experiences with men had contributed to my depression and my feeling of self-worth was at an all-time low. "Beer runs" occurred often at my dad's store and running after the teenagers who were stealing beer became a fun activity for me. One time I ran right up to the car a young man was about to escape in and wrote down the license number of the vehicle. He nor his accomplices had any idea I was standing there in the dark, watching them.

I refused to sell beer to one man who didn't have any identification. He told me I couldn't stop him. I immediately grabbed the baseball bat my father had hidden under the counter and walked up to him and threatened to use it to stop him. Luckily, he backed down.

I was acting fearless because I just didn't care whether I lived or died. Unbeknownst to me, my father heard from Valerie about my risk-taking, causing my parents to question whether they wanted to continue as franchise owners.

One last compelling episode convinced my parents to relinquish their franchise. My brother, who was sixteen years old at the time, and I were working a Saturday evening shift together. I was standing behind the cash register and my brother was on the floor making coffee at the beverage counter, when suddenly a man with a mask on ran in and quickly pointed a gun at me and yelled, "Get it up!" I wasn't sure what he meant, so I raised my hands.

He then yelled, "No! Give me the cash." My brother heard him yelling and walked around the coffee machine so he could see me. He startled the robber, who then pointed the gun at him. All I could think of at the time was to give him the money and get him out of the store before one of us got shot. So I began to throw money out of the register at this masked intruder. I threw paper money and coins as fast as I could. It all landed on the floor, hitting him on the way down. He turned from pointing the gun at my brother, to holding it upright and dodging the money I was throwing at him.

"Lady, keep the change!" he shouted out. He then picked up all the bills I threw at him and shoved them in his pockets and ran toward the door. As I watched him run out, I saw the San Bernardino County deputy sheriff's patrol car driving into the store parking lot. Without hesitation, I ran out of the door and began waving my arms, pointing, and yelling, "He robbed us!"

The deputy stopped his car in front of the parking lot driveway, jumped out and began shooting at the suspect who was running away from the store with his gun in his hand. Before I knew it, the suspect stopped and began firing back at the deputy. I stopped and stood still as the orange flashes from their guns glowed in the darkness before my eyes. My ears were deafened from the sound, but I was compelled to just stand and watch the gunfight. Suddenly, a hand pulled on my blouse and a voice yelled, "Get inside, Laurie!" It was my brother Tommy, desperately trying to remove me from danger.

I was numb and my feet stood firmly glued to the sidewalk below me. My brain was enjoying the allure of this peril. Hearing my brother's voice made me finally realize he had put himself in harm's way to try to save me. I turned around and ran in with him. We both watched through the window as the robber jumped in a vehicle and drove off and the deputy's car followed in pursuit with the siren blaring. The pursuit ended at a rock quarry a few miles away from the store. The suspect escaped, but both he and the deputy had cuts and bruises all over their bodies from the quarry and both ended up at an emergency room. The comparison of wounds would convict the suspect a year later.

Chapter 21:

The Trip from Hell

"James, I need to tell you I've been screwin' a guy I met at the store," I said.

"How long have you been fuckin' around on me?" he said in an angry tone.

"It's been about two and a half months. I thought you might think it was good I found someone to fuck on my own."

"Really? You thought I'd be happy you're cheatin' on me?"

"Cheatin' on you? You have me fuck all your friends."

He ran up to me and pushed me down." You bitch," he yelled.

I sat on the floor staring at him in surprise as he had rarely expressed any jealousy or anger about any of the other men.

He then stepped back and said," But, ya know what? When you go to see him again, let me know. It does kinda turn me on." His swift change from anger to calmness confused me, but I was relieved for the moment.

Our discussions regarding my sexual encounters with Brad were short-lived as it was only a few weeks later when I stopped seeing him. I never told James the real reason I stopped seeing Brad. I just told him he moved away.

One day shortly after that James said, "I've noticed you're a little down, hon. Ya know how I always promised you we'd go to Disney World some day?"

"Yeah. Why?" I asked.

"Well, let's do it. I've vacation in July, and I'm sure your dad will let you take a week or so off. What ya say?"

"Okay."

"We'll take the camper and truck and drive there, so it won't cost us a whole lot."

This news did make me happy and excited to travel, but this was temporary.

I could see the giant, green alligator with huge white shiny sharp teeth running toward John, picking him up with its mouth and swallowing him in one bite as I stood there screaming.

"Wake up! You're havin' a nightmare," James said as he shook my shoulders.

This kind of nightmare began haunting me a few days before we left for Florida. As much as I wanted to go on this vacation, deep down inside I knew James had an underlying, menacing reason for this trip.

The first day out appeared to be a normal family vacation. John in the back seat and me in the front next to James, all three of us excited and happy. But on the second day it was as if a dark cloud began to hover over James.

"I'm starvin'. You're taking way too long to cook breakfast."

"James, it's been a while since I cooked in the camper. I'm goin' as fast as I can."

"Well, ya need to get faster because we need to get on the road. You're the slowest bitch I know."

"Sorry, I'll work on getting faster."

"Ya better or else."

His authoritarian ranting wasn't unusual, but I thought it

might subside a little because we were on vacation. Later in the day when we stopped for a break, his ranting took on a different tone and content.

"Hey, hon, I know my dick isn't as big as Brad's, but I'm your husband, and I'm thirsty, so run and git me a drink, ya bitch. Oh, and we can fuck in the campground bathroom tonight."

By the third day, as we were going through Texas, his rhetoric got even worse. "You're a cheatin' bitch, not worth the dirt on the bottom of my shoes."

I just sat there as he continued to berate me. "My wife cheated on me with a fuckin' worm farmer. His worm was sure in her farm!" he yelled out the window.

Suddenly, he pulled the truck over to the side of the road and stopped. "Git out, ya fuckin" whore!" yelled.

"What are ya doing? Please don't leave me here!" I screamed. John began to cry.

"Ya crazy bitch. I'm not goin' ta leave ya here. Just get in the camper. You're not fit to sit up here with me. And take your son with ya so he'll stop crying."

I wiped my tears from my face, picked up John and walked around and climbed into the camper. Before I could even sit down, James hit the gas and took off. He didn't make very many stops, but when he did, he was still very nasty toward me. At one stop for gas on the border of Texas and Louisiana, there was a small restaurant on site. I got out of the camper carrying John and asked, "James, can I take John and go into the restaurant and get us something to eat?"

"Ya can go in and git a bite ta et for ya and John. I don't want anythin' ta et. The sight of ya turns my stomach sour."

I immediately took John into the restaurant and ordered some food. John and I had just started to eat when James came storming in. "Hey, woman, ya need to come back to the truck right now," he said.

I picked up the food the best I could and complied. He walked ahead of me and held the door. Once we were outside, he began screaming at me. "You took way too long. I waited in the truck by myself thinking you would be back any minute. But, no, you were deliberately taking your time, just to piss me off. You're such an inconsiderate bitch!"

"I'm sorry, James. I didn't realize how long . . ." I said as he cut me off mid-sentence.

"You didn't realize how long it was takin'? Poor excuse."

John and I got back into the camper, and we drove off. I held onto John tightly not only to keep him safe from my husband's erratic driving, but to sooth my emotions.

James drove until we came to the bridge in Louisiana that spans the Bonnet Carré Spillway at Lake Pontchartrain. It was late in the night and very dark. James stopped the vehicle in the middle of the road, "Git up here now!" he yelled. John was sleeping, so I left him on the bed and crawled through the window between the truck and camper. Once I was in the front seat, he handed me a spotlight.

"Shine the light out ta the side of the road while I drive. I want to make sure I don't git too close to the side."

As I aimed the light toward the side of the road, there was nothing but water. He took the spotlight and shined it on the other side and all we saw was water. "I've been driving for a few minutes on this bridge. I thought we'd be across by now."

Coming from California we had never seen so much water, other than the ocean. You could see people were living on the water, which also amazed us.

"I need ya to stay up front with me now, babe. I'm a little nervous 'bout driving on this long-ass bridge."

I continued shining the light onto the water. There were

160

no other cars on the road. Finally, the bridge ended, and we came upon a campground and stopped for the night. The next morning James appeared to be friendlier to me, and I asked him if we could stop in New Orleans, as I had always wanted to see this city. He agreed.

The campground we stayed at was only about twenty miles away from New Orleans, so we reached the city by noon. James decided he would drop me off so he could find a park for John to play in while I went sightseeing. He gave me one hour. I was disappointed that I only had an hour but took it and quickly got out of the truck. He dropped me off at Jackson Square by the St. Louis Cathedral. I was frantic to get in as much sightseeing as I could. I started walking and happened upon Bourbon Street. It was lunchtime, so not a lot of jazz was being played, but I enjoyed walking down the street and just looking at people. Just being in New Orleans was an awesome feeling. I watched the time very carefully, as I didn't trust James would wait for me. In the past, he had dropped me off when we were having an argument and had left me to find my own way home. I didn't want to make him angry. I walked back to Jackson Square, where he had dropped me off. I still had a few minutes left so I decided to go inside the St. Louis Cathedral. It was breathtakingly beautiful. I stood inside and felt safe and comforted. It was as if God had wrapped his arms around me and whispered everything would be okay. I looked down at my watch and saw that my hour was up and walked out. He was there with the truck running, yelling, "Hurry up! I don't want to park!" I ran and got into the front seat of the truck quickly and we drove away. I didn't dare complain it wasn't enough time to see New Orleans, but I was satisfied I got to see it, even if it was just for an hour. I was at peace.

The next leg of the journey was uneventful, and James's

anger seemed to have subsided. We drove from New Orleans to Mobile, Alabama, and slept for a few hours at a rest stop. I slept in the camper bed with John, and James slept in the cab. He didn't exhibit any anger toward me, nor did he show any kind of affection whatsoever. But that wasn't necessarily always unusual in our relationship. It was so hot and humid we really didn't sleep much. When the sun came up, we got up and headed for Orlando.

We found an RV campground just outside of Orlando, about seven miles from Disney World. The campground had a lagoon and an older, kind gentleman named Bill warned us there were alligators. That night I could see their glowing eyes piercing through the darkness. As a result, I kept a very close eye on John and explained to him about the alligators. My insurmountable worry, plus the Florida heat and humidity, caused me to have continued sleep deprivation which deepened my poor emotional state.

On the first morning in Orlando, we got up early and traveled to Disney World. It was July 1978, and there was only the one park open at that time.

John was less than one month away from his third birthday and developmentally disabled. He often feared things we could not figure out. He would just burst into a tantrum or cry horribly, and we had a rough time figuring out what prompted this behavior. This, along with James's continued anger at me, made for a stressful experience for me. As soon as John began to act out, James would scream at me and tell me to make him stop. If I was unable to do so, then he would forcefully pick John up and scare him into stopping by telling him he was going to spank him. Because of this, I was constantly on edge.

There were long lines for all the rides and John was not very patient. James picked out the rides we were going to go on, and

I didn't argue with him until he chose "Mr. Toad's Wild Ride."

"James, I'm not sure John will like this ride. It might be too much for him."

"He'll like it 'cause I say so."

When the ride car entered darkness, John began to cry. James put his arms around him tightly and talked to him in his ear. I couldn't hear what he said, but John stopped crying and was fine the rest of the ride.

Throughout the day, James would shoot me an angry look, but we didn't argue much, as I kept very quiet for the most part. I only spoke when I feared that something would scare John. I went along with James's choice of rides, food, etc. We had purchased a two-day adventure booklet, so after dinner at the park, we left to go back to the RV park for the night.

When we arrived back, Bill greeted us and invited James to go on his boat fishing early in the morning. James loved to fish, so he agreed to go. I remember feeling so desperate I fantasized that the boat Bill and James were in would capsize, and James would be eaten by an alligator. This, of course, did not happen and James returned without a scratch or with any fish.

He did appear to be happy after his fishing expedition, as we loaded back in the camper to drive to Disney World for our second day.

The second day was even more crowded and hotter and more humid. John had several tantrums. I believe James didn't want to appear to be cruel to John in public, so he walked away and left me to handle John by myself. Once as he walked away, I could hear him saying, "You're so stupid. What a joke." I was always able to calm him down in a couple of minutes, amid many stares from the crowd.

Afterward, James would scold me for a few minutes. "I can't believe what a terrible mother you are. You're smart, but really dumb when it comes to handling John." I refrained from reacting, as we were in public, and I didn't want to prompt James to say more nasty things, nor did I want him to take his anger out on me or John later in private.

Since we were both working at the time, we had enough money to afford to buy John lots of drinks and a couple of toys. These items seemed to help keep him calm at times, but if the crowd became extremely loud, he would cover his ears and run for cover screaming. At the time, I didn't realize John was not only developmentally disabled but also autistic and taking him to such a noisy, crowded place was not fun for him. In 2013, John's disability was listed under the definition of autism spectrum disorder. In 1978, autism was not a well-known disorder compared to today. The public in general did not understand or recognize John as disabled. To the general public, it appeared as if he was a spoiled brat and I was an inadequate parent, which is also how James classified me.

Chapter 22:

The Decision

"I want ta have another baby," I said to James shortly after John's third birthday.

"I guess, ya crazy bitch. I really love baby-makin' sex," he said, elongating his words.

I thought having a second child would help our marriage. My faulty logical thinking was that if this child was not disabled, James would be happier, thus we would both be happier. So I went off the pill and we found out we were pregnant in April 1979.

James's parents were thrilled with the news about having another grandchild. My parents were not as thrilled, as they had witnessed firsthand James's dissatisfaction with John. They, as parents do, worried about the future with James and I and two children, one being disabled.

The pregnancy went well, except for extreme heartburn I experienced quite frequently. The doctor determined the due date to be November 16, which happened to be the same day as James's birthday.

Our life together seemed hopeful but began to change while

I was in my sixth month of pregnancy. James began coming home early from work a couple of times each week. I was happy to have him home, especially when I was pregnant, but when I asked how he was able to do this, his response was, "No worries, my buddy clocked me out."

If I began to question further, he would get angry, so I backed off. As time went on, getting home early became a daily occurrence. My parents had given up their Circle K franchise, so I wasn't working. James was our only source of income, and I feared this behavior could jeopardize our financial stability.

Unfortunately, my fears became a reality and James was fired from General Dynamics for falsifying his timecard. The Aerospace Workers Union vowed to get James his job back, but it was going to take three to six months. Our medical coverage was stopped immediately and, with me being pregnant, this was a problem. We visited his parents and told them our predicament, but they were not in any financial situation to help us. My parents were on a camping trip at the beach and James suggested we go visit them there.

I was extremely embarrassed to admit to my parents that James had been fired from his job. I expressed my concerns to James.

"I will talk to your dad and tell him what happened. Don't worry, honey. It'll be fine."

"Good. Dad would probably rather hear the news from you, because I will cry if I tell him.

"Okay. I'll fess up to my mistake. I am thinkin' he'll respect that."

When we arrived at the campsite, James did what he said he would do. He told my dad by himself, while I visited with my mom. Whatever they said to each other, it seemed to work.

"Don't worry, sweetheart. Your mother and I will help you

guys out financially," my dad said in his usual comforting tone of voice. I breathed a sigh of relief, taking in the calming smell of the ocean spray.

Over the next few months, I was able to apply and receive Medi-Cal coverage for my delivery costs and was able to continue seeing my doctor. In addition, we qualified for food stamps. James went to work for our preacher's family gas station for a few weeks, and then landed a job working at the Food Machinery Corporation. Expecting a new baby made life tolerable and once again, I had hope for the future.

On the morning of November 16, I was awakened by contractions like those I had experienced with John weeks before I delivered him. I had a scheduled doctor's appointment that morning. My mother and her best friend, Bonnie, drove me to my appointment where I expressed my concerns about delivery to my doctor. Dr. Ruiz was very supportive and assured me this delivery would go smoother than my first one.

I was scheduled to have a sonogram at 1 o'clock that afternoon. At the conclusion of this test, the technician recommended I check in at Labor and Delivery, which I did. After assessing me, Dr. Ruiz was summoned. I was quickly rolled into the operating room where our second son, Michael, was delivered by C-section on Friday afternoon, November 16, 1979.

James arrived just in time to see his son minutes after his arrival. Mom and Dad, Anna and James Sr., all came along wi00000th James into my hospital room to welcome Michael. Not long after everyone left, so did James. He only came back once to see me two days later for a brief visit. I longed for James to be there to share in this experience, but to no avail.

Michael and I remained in the hospital for five days. My cousins visited, my sister came quite often and on the day of our discharge, my mother picked us up and took us to her house for the first night.

I would find out after I arrived home that James partied with several men and women in our home, including Mitch. This was the beginning of James's affair with Linda. His attitude regarding this affair was one of arrogance.

"I deserve happiness and she's makin' me happy. You had Brad and now I got Linda. We're even."

His words made me feel guilty for his behavior—once again. In the meantime, I continued to recover from having a Cesarean section and focused on my children.

I often had phone conversations with my mother and on one occasion, I had a weak moment and complained to her about James's affair with Linda.

"Mom, James is having an affair."

"Well, is your marriage important to you?"

"Of course it is."

"I agree with you. Marriage should be important to you. So you should do everything you can to preserve it. You have two children to consider also. This will require great patience on your part. You should ask him to discontinue his affair and if he does, then he deserves your forgiveness."

This was the first time I had revealed any of the troubles in our marriage to her, so she had no idea of the complexity of the real problems that existed. Her words convinced me I was making the right decision to stay married to James. She would regret her advice later when she discovered the myriad of issues I was dealing with—the affair being a symptom of James's mental issues and not the real problem.

Chapter 23:

Cancer Comes to Visit

The Dragon's eyes were looking straight at me. I stared right back, practicing for my reaction to what James was going to tell me. He was sitting right across from me jabbering about the weather. "When is he going to tell me he is leaving me?" I thought to myself. Part of me wished he would leave me and go live with Linda. My mind pondered as to the real reason he was here.

On this day, he had arranged to meet me for lunch in Riverside at my favorite Chinese restaurant. He only did nice gestures if he wanted something. I was working now as a clerk in the Elections Department for Riverside County, so I could supply him with money for his extra spending and his amphetamine use. I didn't like the idea of leaving my newborn son with a sitter, but I had grown impatient with James's affair with Linda and couldn't sit home alone anymore. He often lied about where the money was going and, frankly, I didn't question it to avoid any confrontations with him.

The waiter took our order and immediately I asked, "Okay, James. What's going on?"

"Well, I need ta tell ya something."

I braced myself for the words "I'm leaving you for Linda."

"My mom has been diagnosed with cancer. The doctor told her he believes it started in her cervix, but it's spread to other parts of her body. It doesn't look good, babe."

I had prepared myself for a fight. This news completely shocked me. Anna was truly the only Hawkins family member I trusted. The thought she might die soon frightened me and tears began to run down my face. James touched my hand as it rested on the tabletop.

"This is bad news. I'm not sure what's gonna happen. I just . . . want her ta stay around. Ya know?" Instantly, my thoughts shifted from our problematic relationship to Anna and her illness.

"Oh, I'll fight this cancer and win," Anna told me when I saw her the next day.

"I sure hope so."

"The womenfolk in our family're strong. We've no other way to be. We fight and win," she said.

Anna's first surgery was performed in February 1980, followed by several rounds of radiation, which severely weakened her body. As time went on, her shoulders slumped, her hair fell out, and her skin turned gray.

We visited her often and each time, I would sit on her bed, and she would say, "I'm stayin' strong. My grandkids give me the strength to go on. But if'n I don't, I need you to keep me alive by tellin' those boys 'bout me. They're the reason I live. If'n I can't be on this earth anymore, then I'll live on in them. Ya need to protect them. They're what's important. Promise me." No matter how many times she asked me, I always promised.

During the months after her treatment began, she spent a great deal of time in the Loma Linda University Hospital. James

170

and I and our two boys went to visit her as often as we could. These visits took up most of our spare time, so my husband's escapades slowed way down, as did our domestic quarrels. Our weekends were spent going to the hospital and one of us going up to visit her while the other stayed outside on the hospital grounds with the kids. Anna's hospital room had a window allowing her to see the boys, since the hospital did not allow them on her floor.

Anna grabbed my hand and squeezed. "My . . . fight is almost done . . . I'm gonna be fine, just fine," she said as I stood at her bedside the last time I saw her alive.

"Anna, don't say that," I told her. James was outside with the boys and James Sr. was out having a smoke. Anna and I were alone.

"I . . . must . . . tell ya . . . I know I . . . don't have much time. You gotta be strong for your boys. I . . . love . . . my son. But . . ."

"It's okay, Anna. Please save your strength. I do understand. John and Michael are my life, and I will do whatever it takes to protect them."

She closed her eyes for a couple of minutes. When she opened them again, she squeezed my hand again and smiled. She and I both knew she was near death, but somehow both of us were at peace with this inevitable end.

That night I didn't sleep very well. We had a night light in the hallway and at around three in the morning I saw a shadow. I thought it was John, so I jumped out of bed and ran into the hallway. I stopped about a foot from the shadow when I realized it was not John. The shadow put its hand up motioning for me to stop. We both stood motionless for about a minute, when suddenly it disappeared. A wave of sensations transmitted the message to me that this shadow was Anna. I stood still for another minute questioning myself, "Am I awake or is this a dream?" I determined I was awake, and then wondered the significance of this event. This was the first of several times Anna's soul would visit me.

Early the next morning, we received a phone call from Fiona stating Anna was very near death. We arrived at the hospital just minutes after she passed away. It was September 2, 1980.

Fiona and Gina had spent the night with Anna and were there when she passed. Fiona told us, "Her passing was so peaceful. Gina and I started holding her hands around three in the morning. That's when we noticed she was starting to slip away. I think we grabbed her hands to try to hold on to her. I can't believe she is gone, but at least she is out of pain."

James began to sob quietly, and I put my hand in his hand as Fiona grabbed him and they both sobbed together. It was comforting to me to see him display normal emotions.

The next week was a whirlwind. James and I, along with his two sisters, helped his father make all the arrangements. His father gave us the money to go out and purchase new outfits for the funeral, so we all looked respectable. It was a deep loss for me, as Anna and I had a close connection. We both lived with abusive men. Anna and I didn't discuss our marital situations a lot, but her eyes often sent me messages of support and empathy. I believe deep down inside she knew something was wrong with her son. She understood motherhood and encouraged me to always protect my children. Her role as a mother was part of her soul and transcended death where her spirit was present to guide me and help protect her grandsons.

Chapter 24:

A Child is Born

I saw her vehicle and gave into the urge to follow her. I wanted to torment her the way she had been tormenting me with her phone calls. My little Pontiac Sunbird sped up quickly and before I knew it, I was right at the bumper of Linda's older Ford Country Squire station wagon. Because I was traveling so close behind her, she turned her head to look. Her long dark straight hair was covering part of her face. I saw her move her hair away, and a look of surprise came on her face when she realized it was me following her. She swerved and stopped suddenly, trying to make me run into her car. I braked without hitting her car and proceeded to drive beside it, causing her to drive on the shoulder of the road. I stuck my head out of my window, looking at her with as mean a look as I could muster. Without caring about my own safety or hers, I swerved my car toward her trying to make her go off the road. It was at that moment, I noticed she had two of her children with her. A look of fear and shock emanated from her face. My own act of anger scared me, and I drove back on to the road and sped away. My heart was racing but I was left with a weird feeling of satisfaction.

"I'm pregnant, and it's James's. Ya need to let him go," Linda often said as I picked up the phone.

"I'm not forcing him to stay with me. He can leave anytime."

"Bitch! He says you won't let him go!" I usually hung up the phone at this point.

After Anna's death, James and Linda resumed their relationship. It was a few months later when I found out there was a child on the way. To complicate matters, Linda was married with three children. James denied the child was his, and Linda's husband, Steve, according to James, appeared to have no idea the child wasn't his. The only reason I had any knowledge regarding the child was Linda's relentless phone calls to me during the first trimester of her pregnancy.

Her phone calls usually came when James was not at home. One time she called and left the phone off the hook after calling me "Bitch!" That time I stayed on for a few minutes to see if I heard James's voice in the background because he was not home that evening. Unfortunately, all I heard was the opening and closing of a door to a small store or a bar and muffled conversations. I couldn't distinguish any one person, so I finally hung up.

A short time after the phone calls started, Linda's husband came to see me. I hadn't met him, but James had told me his name. My doorbell rang, and I answered it.

"Hi, Laurie. We've never met, but my name is Steven Gallagher. Can I speak to you about Linda and James?"

I didn't want to invite him inside of my home, so I said, "Okay. But let's talk on the porch."

He appeared to be calm and reasonable as he began to speak. I believe he was under the assumption I didn't know about their affair.

"I've gotta come right out and tell you. James and Linda are cheating on us. I think they started their little fling a couple of months ago."

I just listened and nodded my head as he spoke. He made no mention of the pregnancy. I think he realized while he was speaking that I was already aware of their affair.

"Did you know about this?" he asked.

"Yes."

"Are you okay with this?"

"Of course not. But what can I do except divorce him?"

"Are ya going to?"

"That's a matter for discussion between my husband and me, not you and me."

Steve was tall and more handsome than I had imagined. He was dressed in a collared shirt and dress pants, and it made me wonder if he was on his way to work.

"I think you and I have nothing more to talk about, so if you don't mind, I need to get back to my kids."

"Oh, okay, I need to go now anyway," he said as he looked at his watch.

I was a little surprised, as I watched him walk from my porch, through my yard, and get in his truck and leave. I thought he might be a little more persistent in asking for details as to how and when I found out. After he left, I surmised his only reason for coming to see me was to tell on my husband. He appeared to be deflated when I revealed I already knew. I never heard from him again.

The evening after Steve's visit, I revealed the encounter to James. He didn't seem worried about it and told me, "He's a jerk and I think she's gonna kick him out."

About a month or so later, I noticed James was not seeing Linda as often and one day I asked, "Are you and Linda still hot and heavy even though she's pregnant?"

"She keeps insistin' that baby's mine. I'm not into her anymore. We are through, babe. I just wanna be with ya."

A few months later, I received a phone call from a woman who only identified herself as a friend of Linda's. She told me Linda had just delivered a baby girl at the San Bernardino County Hospital and, before I could say anything, she hung up.

Immediately after finding out she gave birth to a little girl, I decided to go to the hospital and see the child for myself. I told no one where I was going. I told James I was running to the store and left the kids with him. I parked my car far out in the parking lot so I could survey it to see if Steve's truck was there. I approached the building cautiously but didn't see any sign of Steve. I stood in front of the viewing window staring at the beautiful little girl. I had so longed to have a girl, but instead, this nasty woman who was sleeping with my husband had a girl by him, I thought as I stood there. This sweet girl had dark hair like James and her mouth and chin resembled his. I knew in my heart this little girl was his offspring. As I drove home, I became angrier and angrier at James for denying the obvious. I stormed through our front door and said, "James, I got a phone call today telling me Linda gave birth to a baby girl. I went to the hospital to see the baby, and I think she's yours."

I was waiting for an angry response, but instead he said, "I dunno why you went to see her. You're gettin' yourself all worked up. All new babies look the same. That baby's not mine. I don't care about Linda, and I don't care 'bout her baby. I don't want to talk 'bout it anymore."

Chapter 25:

The Class Reunion

"**I** saw you! Ya didn't think I did, but I did!" he yelled.

"What're you talking about, James?" I asked.

"You were flirting and waving your ass at those guys. You're such a whore," he said as he pushed me against the wall in our hallway.

"Really, James? You're mad at me about my flirting when you spent the entire evening following Lila around like a lovesick puppy dog?" Lila was one of his old flames he reunited with at the class reunion.

I crouched down and waited for him to hit me. When he didn't, I yelled, "Go ahead and hit me. Ya know you want ta!"

"You're such a bitch. You embarrassed me tonight. Lila is a perfect lady. She isn't a whore like you."

In May 1981, an invitation to our ten-year high school class reunion arrived and we made plans to attend. Our neighbors, Mitch and Carrie, invited us to ride in their car to the event. Carrie and I planned a shopping day to go out and get dresses. We were excited to find dresses that would enhance our appearance, as now we were women and not teenagers. We began our shopping excursion by visiting small dress shops in the mall, but quickly switched to Sears and J. C. Penney when the dresses we chose—which were labeled our sizes—got stuck around her neck and mine fell to the floor. When this happened, we had a very good laugh and decided the more mainstream stores were better places to find our proper sizes. We did finally manage to find dresses that fit us both and enhanced our looks. Then we planned our hairstyles, makeup, etc., and waited anxiously for the date to arrive.

On the day of the reunion, we all happily got ready and headed in our car together to the Riverside Convention Center. Once we arrived, James discovered Lila was there unaccompanied, so he spent most of the evening following her around. Several of the male classmates who had never bothered with me in high school took notice, complimenting me and making me feel special. This attention afforded me an opportunity to temporarily forget about James and his disgraceful attention for his old flame. Mitch and Carrie mingled with the crowd, separately from us, as I believe they didn't want to get involved in our marital dispute. At the end of the evening, I felt like I had enjoyed the evening despite James's behavior. We appeared all to be happy as we left the event.

When we arrived home, for the first time in our marriage, I truly feared for my life. After our quarrel he left the room. I sat on the floor sobbing. I heard him in the bathroom and then watched him head for the bedroom. I was so angry at him I couldn't make myself lie down next to him, so I made a bed for myself on the couch. I had trouble falling asleep, but finally did. I don't know how long I had been asleep, but I awakened to the sound of heavy breathing. I opened my eyes to see his red, angry face hovering over me. He didn't say anything but grabbed me by the neck and held me in the air over him. His eyes penetrated my soul. I couldn't breathe . . . I remember waking up on the floor alone in a puddle of my own urine. I could hear him snoring. He had gone back to bed.

Once again I had fallen victim to his erratic behavior. When he awoke the next morning, he acted like nothing unusual had transpired the evening before. There was no mention of anyone's behavior nor any conversation regarding the class reunion. I certainly didn't want to mention the subject. All I could think about was the intense and crazy look in his eyes as he held me by the throat above him. I was too scared to even contemplate the idea he could murder me. I asked myself, "Did he even check to see if I was alive before he went to bed last night?"

This incident instilled even more fear and insecurity within me regarding my interactions with other men when James was around. James, on the other hand, seemed more determined to arrange sexual encounters and watch me squirm to make sure I had his approval. These arrangements were throwing me into a downward emotional spiral, and I found myself beginning to lose "me."

Chapter 26:

Birds of a Feather Flock Together

"Man, I never want to go through a beating by Denny ever again. If he even gives me the same look, I will run out of the door so fast . . ." Belinda told me in the car one day on our way to college.

"Belinda. He beat you?" I asked.

"Yeah. It was so bad, I was admitted to the hospital. My eyes swelled shut. My jaw was broken. I was a mess," she said.

I could feel her pain. The sadness in her eyes prevailed as she told me her story.

"I married Denny when I was seventeen. I was too young, just like you. I was oblivious to all the warning signs. I thought I was in love."

"I'm not sure we really know what love is at that age," I added.

"My parents were against my marriage, which made me more determined to marry him. He pushed me around a few times now and again, but after I gave birth to our first daughter, Janice, is when he began hitting me."

"Belinda, James didn't begin hitting me until after John was born. I wonder why?"

"I'm not sure I know the answer to that question. All I do know is that's when his physical abuse toward me began. At first his fits of violence left me with a few bruises and an occasional black eye. He would apologize profusely and promise not to do it again. I have always accepted his apologies," she continued.

"It feels like James is beginning to get more violent with me."

"You need to be careful."

"I know, but he is unpredictable."

"I know what you mean. When Denny isn't angry at me, he's great. When he lets his anger consume him, is when we have a problem. It was not long after our second daughter, Debbie, was born, when he beat me so brutally."

"Wow, Belinda. I'm so sorry. You didn't leave him?"

"No. I blamed myself. My mom and dad were horrified and did not want me to go back home with him. Somehow, I convinced them he was willing to work on his anger issues. I have forgiven him, but I'm not sure I can ever fully trust him again. He seems to be working hard to control himself, but we'll see."

Belinda and I were kindred spirits. I believe it was no coincidence we met when we did. After the US presidential election of 1980, I was laid off from the Riverside County Elections Department and sought out employment in the field of education. I was hired as a teacher's aide at North Tamarind Elementary School in the fall of 1981. Belinda had been working as a teacher's aide there for a few years before I arrived.

Once we began talking to one another, it was like we had always known each other. Through our conversations we discovered we were both attending the same college, and both had the goal to become teachers. After a few months, we began to reveal the darker sides of our marriages. Having a friend with a similar struggle became one of the lifelines I dearly held on to, preventing myself from totally losing "me."

Belinda's strength emanated from the depths of her soul. You knew you were in good company when you were with her. At the precise moments I needed her strength she would look downward at me and say, "You can overcome anything, lady. And if you can't, I've got your back."

Her normal stance appeared strong, resting on a firm bone structure. Her black hair was cut short, and her voice was low and strong. Her smile showed strength and warmth at the same time. Her hand on your shoulder felt like an angel's touch.

Belinda and I both found one another when we were both at a very dark and painful point in our marriages, but our friendship helped ease some of the pain. We could talk to one another like no one else. We had an understanding we shared. I think we both knew these marriages were not long for this world, but for the time being we had each other to vent to and offer emotional, empathetic support. We saw each other almost every day and neither husband recognized the significance of our relationship.

"Good morning, girl. How did you get those two black eyes?" she asked.

I replied, "Oh, I ran into a door in my house."

"Oh really?"

"Yes."

"I don't believe you."

"Why?"

"Because I can tell you are covering the truth up, because I've done it. So you can tell me or not. It's up to you."

"Okay."

"Okay what?"

"He hit me."

"Who hit you?"

"James."

"I suppose he told you that it was your fault he hit you."

"Well, I wouldn't shut up."

"That's bullshit, and ya know it."

"I know. But . . ."

"You know what he does to you isn't right. Just know I'm here for you when you need me."

"Thanks. I'm good for now."

"I have some makeup in my purse. I'll help you hide those black eyes."

Her support was crucial in my survival. In our world, God had to be a woman. We didn't want a male figure to have supreme power over us. It was hard enough to have men overpowering us on earth, let alone in heaven. We portrayed our God as kind, giving and sympathetic to our human plight with men on earth. We poured our hearts out to each other and prayed to our female God when we both were feeling there was no hope.

"I left the son of a bitch," she told me one morning.

"Wow. Good for you. Is there anything I can do to help you?" I replied.

"No. Not right now. I just wanted you to know. I'll see you at work. So far, he hasn't reacted much. The girls and I are staying with my parents."

It was New Year's Day, 1983, and I was so happy for her. She was starting a new year and a new life. I spoke to her every day for several weeks. She never once questioned her decision. Denny surprised everyone when he didn't contest the divorce. I don't think he was shocked.

Chapter 27:

Starvation, Anyone?

I craved affection and moments of calmness. In our bed, he would roll over and caress me. As soon as I believed this was a kind, loving gesture, James would turn it into something bizarre. Our moments of intimacy became an experimental playground for James, as he began to find objects to use on me to replace his penis. His kind affectionate touches became violent thrusts of rage and abnormality. I often just lay there, when possible, thinking, "How did this happen? Why did he choose me? How will I ever be able to be free of this torment?"

I fantasized someone in the neighborhood calling the police on him during one of his extreme episodes. Not all of these occurred inside our house. One night at two in the morning, one of these outside incidents unfolded. A man who lived a few doors down from us had just left after a sexual arrangement involving me, orchestrated by James. I was headed for the bathroom to get ready for bed when he stopped me.

"Did ya enjoy that?" he asked.

"Not really."

He pushed me down and started yelling, "Whore!"

The next thing I knew he grabbed my shirt and ripped it off my body. Then he pulled the bra off without unhooking it. The fastener ripped my flesh as it was pulled off. He turned around and grabbed my feet pulling my pants off and shredding my underwear with his bare hands.

"Ah! Look at ya. Naked whore. I think the whole neighborhood would like ta see ya this way."

He threw me over his shoulder, walked through the front door and tossed me onto our front lawn. The porch light was on, spotlighting my undisguised body. I watched as James went back into the house. I could hear the door locking as I lay there horrified. I raised my head up and looked to see if anyone was around, praying someone would call the police or come and rescue me. Nothing but darkness and silence surrounded me. I pulled myself up and ran to our camper and truck. The camper was unlocked. I went in and found some clothes to put on. As the sun started to rise, I emerged slowly and quietly. I made my way to the front door, hoping I could get into the house to check on my kids. I put my hand on the doorknob. It turned, and the door opened. Silence. I breathed a sigh of relief. Everyone was asleep as if nothing had happened.

I was beginning to feel trapped and was tiring of the power he continued to hold over me. My thoughts were filled with fantasies about leaving James and meeting someone who really treated me like a true lover. "I will go to the airport and buy the boys and me tickets to another country. I will change our names and start a new life in a place where he will never find us. I just know wherever we go I will meet a man who really loves and appreciates me. I know there is someone out there waiting for me," I told myself that night.

"Look at how cute John and Michael are when they play together," I said to James the next day.

"I see how much ya love those boys. If'n you're ever thinkin' 'bout leaving me . . . I will take those boys back to the hills of Kentucky and you'll never see them again. So, if'n you're even havin' those thoughts, I'm warnin' ya. Ya hear me?"

"I wasn't even talking about any of that. I just was thinking . . . how cute our boys are."

"Oh, I know what you're thinkin', ya liar." Even normal conversations between us began to take an abnormal turn.

I was being physically and emotionally exhausted. I not only lost my appetite for life, but also for food. I picked at my food, moving it around on the plate, pushing it closer together to make it appear I had consumed some of it. No one, including James, paid much attention to my eating habits until my weight loss became noticeable.

My mom was the first to notice. "My dear, you need to eat more. What's going on?" she asked one day.

I was afraid to let her in on the real secrets of my life. I convinced myself I was protecting her from the horrible truth of my life with James.

"Mom, nothing is going on. I am just working, going to school, and taking care of John, Michael and James," I said.

Her face was filled with worry. "Are you sure?"

"Yes, Mom."

Mom was intuitive and knew something was going on in my life I didn't want to share with her. She also knew if she applied pressure, it would just contribute to my stress.

"Well, I love you and just want you to have a little more weight on those bones of yours."

Soon, the weight loss began to weaken my immune system, and I became sick with colds more often. At times I would end up in the doctor's office and was questioned about my lack of desire for food.

One day when James and I were visiting my parents, my mom told James, "You need to make sure our girl is eating. Look how skinny she is getting."

He promised my mom he would and the next day when we were out running errands together, I mentioned I was hungry for a taco. He made a very sudden turn into the driveway of a fast-food restaurant and pulled up to the drive-thru speaker and ordered two tacos for me.

"I'll git ya anythin' ya want to eat, hon, I want ya ta gain some weight back. I'm worried." Little did he realize his behavior was the reason my desire to eat had disappeared.

John was now seven years old, and Michael was three. I was doing my best to make sure their needs were being met and I had managed to stay in college and hold down the job as a teacher's aide. I believed in my mind everyone just thought I was busy and wasn't taking time to eat. I continued to live underneath a cloak of darkness.

To add to the stress of it all, college tuition was a financial burden because James did his best to spend any extra money we might have saved. Also, since Anna's passing, I was in the habit of visiting James Sr. once a week to assess his needs. One day while I was there, I made the mistake of complaining about his son's spending habits.

"Ya know, your son spent my college tuition money on a bow and arrows," I said.

"So do you need me ta give ya money for your college?"

"If ya can. That'd be great. I'll pay you back as soon as I can."

"Well, sweetheart . . . you know I'm lonely since Anna passed."

"Yeah . . ." I said nervously.

"Well . . . if'n you stroke . . . me . . . I'll not be expectin' any of the money back. Strokin' me will be your payment," he said as he unzipped his pants and pulled his penis out.

I could hear my boys' voices as they played outside. "If'n ya do this, I'll pay your tuition 'til ya graduate."

At this point, my determination to finish my degree outweighed my disgust. In the back of my mind, hidden from even myself, were the thoughts repeating over and over, "The only path to exiting this horror is to obtain my bachelor's degree and a teaching credential. Then I will be able to support us financially without James."

This offer would ensure my goal would be reached despite James's frequent spending sprees. He bought motorcycles, bicycles, TVs, etc. My hand reached and touched his penis. I closed my eyes and stroked as quickly as I could. As soon as James Sr. let out a small moan, my hand became sticky and wet. I pulled it away quickly and ran into the bathroom to wash. I came out of the bathroom to see James Sr. smiling.

"Thanks, sweetheart."

"Okay, I have ta leave now."

I opened the front door and yelled for my boys. All I could think about on the way home was the old saying, *the apple doesn't fall far from the tree.*

Later I informed James regarding his father's requests, "James, your dad says if I give him hand jobs he will pay for my college." I was a little disappointed and surprised at his response, but I shouldn't have been.

"Oh, well, the old man is lonely since my mom died. It won't kill ya ta do it."

Later, my psychologist would confirm that I was planning to leave James all along, and I was determined to finish my degree because it was my ticket out of the marriage.

I finally completed enough college units to qualify as a substitute teacher. I resigned from the teacher's aide position and began to work as a substitute teacher. I began to feel less trapped, and I began to eat. I even took cans of liquid nutrition to work with me, as substitute teaching required more energy from me. Physically, I was doing better.

Once I began receiving paychecks at this higher pay, James coerced me into acquiring several credit cards. As soon as they arrived, he immediately took a trip to the local electronics store, as well as several photography supply stores and purchased thousands of dollars of camera equipment and black room supplies.

At the time I was surprised by his sudden interest in this hobby but believed it might be a good thing. His focus on finding friends for me to have sex with ceased, and he became totally engaged in this new activity. His time at home dwindled. For me this translated into him not being at home abusing me, and I was a tad bit happier.

Life in our home would take on a temporary appearance of normalcy at times; however, the children and I still lived under the duress of waiting and wondering.

As 1984 began, the shift back to angry episodes and violent acts returned. It was about this same time I became aware the San Bernardino County District Attorney's Office had ordered James to take a paternity test and it revealed he was the biological father of Linda's daughter, Kirsten.

As he opened the letter and read it, he yelled, "If'n I have to pay child support to that bitch, then she's gonna let me see the girl." He never asked me my thoughts on the matter and there was never an apology about his affair with Linda.

Finding out that Kirsten was his daughter did not benefit our two boys. They suffered from exposure to his more frequent angry outbursts. There were times his violent nature spilled out onto them. One time, when I was in another room folding clothes, he connected his belt with John's legs and left welts. I was horrified and vowed I would protect John from that point on, no matter the cost to myself. I didn't send him to school the next day but asked my mom to watch him. I worried all day, expecting my mom to find the welts, but she didn't mention anything when I picked him up.

From that day forward, I would step in the way when I feared he was going to strike John or Michael, yelling, "You're not going to hit them anymore!"

"Well, I guess I'll give ya a whoopin' instead."

"Go to your room, boys, and shut the door," I would tell them. Once they left, James would strike my legs with the belt, three or four times, always hard enough to leave welts.

When he finished, he would say, "If'n ya disciplined those boys, they wouldn't be brats." I often wore clothing to cover my legs, so no one noticed the belt marks.

It was during this same year James renewed his interest in me into having sex with other men. Once these sexual encounters began, a new twist was added. Beating me afterward was embedded into the routine. I began to realize I was damned if I did and damned if I didn't, so I became more vocal.

"I do not want to have sex with your buddies anymore!" I yelled at him one day. He looked at me, rolled his eyes and walked away without saying a word. I had hopes he was reconsidering and would not force me to commit these acts anymore. But, in a few days he arranged another encounter and forced me to participate. I began to question who was crazier, him or me? He was beating me anyway, so why was I complying? Was it the unknown potential of his violent nature frightening me?

Chapter 28:

The Wolf in Sheep's Clothing

"**I** want a turn please, Mr. Hawkins!" shouted Bobby.

"Okay, Bobby, as soon as I finish givin' Sally her horsy ride," said James.

I could hear oodles of giggles coming from our two boys as well as two kids who lived nearby. Children from the neighborhood were often at our home when James was there. They gravitated toward him as if he had cast a magic spell over them. One neighbor girl in particular, Sally, was especially fond of him. Her mother had known us for years and trusted Sally was safe in our company. I, too, thought Sally was perfectly safe. She was extremely affectionate with James, but I thought nothing of it at the time, as her father and mother were divorced, and she seemed to crave adult attention. I was also aware both of her parents were having severe problems from substance abuse. Della, Sally's mom, because of her issues, was living with her sister and brother-in-law, whose home was only two doors away from ours. Therefore, I believed Sally was just a very needy child and James was more than willing to make her feel more secure. I didn't suspect anything else and thought it was all innocent.

Later, when I had the opportunity to read the police reports, they revealed that those innocent moments of affection I witnessed were anything but innocent. For example, when he was cuddling her on our couch, it was revealed in an interview with Sally that one of her hands was placed on his erect penis, just out of view, somehow. The torturous thing for me was, "Why didn't I see it?" I have had many sleepless nights trying to answer this question.

Even I wasn't aware of all the layers constituting the man called James. He had many disguises hiding in his psyche.

James was very talented at portraying his image as a kind, well-meaning person. No one in the neighborhood, not even Mitch and Carrie, were aware of his dark side. Whenever children in the neighborhood were participating in fundraisers for their school or club, he would step forward and buy first and convince others to do the same.

One winter there was a severe windstorm that knocked down trees and created a mess in everyone's yard. The day after the storm subsided, James was out assisting everyone with their yard clean-up. He always volunteered to play games with the neighborhood children and was the first to organize baseball games in the street. All the neighbor kids seemed to enjoy his company, including Sally.

James worked diligently on keeping up this pristine image he projected to the outside world. This image was designed to protect him against any statements to the contrary made by me, the main keeper of his secret.

His image would begin to tarnish in May 1984, when James became obsessed with buying a purebred German Shepherd puppy. He found a breeder who had a litter of puppies due in June. He left a $100 deposit with her and told me afterward, when he arrived home. He was so excited and wanted me to share in his excitement. "Guess what I did today? I put a deposit on a purebred German Shepherd puppy.

"Oh, a puppy. I can't wait to see it!"

"Oh, it isn't a dog for ya or the kids. It'll be my dog. I'm goin' to train it as an attack dog. Ya can't baby him, like ya baby our kids. I'll take care of him. Ya don't get ta be 'round him at all. He'll be penned up. I'll be his master."

"So he won't be part of our family?"

"No! He's my dog. He'll follow my commands. I'll train him only to respond to me and no one else. Not even you, Laurie."

"Oh . . . okay."

My heart was broken. I had always loved dogs, especially puppies, and to think one was coming to live in our home and I wasn't allowed to love on it added to my feelings of hopelessness. I thought to myself, "How could he be so selfish and mean?"

When he brought the beautiful German Shepherd puppy home, he did as he told me. He limited my access to him. He alone named him and cared for him. He named him Sirius, after the Dog Star. Due to the amount of time James stayed away from home, he quickly changed his mind regarding my interaction, and I was allowed to care for him, but he gave me strict instructions on the amount of affection I could give his dog. I didn't always adhere to his rules and secretly loved on Sirius, especially when he was a puppy, when James was not around.

When Sirius turned six months old, James began to attack-train him. He focused on training Sirius and researched the subject thoroughly. He diligently worked with the dog and showed him a great deal of attention. I, however, didn't enjoy watching him train a dog to attack, especially because I feared he might be inclined at some point to turn the dog against me. I feared it might be just one more tool to add to his repertoire of ways to control me.

James developed a routine where he walked Sirius in the neighborhood. At times, I had the opportunity to observe him walking the dog as he wandered down the street. It often appeared as if he would deliberately head toward the yards with dogs, often zig-zagging to do so. He would allow Sirius to bite and bark at the dogs behind the fence, then pull him back with the leash when the encounter got intense or the neighbor noticed.

One evening in the late spring of 1985, James pushed a little too far with his dog at the yard of the house behind us. This neighbor had just moved in and didn't know James. All he saw was a man encouraging his large dog to attack his smaller dog through his fence. He rushed out with a baseball bat and caught James by surprise. He didn't anticipate the actions of this neighbor and as a result came home with a huge bruise on his forehead. It frightened me, so I called the police. I was not expecting the response I received.

"My name is Laurie Hawkins, and I would like to report an assault on my husband James Hawkins. We live at 14660 Shadow Street."

"Mrs. Hawkins, how badly is he hurt?"

"Well, he has a huge bruise on his head."

"Is it bleeding?"

"No."

"Well, we are aware of the situation and please tell your husband he needs to stop deliberately antagonizing other people's dogs," she said in a stern voice and then disconnected with me.

I put down the phone and turned to James and said, "The dispatcher says you need to stop antagonizing other people's dogs."

"She can fuck herself," he said as he stood holding an ice pack on his forehead.

Inside I silently cheered. Someone had finally stood up to him. What I didn't realize at the time was that the sheriff's department had already begun investigating James.

Chapter 29:

The Choice:
For the Good of the Family

A nervous feeling in the pit of my stomach erupted as I realized I needed to tell my family about Kirsten. I stared at the phone for a few minutes, contemplating how I would reveal this information. I knew I needed to tell them, because James had told his dad. According to James, his dad congratulated him on fathering another child. I wasn't surprised, but counteracted my loathing for both men by thinking about what Anna would have thought about the whole situation.

My mother and I conversed on the telephone quite often, but I very rarely shared any part of the nightmare called my marriage. I had previously revealed to her a small amount of information regarding James's affair with Linda, but nothing about Kirsten, as James had vehemently denied she was his child. I finally decided telling my mom on the phone first was my best approach. She would tell my dad and soften him before I saw him face-to-face.

I told her about Linda's pregnancy and the birth of Kirsten.

I went on to tell her how James had denied the baby was his, but now we had an official letter confirming he was the father, and we had decided to have her visit us twice a month. She asked me how I felt about the situation.

"I'm not sure how I feel, but Kirsten did not create this problem, so I'm willing to have her visit. I . . .'m really angry at James."

"Well, let me ask you the same question I asked you the last time we discussed this issue. How important is your marriage to you?" she asked.

"Well, it's important because I want to keep my family together, I guess," I said.

"Well, you know James is still mourning his mom's death. Maybe this was the only time he will cheat on you. So these situations happen, and maybe just this once you must forget about your feelings and do what is good for your family. I know it stings because your pride is hurt, and I'm sorry about that."

I appreciated her point of view, but my motive was just to give her the information. I wasn't ready to reveal my secret life to her just yet. I knew if she possessed all the facts, her advice would have changed drastically.

A few months later James handed me more correspondence from the District Attorney's Office. It was a court order specifying James Hawkins pay $150 per month for the support of Kirsten. In addition, he was also ordered to pay $2,000 to repay the county for funds that they had allotted to Linda through the welfare system for the support of his child. This was a huge financial burden on our family, as we didn't have extra money at our disposal.

The next day James said to me, "I've decided we need ta get a loan ta pay the two grand those bastards are makin' me pay. I need ya ta sign the loan papers." I wanted so badly to say no, but

I remembered my mother's advice and decided this was just one more of those things I had to accept.

I wasn't happy at all about the whole situation but did like the idea of having a girl stay with us, even if she was Linda's child. I kept repeating to myself none of this was Kirsten's fault. The visitation schedule agreed upon by James and Linda was that Kirsten would be with us from Friday evening to Sunday afternoon two weekends a month. Also, we were planning a camping trip, and requested she come along with us. Linda agreed to this arrangement.

The first six months of 1985 proved to be an extremely challenging time in my life and certainly a recipe for disaster. I was taking the final courses to complete my bachelor's degree while managing a household and two children, one of whom was mentally challenged. To add to it, a third child's visitation schedule—a child conceived out of my husband's affair. Then fold in adjusting my household budget to accommodate the extra bill called child support. Mix in a full-time job, blended with the stresses of dealing with a very angry, crazy, and abusive husband, and you have the perfect recipe for emotional chaos. My brain was constantly seeking a solution to end this bedlam. I kept asking myself, "How can I escape this disaster?" I began fantasizing my escape.

The few moments a day when I was left alone with my thoughts were frightening. It was during this time I carefully plotted the murder of James. My weapon of choice was my heavy iron skillet, the one he insisted I use to make his favorite dish, biscuits and gravy. In fact, sometimes I imagined the skillet was just taken from the stove filled with hot gravy, enhancing the element of torture. The impetus for this fantasy was a news story of a woman who was the victim of domestic violence over several years, who smashed her husband's head while he was sleeping. She hit him repeatedly with an iron skillet until she was sure he was dead. She was charged with murder but was found innocent due to temporary insanity. Her attorney demonstrated she had withstood years of abuse from her professional footballer husband, until one day her mind had snapped, and she killed him. She was a woman of small stature and, like me, had feared for her life. I convinced myself the only way to murder James was while he was sleeping. My dilemma? I would have to strike him hard enough the first time to knock him out and then be able to sustain hits hard enough to accomplish such a feat. But . . . there was one drawback; if I didn't kill him, *he would kill me.*

I sat in the living room with my two sons waiting for James to bring Kirsten for her first visit with us. I watched as these two precious gifts from God played happily with their toy cars on our carpeted floor. "A little girl is coming to visit us. She is your sister," I told them.

Michael was now five years old and quite verbal and curious. He asked questions, but thankfully none of them about why she was his sister. John was nine years old, but his language was still quite limited, so he posed no questions.

My eye caught the swift approach of a vehicle. It was James. I could see him helping Kirsten out of the car. Her little face was pointed downward as she exited the car, so all I could see was her long, dark hair. She was carrying a baby doll under one of her arms. As she walked up the two steps of our front porch, I saw her look up at me as I opened the screen door. Her face was engulfed with a huge smile. "Hi!" she said. This was the sweet face I had seen in the nursery window at the hospital almost four years earlier. Her eyes glowed when she smiled. The boys greeted her as she walked through the door.

"Hi, Kirsten! I'm Michael. Wanna play?" Michael said,

while John giggled, turning his hands over and around one another repeatedly.

James and I sat and watched them play. At one point Kirsten approached me and asked if I was the mommy. She then crawled into my lap and gave me a great big hug. I thought to myself, "How did those two mean souls make such a beautiful child?"

Whenever Kirsten visited, James was on his best behavior. I believe he toned down the abuse just in case Kirsten might communicate to others about life in our household.

Kirsten and I really enjoyed each other's company. She loved the attention I gave her, and I loved the respite from James's cruelty. We were all living in the facade of a life created by a madman.

Chapter 30:

Calm Before the Storm

Anna sat beside me, her smile so delicate and kind, radiating like a lamp without a shade. This is how the dream always began. This repetitive dream started in May 1985.

"Why did you bring me here?" I asked.

"I wanted ta warn ya," Anna said

"Warn me about what?"

"Somethin' is goin' ta happen . . . soon. I want ya to be strong. You're goin' to have ta make some tough decisions. I brought ya here so I can tell ya I'll always love ya no matter what ya decide ta do."

I remember nodding my head, and then a feeling of warmth surrounded me. I glanced around to see the beautiful white cabinets with wood-framed glass doors on each side of the fireplace. A small statue of Martha Washington was visible through the glass door. The smell of the ocean breeze surrounded my nostrils, reminding me I was in a safe, secure place. My soul recognized this atmosphere as the home of my mother's mother, my grandmother.

"But I need ya ta do something for me."

"I will do anything for you, Anna. I love you"

"Please tell each of my children, one by one, about my visit with ya."

Suddenly, her smile disappeared, and her voice changed into a louder, stronger tone.

"Tell them they must stick together and help one another no matter what happens. *They must stick together!*"

Those words resonated deep inside of me . . . the smell of Anna's cigarette smoke encircled my head as I opened my eyes and realized I was dreaming.

The first time she came to me in the dream, James lay beside me sleeping soundly. I tapped him and woke him up. When he realized why I awakened him, he just told me to go back to sleep.

I had trouble going back to sleep and finally got up around six in the morning. It was a Saturday morning, so everyone slept in. When James got up, I told him in detail about the dream and gave him the message from his mom. His response was rather casual, but not dismissive.

"James, you know I have a gift when it comes to connecting with the spiritual world. Remember the night before your mom passed away? A spirit . . . maybe hers . . . came and visited us?"

"Yeah, I remember. I believe she came to ya in your dreams. My mom has a strong spirit. I know that."

"Okay, then you know I MUST relay your mom's message to your sisters in person."

"Yeah. I know. Talkin' to Fiona's easy. But I don't know when we can take the time to go visit Gina."

"We have to."

"We'll see."

His sister Fiona lived nearby, but Gina and her husband, Gregg, and their daughter, Christina, had moved to Santa Maria.

I planned a lunch date with Fiona to deliver her mother's

message. She and I didn't do lunch often, so she was very curious when I told her it was important I meet with her. She was already there when I arrived. She was seated in a booth where she could see me the minute I walked into the place. Her nervous smile invaded her eyes like a spreading virus. As I reached the booth, she lifted her pudgy body to greet me with a hug. We began with usual small talk but were interrupted by the waitress. Fiona fidgeted with a spoon the entire time the waitress stood there asking us for our drink order.

As soon as the waitress turned around to walk away, Fiona asked, "So what is this about, sweetie?"

"Well . . . your mom came to me in a dream."

"And . . .?"

"She gave me a message to give to each of her children."

"What message?"

"She told me that something big's going to happen and when it does, she wants the three of you to stick together and support each other no matter what."

A tear pushed out from her left eye. She wiped it away quickly.

"What's gonna happen? Did she say?"

"I have no idea. The only thing she said was I was going to make some tough decisions and she would support me in those decisions."

"Wow. I wonder what all of this means?"

She wiped away another tear. The waitress reappeared and took our order quickly and left.

"I've always stayed connected with Brother and Sissy, and that'll never change for me, no matter what."

As I left the restaurant, a sense of partial relief came over me. I was the courier of a message from the spirit world, but I wasn't finished.

Plans to visit his sister Gina kept falling through. After a couple of weeks went by, Anna visited me again. This time she was forceful in her request for me to deliver the message to her children. I was pretty sure Fiona had communicated with Gina about her lunch date with me, but for some reason, I was the one who needed to tell her in person. Once again, I requested we plan a visit to Santa Maria. And once again James told me, "We'll see."

For once I understood why James was hesitant about squeezing in a trip to see Gina. He was working full time, I was finishing classes to complete my bachelor's degree in Liberal Studies at CSUSB, and we were wrangling three kids every other weekend, so making the visit to Santa Maria, even on a weekend, was almost impossible.

Finally, graduation day came for me on June 24, 1985, and we still hadn't made the journey up north. A few days later, Anna reappeared in the same comfortable scene, but this time she didn't sit by me. She stood over me and spoke in a louder, more animate way.

"You have not delivered my message to all of my children! You're running out of time!" When I awakened from this dream, I made a desperate plea to James.

"James, we have to go and visit Gina! Your mom came to me again. This is her third visit. She says I am running out of time. I don't know what it means. I'm really scared," I said as tears began flowing from my eyes.

"Okay, I think we can squeeze a short visit in. Let's go this weekend."

The three-and-a-half-hour drive to Santa Maria seemed to take forever. The burden of carrying this message had taken its toll on my stress levels. Thankfully, we didn't have Kirsten, and the boys were very well behaved. They were enjoying the trip. They loved to play with their cousin Christina. When we arrived, Gina and Christina ran up to the car to greet us. Gina grabbed my hand and said, "I'm so glad you're here. Fiona told me Mom has been visiting you in your dreams."

Christina and the boys giggled with delight to see one another and quickly disappeared into the backyard to play. Gina and her husband Gregg had been married for seven years. He was her one and only boyfriend, and they had met in high school just like James and I. Gregg had studied to be a health inspector and was offered employment with Santa Barbara County at their location in Santa Maria, so they moved there in 1984. They purchased a spacious two-story brand-new home which had plenty of room for us to visit. This was our first visit since they had moved, and I was in awe of their beautiful home.

Gina and I paused our conversation until later, so she could give James and me a tour of her home. Gina had a talent for interior design and everything inside was eloquent. As soon as she finished her tour, she said, "Brother, can you please go outside and check on the kids, while we talk?"

As soon as he left, Gina said, "Okay, Fiona said Mom talked to you in a dream?"

I proceeded to give her the same message I gave James and Fiona.

"Well, Mom loved you. I just hope everything turns out okay. It makes me a little nervous."

Gina and I sat for a few more minutes reminiscing about our days in high school together and how things had changed. Gregg came home about an hour later and we all enjoyed a family dinner together. This visit was the first and last visit for James, Michael, John, and me.

I would never fully know the impact Anna's message had on her children; however, the true meaning of her message was soon to become a reality for me. I believe I sensed her warning was related to James and me, but I had no idea the extent of change that was about to happen. In my heart a small spark of hope, encircled by fear, had begun to emerge.

Chapter 31:

The Beginning of the End

Packing a pink t-shirt was new to me. This camping trip was to be the perfect family vacation, a new beginning. I was looking forward to this trip for many reasons, one being, James sometimes treated me better when we vacationed, and with Kirsten joining us this possibility doubled. I anticipated more work with the addition of a third child, but her smile lightened the load.

We packed the night before, and early the next morning we loaded into our camper and truck and started our journey. It was a little cramped, but all the children appeared to be comfortable and secure. James drove and seemed more distant than normal. His mind was operating in a different arena from his family.

We were headed for a week of camping in the High Sierra Mountains. It was to be a week of fishing, hiking and relaxing. Just being in a different environment, one in which there was a possibility of having some fun, gave me a sense of joy. Once we arrived at the campground, all three of the children leaped out of the truck giggling. Their giggles were contagious, even infecting James.

There was one discerning cloud hanging over this trip. I was irritated with James's attitude regarding the whole situation with Kirsten. He acted as if this was a normal situation and exhibited no remorse regarding his affair with Linda. He gave no help when it came to the care of Kirsten. He just expected me to take on the extra work without any help from him, even though Kirsten was the result of his act of adultery. One time, the boys were running around while I was inside the camper helping Kirsten change her clothes. "James, can you please check on the boys and make sure they don't wander off?" I called out.

"I'm busy. Besides, young'uns are your job, woman."

"Well, then come finish helping your daughter."

"Oh, hell no! That's for sure your job."

Other times, I would ask for his assistance regarding Kirsten's care and he just gave me the look, clearly communicating with his eyes I was crossing the line. He treated me like I was a servant, and I had no rights to any feelings regarding resentment. I did what I had been conditioned to do. I continued to do whatever it took to keep James happy, giving way to my co-dependent nature.

Throughout the marriage, I kept hoping he possessed a small shred of decency inside himself and could stop his abusive behavior, but as time went on, this belief faded away. I would learn later that he did not possess the ability to love or think about how others felt. It was always about himself and what he wanted to believe or accomplish.

This vacation marked the beginning of our new adventures as a family of five, or so I thought. Like all good times it swiftly came to an end, leaving memories etched in my mind. Memories of happy little kids holding fish they had caught, smiles through faces smeared with dirt, and delicious meals cooked outdoors. James even appeared to be happy at times, and his nastiness toward me was at an all-time low. I pondered several possibilities.

"Is there hope for our marriage? Is that the spark of hope I am feeling in my heart? If so, do I really want that hope? If I allow myself to embrace this hope, would it just be crushed again?" These were the questions I asked myself. Anna's warning loomed in the back of my mind. The steps leading to the core of her message had begun, I just didn't know it.

A few weeks before our trip began, James drove to a photo-processing center and dropped off a roll of film. This roll of film contained photos capable of incriminating him in a crime. James was intelligent, and I am sure he was aware that there was a high possibility his photos would be turned in to the police, and he would be arrested. On the other hand, the sociopathic portion of his brain was extremely arrogant and believed that even if he was arrested, he was above the law and immune to any conviction or associated penalties. These thoughts might have weighed heavily on his mind during our family trip, I have no idea. I was too wrapped up in his emotional web to even notice if he was looking over his shoulder.

Chapter 32:

The Day that Changed the Course

Summer had settled in, and it was too hot to do anything but sit inside the house. Our water cooler was blowing a cool breeze on my face as I watched John and Michael play with their toys in the middle of the living room. James was sitting on the couch across from me and dozing off into a quiet slumber. Our lunch was resting comfortably in our stomachs, and we were enjoying this Saturday afternoon. Suddenly, there was a brisk knock at the door. I jumped up to answer it. I pulled open the door to find three San Bernardino County Sheriffs standing on our front porch, holding their badges out directly in front of them so I could see them.

One of them said, "We have a warrant to search the premises." He held a paper up and waved it. Shocked and afraid, I opened the screen door and held it as they forcefully walked in, "I have done nothing against the law, so please go ahead and search," I said.

I stepped back and my eyes peered over at James to see if he was going to speak to the deputies. Nausea flared up inside of me like lava in a volcano when I saw him sitting with his hands over his face and trembling like a child who had been caught doing something wrong. It was at that moment I knew they were here for him and not me.

The number of officers entering our home swiftly multiplied and the situation became extremely chaotic. My two young sons stood there hugging each other and their eyes told me they were very frightened by all this mayhem, so I quickly asked one of the officers, "Can I please take my sons over to our neighbor's house?"

He nodded in a yes motion, so I gathered them up and walked them to Mitch and Carrie's house. She had noticed the police cars and opened the door as I approached. Before I could even utter a word, she said, "Of course they can stay here while all this is goin' on."

I ran back to our front door and slowly opened it and stepped inside. James was nowhere to be seen, and I could hear items being tossed and drawers being opened throughout the house. Suddenly, I heard my chihuahua growling. She often slept in our bed under the covers, so I quickly entered the bedroom to find one of the officers holding a gun aimed right at her head. I quickly yelled out. "It is just my little dog. I can get her if you allow me to."

"Okay," he said as he put his gun back in his holster. I quickly grabbed her and put her in the backyard with Sirius.

As I cautiously re-entered the house from the backyard, a female deputy approached me. "Hello, Mrs. Hawkins. My name is Deputy Bower. Can you please come outside with me so I can ask you a few questions?"

I agreed and, as I walked with her back through the living room, I asked, "Do you know where my husband has gone to?"

"He is out in one of our patrol cars being questioned," she said. Thoughts were racing through my mind: "What is she going to ask me about? Has James wound up in a drug deal gone wrong? Has he stolen something from work?" I tried to prepare myself for her questions, but I would soon find out there was no preparation for her interrogation.

Deputy Bower led me to our driveway and stopped in front of our Chevy Sprint. She opened her briefcase and took out a photo with the picture side down. Next, she looked me straight in the eye with a very stern look and flipped the picture over. Without any warning my legs abruptly turned into gelatin, and I immediately fell to the ground upon seeing this photo taken by a deranged individual, my husband. I was viewing an image forever forged in my mind. I saw Sally sitting on top of our microwave oven with no clothing on her bottom half, with her legs wide open showing her vaginal area. The hard pavement was hot and blistering, but the reality shown to me in the picture was even more painful. Then, a cool, caring hand caressed my hand, gently pulling me up from the ground. I gazed upward to see Deputy Bower's face. Her stern look had transformed into one of kindness and compassion. Once I was standing again, she said to me, "I'm so sorry, but I had to find out if you knew, and your reaction tells me that you didn't."

My mind was still swirling with confusion.

"Laurie, often the wives are accomplices to their husbands' crimes, but I know now you were not. It is apparent to me you had no idea he was molesting Sally."

"I . . . had no idea," I stammered.

"I only showed you one of the photos on the roll he dropped off at the photo-processing facility. We absolutely know it was James who picked up the developed roll of film because we have video of him."

"Wow. I'm in shock. I can't believe . . . he did such a horrible act."

"We also know he was alone."

Just as Deputy Bower and I were finishing our conversation, the deputies inside my home were carrying out multiple boxes of photos and photo-developing equipment. James was still sitting in the sheriff's vehicle, and I was still standing outside. My mind was overwhelmed with many thoughts. "What am I going to do next? What am I going to tell my children, my parents, my entire family? Is this the event my mother-in-law's spirit warned me about? Am I really strong enough to withstand this life-changing event?"

I stayed outside with Deputy Bower until the search was completed. "I am going back to the station now. Hang in there. James has been arrested and will be taken to the county jail," she said as she hugged me. Before I knew it, all the deputy sheriffs and their cars were gone. There I stood in the middle of our driveway, alone.

As I watched them all drive away, my mind quickly shifted to my children. I ran to Mitch and Carrie's house and tried to explain to Carrie what had just occurred. Holding back tears I said, "Carrie . . . they arrested James . . . for molesting Sally."

"Oh my God, I'm so sorry. It must be a mistake. I'm sure it'll all work out."

"I'm not sure about anything at this point. I just know I can't stay here tonight." I burst into tears. She grabbed me and hugged me tight.

"I want to go stay with my mom and dad. But how do I tell them James was arrested for such a hideous crime?" I said as I cried.

"If you want, I can drive you and the boys over to your mom and dad's house," she offered.

I agreed and upon arriving at their house, I knocked on the door briefly and walked in with Carrie and the boys following me. My mother jumped up from her chair in the living room and quickly asked, "What's wrong?"

I responded quickly by bursting into tears and grabbing her in an embrace. Carrie began speaking to my mom explaining about what she knew had happened. My father came from another part of the house into the living room and both boys ran up to him. I hugged Carrie and thanked her, and she left.

My mom escorted the boys to another room. Once they left the room, I was alone with my dad. "What the hell happened?"

"All I know is deputy sheriffs came knocking at our door with a warrant in their hands. Dad . . . they tore our house apart and arrested James. They showed me a horrible photo . . ." I broke down sobbing.

"It's okay, sweetheart. The good thing is you are here with us now. You're safe," he said as he put his arm around me.

"I know, Dad. That's why I'm here. I . . . dunno . . . if . . . I can ever go back there again. There's a lot I haven't told you. It isn't good. The female deputy sheriff told me he has been molesting our neighbor girl, Sally. Dad . . . I think he might be guilty."

"Okay. This is a lot to process in one day. Why don't we just have a quiet dinner and a calm evening together as a family. Tomorrow is a new day. We can sort all of this out in the morning."

Over the next few hours, not one of us really discussed the situation much. I helped my mother make dinner and then we discussed sleeping arrangements while we ate. We were all in shock, and talking about mundane things like sleeping arrangements made us feel like there was some normalcy.

I bathed the boys and put them to bed. I was exhausted, so I went to bed around nine. The boys were together on the bed in the guest room. I was sleeping in the den on the sofa bed. Dad assisted me in putting the telephone next to my bedside in case James was to call. Sure enough, two in the morning, the phone rang. As I picked up the phone, I was expecting to hear James sound remorseful and show some concern for the boys and me. Instead, his concerns were all about himself. His voice was strong and commanding.

"Tomorrow I need you to go with my dad and bail me out of here."

"Okay."

"I hate it here, I want out. You're gonna go first thing in the morning, right?"

"Okay."

There was no question regarding how the boys and I were doing. His continued comments were all about himself and how unfair all of this was to him. After a couple of minutes, he said, "Well, I gotta get off here, they only give ya a couple of minutes. Just make sure ya do what I said and go with my dad tomorrow. Okay, hon?"

"Okay."

We both said quick goodbyes and I hung up. I was now wide awake, and my mind would not shut off. Now I was angry at James. I had always abided by the law and now I was married to a man who had broken the law. Not only had he broken the law, but he had also hurt a precious child beyond reproach. The picture Deputy Bower showed me was clearly evidence James was guilty as charged.

The next morning James's sister Fiona came to my parents' house. I answered the door.

"Hi, sweetie. Are ya ready to go bail brother out of jail?"

She sounded way too cheerful for my comfort. "Y. . . es," I replied.

"I left the car running. Dad is goin' with us."

I scooted into the back seat. "Hi, my sweet girl. How are

you holdin' up? We're gonna get through this. You're tough. You'll help my son stay strong. We Hawkinses stick together, ya know," James Sr. said.

When we arrived, Fiona and I went into the office, while James Sr. stayed in the car. Once we sat down with a bail bondsman, he began to ask me questions.

"Mrs. Hawkins, what day was he arrested?"

"Uh, yesterday, August 3."

"What are the charges against him?" he asked.

"Molestation?" I said sheepishly.

"I need the legal charges, mam," he said.

Fiona spoke up. "Lewd and lascivious acts with a minor."

The bail bondsman told us he needed to leave the front to do some research. While he was gone Fiona asked, "Are ya going to use the house on Shadow Street as collateral for Brother's bail?"

Unexpectedly somewhere inside of me, a burst of courage spouted out from my mouth, "No," I said adamantly.

I expected her to begin pleading with me to use our house for his bail. Instead, I was surprised at her reaction. She told me, "Okay, let me talk to my dad."

She went outside to the car and spoke to my father-in-law. She came back just as the bail bondsman returned.

"The bail for James Hawkins is $5,000."

"Okay," Fiona said as she handed him a credit card.

I breathed a sigh of relief. As soon as Fiona signed the credit slip and it cleared, the bondsman said, "You're all set. His release will occur tomorrow morning at nine." He handed Fiona the paperwork and we walked out.

All I could think about on the walk to the car was how proud of myself I was for saying the word "No." I was beginning to build up strength. When we reached the car, I got into the back seat and remained silent all the way back. James Sr. and Fiona spoke briefly about the transaction to each other, but neither addressed me. They dropped me off at my parents' house. Little did I know this would be the last time I would ever see them.

As I walked into my parents' home, my boys ran up to me, surrounding my body with their loving hugs and kisses. My dad started to ask questions.

I interrupted him and said, "I told Fiona there was no way I was using the house as collateral for his $5,000 bail. His dad paid it and he's getting out tomorrow morning at nine."

"Are you picking him up?" my mom asked.

"Probably. But I can't go back to our house with him. I just can't."

"Well, why don't you book a room at the Motel 6 down on Sierra and Valley. It's only a mile from our house and three miles from yours. It's close enough to visit if you decide not to stay with him there. You can use it to talk about what happens next. It could be a neutral place, where both of your emotions won't be as stirred up as they would be in your house," Dad said.

"I like your idea, Dad. I think I will call and reserve a room now. The thought of taking him back to the house sickens me."

James called that evening and was elated bail was posted for him. I told him about the motel room. He didn't sound very happy about it, and asked me, "Why?"

I explained it this way, "Well, ya know those deputy sheriffs searched our home, and they were not very careful about it. They threw things everywhere. I need time to clean it up before we return there."

He seemed to understand and agreed to going to the motel room. He then asked, "Ya will stay there too, right?"

"Sure."

My emotions were all over the place. I wasn't sure I wanted to even be near him at all, given the nature of his crime. I think

I knew deep down inside that this was the one crime I couldn't live with or forgive, but I needed to work through this fact and come to terms with it myself. I was about to break up my family.

The next morning I got up, helped my mom feed the kids breakfast. While I showered and got dressed, Mom and Dad kept the boys busy. Having my mom and dad supporting me, gave me the boost of strength I needed, especially on this day. But the real source of my strength was in the precious faces on those two little boys whose future depended on me, their mom.

When I arrived at the parking lot of the jail, I parked and walked to the front door area. A deputy approached me. My knees went weak for a moment. "Can I help you?" he asked.

"I'm here . . . waiting for my husband to be released," I said nervously.

"Well, you can't wait in here. You need to go wait on the benches outside," he said.

I walked out and sat down. There wasn't a lot to look at, just cold stone floors, a deputy at a desk, and the concrete below my feet. I sat there, waiting. What was I going to say to James? "Hi, how was your night? Hi, I can't believe you molested Sally, you bastard." I continued to sit there for what felt like an eternity. Finally, at about nine thirty James came walking out.

He grabbed me tightly and whispered in my ear, "I'm so happy to see you."

I didn't and couldn't say anything. I grabbed his hand and led him to the car. I got in the driver's seat automatically. He shot me a confused look and then got into the passenger side. As I turned on the engine of the car, his mouth turned on.

He began to chatter nervously. "That jail is horrible! I can't believe I had to stay there for two nights. I never wanna go back there. They treated me like I was dirt. I talked to my dad, and he told me he was going to hire an attorney. I think I was molested

218

by someone when I was young, which is why I did what I did. My dad thinks we can win the case."

I finally found my voice and said, "A lawyer told him they could win your case?"

"I think so. I hope so. I think they just wanna scare me. Those charges ain't gonna stick. I wish I could remember who molested me. If'n I give 'em a name it might help win my case. I hope I can meet with the lawyer soon. I can't believe this happened to me."

I could feel my face warm up with anger. I told myself to focus on driving and ignore his chatter. Somehow my heart still hoped to hear words of remorse for what he had done to Sally. But not one word came out of his mouth regarding his victim. Nor did he even appear to recognize the impact his actions had on his family. As we approached the motel, he spouted out a command, "Hey, hon, you gotta go ta the store and pick me up some of that cream for sore muscles. I'm really sore from sleeping on that lousy jail bed."

As I exited the car to go check him into the motel, I could feel the anger bubbling up into my face again. "How dare he order me around as if everything was still the same," I thought to myself. Nothing was the same. I went into the motel office and checked in. I drove to the assigned parking spot, opened the door and we both entered the room.

"Don't forget to go an' get me somethin' for my sore muscles. I really need it. I'm so sore," he said the minute we entered.

"I guess I'll go right now."

While walking through the store, I began to gather up the courage to finally stand up for my children and myself. In my mind, I tried to view a picture of life with him after this incident. All the options were unacceptable to me. There was no room in my heart to tolerate living with a child molester. I found the cream he requested, purchased it along with a few snacks, then returned to the motel.

As I entered the room, he was lying on the bed, so I handed him the cream and sat down in the one chair in the room. I was ready to have a serious conversation, but he was not.

"Honey, come an' rub this cream on my legs," he said in an all-familiar commanding tone of voice.

His request immediately signaled to me he thought nothing had changed in our relationship. I don't know exactly why, but I complied. Even the smell of the muscle cream couldn't cover up the stench I smelled just being in the same room with him.

"Hey, when ya get done, come and lie down here with me. I really missed ya."

I was so infuriated, making myself lie next to him was almost impossible. It was at that moment I came to the realization I could never be with him again. I also knew for my own safety I dared not let him know what I was thinking.

I told him, "I would like to lie down with you, but I need to wait until later. I need to get back to our children. I told my mom and dad I would be back to pick up the kids so you could see them."

His reaction didn't surprise me. I held my breath hoping to get out of the room without him hurting me. He said, "Okay, I get it. Ya need to go back to see your mommy and daddy, you little bitch. You've always been stuck to them. Ya always choose them over me. Go on, get outta here."

His eyes donned his usual mean look. He raised his body up, grabbed the tube of muscle cream, and pitched it across the room. It hit the wall with a dull thump. I tried my best not to react to his behavior. I didn't want to be the next thing he pitched across the room.

"Ya know I'll be back. You wanna see the boys, right?" My

words seemed to calm him down.

"Oh, yeah, I wanna see my boys."

"Well then, I need to leave and go and get them. You know I wasn't about to bring them to the jail. I will be back in a little while with them, and I'll bring lunch for all of us."

I said those words with such calmness, I even surprised myself. I put on a performance as if I were playing the role of a devoted wife in a play. I kissed him goodbye and said, "I won't be gone long."

I walked toward the door with a smile on my face. With each step I took, the idea he might see right through me, quivered inside me. But, lucky for me, he was focused only on feeling sorry for himself and not paying close attention to my behavior. As I pulled the door closed, I stood still for a moment and breathed a sigh of relief. "This is it," I thought to myself. I had just made the decision to leave James forever. Was this the decision Anna talked about in my dream? She had told me she was behind me no matter what decision I made. I looked upward into the sky as I walked to the car. "Well, here we go, Anna. I believe this is it," I said out loud. I had kissed him goodbye for the final time. He didn't suspect anything. On the drive back to my parents' house, I rolled the window down. I could feel the hot breeze on my face. It was whispering, "You are free. You did it!"

As I walked through my parents' door, I was relieved, but terrified at the same time. What were my next steps? I must have had a look of confusion on my face, because my father looked up at me from his chair and asked, "What's going on? What did you and James talk about? Are you staying here or going home?" His questions overwhelmed me. They stung like pellets striking my body as I sat down on their couch. I looked at him and tried to talk, but all that came out was a cry. Uncontrollable tears burst out upon my cheeks. I pulled myself up from the couch and ran into the room where I had been sleeping. As I stood there in the middle of the room sobbing, my hand went into my pocket and touched something. I pulled it out and it was a business card for a psychologist that someone, not sure who, had given me in case James wanted to seek psychological help. I was emotionally out of control and needed someone outside of my circle to talk to about my situation. The telephone was there, so I looked at the card and dialed the number. A receptionist answered the phone, and I began to speak through my sobbing, "My husband was arrested for child molestation . . . I need help . . . I don't know what to do . . ."

She stopped me and said, "Let me get the doctor on the phone, hang on." A moment later, a very calm voice came on the other end.

"Hello, this is Dr. Johnson. Please tell me a little bit about what's going on."

"My husband was arrested for child molestation, and someone gave me your card . . . to get him help? . . . I feel like I am being pressured by him and his family to forgive him . . . he thinks everything should be the same between us, I can't do it anymore . . . I have two children to think about . . . I don't know what to do . . ."

When Dr. Johnson began to speak it was as if someone threw me a lifeline. "First of all, I won't see your husband, but I will see you. Now listen very carefully to what I am about to say. Do you have a pen and paper handy?"

"Yes." My dad always had a pen and paper by every phone.

"Do the following. Number one: go see an attorney and file for divorce. Number two: stop all communication with him or his family starting right now. Take no phone calls from him or anyone in his family. Do not meet him or any member of his family at any time or anywhere. Number three: come to

222

see me at my office this afternoon at four o'clock. I will put my receptionist back on the phone to give you directions to my office."

I listed the three instructions on a piece of paper. As soon as I hung up the phone, I walked out of the bedroom with the paper in my hand and immediately asked my dad to help me search for a divorce attorney.

When my dad and I looked through the phone book we only found one divorce attorney we were familiar with in Fontana at the time. No one in our family had ever gotten a divorce, so this was uncharted territory for us. I knew that one Fontana divorce attorney because I'd taken some college courses with his nephew. Alex had spoken highly of his uncle as he was planning to be a lawyer like him someday. His name was Jay Roberts.

When we arrived at his office, he was able to meet with us immediately. I explained the situation to him and reassured him I didn't need any time to think about filing for the divorce. My mind was made up. His reply was to quote the amount of his retainer, which was $1,500. I looked over at my dad. He already had his checkbook out and had begun to write a check.

As we left there, I did a mental check off in my mind. I had completed one of the tasks given to me by the psychologist. I thanked Dad for coming with me and paying the retainer fee. Now it was time to work on the second task.

"Dad, I need you and Mom ta know I'm not going to take any more phone calls from James or any member of his family. So when they call, I need you to tell them I will not speak to them."

At three o'clock, I left my parents' home to go to my appointment with Dr. Johnson, the psychologist. This was the third item on the list he had assigned me. I was now operating without emotions, like a machine. A machine with a mission.

Chapter 33:

The Appointment

"Come and see me." Those words played over and over in my head, comforting me as the broken line on the freeway whisked before my eyes. Once I arrived at the office in Montclair, I parked, took a deep breath, and walked into Dr. Johnson's office. I didn't know what to expect, but one thing I did know was he had said exactly what I needed to hear at a critical moment in my life. Keeping this appointment was the third item on the list of tasks he had given me that morning. I checked in with the receptionist and sat for just a couple of minutes before she called my name. As I entered his office, I immediately took notice of its size. It was very large and had several bookshelves filled with books. Dr. Johnson was seated at his desk with his back to the door. As I walked through the door he stood up and turned around. He was a smaller man in stature, but his bearded face revealed large kind eyes and a welcoming smile. He reached out, shook my hand, and introduced himself.

"Hello, Laurie, I am Dr. Johnson. Please take a seat," he said, pointing to a chair next to his. As I sat, he asked, "How are you doing now?"

"Much better than this morning. I did everything you told me to do before I came to see you."

He responded with a quiet short laugh and said, "You did?"

"Yes, I filed for divorce, have cut off all communication with my husband and his family, and now I'm here to see you."

"Well, you are the first person who has done everything I asked them to do!"

"I am?"

"Yes, indeed."

His warm smile made me feel at ease, and I began talking about my life before and after James. Dr. Johnson did a lot of listening and note-taking. After about a half hour of me talking, he began to ask me a few questions.

"How old were you when you met James?"

"I was seventeen."

"How did your family react?"

"They were okay with him at first, but as time went on, they questioned how quickly we decided to get married."

"What made you decide to marry him?"

"I thought I loved him and was afraid of losing him."

"You're not afraid of losing him now?"

"No. What he did to the little neighbor girl disgusts me."

"Tell me a little about your marital relationship before you knew he molested the neighbor child."

"It wasn't good. I tried to please him, but it didn't feel like I ever could. Sometimes he hit me. One time he almost choked me to death. Sometimes he was nice to me, but most of the time he was mean."

"So what I hear you saying is your marital relationship was not going well before his arrest."

"That's true. I tried to stay busy. I went to college, worked, visited my parents, went to see friends, especially when I knew he was going to be home."

"It sounds like you might have wanted to leave him even before this incident occurred."

"Yeah, probably. His arrest has given me the strength to proceed with getting out of a terrible relationship. His threats to take my children or kill me always seemed real. I must admit the last few months have been almost unbearable for me. I was even fantasizing how I could kill him."

"Well, in my opinion, it sounds like you have made the right decision to divorce James. Acquiring your bachelor's degree was one of the steps you were taking to push toward a future without him. I believe you, and I need you to have more sessions so we can help you work through these complicated issues you are dealing with at this time."

"Yes, I agree. I already feel better."

"Well, I'm still amazed you followed all of my instructions," he said with a giggle.

I left his office with a renewed sense of self and the confidence to withstand the next steps of the journey called divorce.

Each session gave me more and more strength and confidence. He guided me through every obstacle. The first time we were discussing James's mental illness, he pointed to the bookshelf, and said, "Grab the blue book on the third shelf. The one in the middle. Now turn to page two hundred forty-four and read the first paragraph out loud to me."

"Sociopaths do not possess a conscience . . ."

When I finished reading the paragraph, Dr. Johnson asked, "Does any of this paragraph describe any of the behaviors you witnessed in James?"

"Yes."

"Well, now you and I both know what kind of personality disorder you were dealing with. We will continue to research together because I have an idea there are other layers to his mental illness."

"Wow. I knew he was not normal at times, but I had no idea he was that mentally sick."

"Now, it's my job to not only help you heal from this trauma, but also give you some strategies you can use to protect yourself emotionally and physically."

As our sessions continued, he dove deep into my emotional responses to James's behavior and how to manage them. He boosted my confidence each time I had a session. He spoke to the source of my emotional strength—a strong family support system empowering me to withstand such a trauma. A trauma which changed everything and drove me to rethink and reprogram my emotional state of being.

In addition, Dr. Johnson assisted me in strategizing each step of my divorce, and prepared me to make a better choice in any relationships I might have in the future.

Was it a coincidence I ended up with his business card in my pocket on the day I was most in need? I truly believe there are no coincidences regarding the major events in our lives. What would have transpired had I not had Dr. Johnson's card in my pocket at that moment in time? One can call it spirit guides, or angels, or whatever explanation suits one's beliefs, but there is one thing I am sure of—there was an inner voice compelling me to make the right decisions at the right time.

Chapter 34:

The Chase

I sat and stared at the food on the plate in front of me.

"Sweetheart, you need to eat," Mom said.

"I know, Mom, but I just don't have an appetite."

The emotional chaos I had experienced the last few days had calmed down into a state of numbness. The anger, fear, and anxiety were gone, but I was left with no feelings at all. My talk with Dr. Johnson earlier in the day had calmed my emotions, but now I was emotionless. I pinched my arm to see if I could feel it. Nope, not really. I pinched harder. I could feel it, but barely. After dinner, the boys played quietly. The phone rang several times, but none of us answered it. My parents and I sat together staring at the television. Little did we realize this was the calm before the next storm.

The next morning, Tuesday, August 6, the phone rang, and my father answered it. He was only on it for a couple of minutes, and all I heard him say was, "Yes, yes, I understand. Thank you for letting us know." As he hung up, he turned around and told my mother and I: "Get the kids, put your shoes on, and everyone get in the car as quickly as you can. I will explain when we are in the car driving." He looked frightened, so neither I, nor my mom, questioned him. We rounded up John and Michael and whisked them into my parents' car and off we went.

As we pulled out of the driveway, I asked my dad, "Where are we going?"

"I've no idea."

"Who was on the phone?"

"It was Fiona. She told me we all needed to leave the house immediately."

"Why?"

"I will tell you more when John and Michael are not listening,"

His statement led me to believe it had something to do with James.

"Where are we going, Grandpa?" Michael asked.

"We're just taking a ride."

"Sweetheart, do you have a friend or acquaintance who might be willing to let you and the boys stay at their house for a few hours? A place James has never been to or wouldn't guess you would be there?" Dad asked.

"James has never been to Mary's house; she is the mother of my friend Lucy from college. He's never met her or been to her house."

"That sounds good. Please tell me how to get there," he said with a frightened voice, one I had only heard when one of us was sick or injured. I instructed him how to get to Mary's house. She lived on the east side of Fontana about six miles from where my parents lived. When we arrived, Dad asked Mom to wait in the car with the boys. As he and I walked up to Mary's door, he explained to me what Fiona had told him.

"Fiona said that early this morning James called her from the motel, and he'd come to the conclusion that you weren't coming back. He told her he gave you plenty of time to return.

He tried to call several times last night, but no one answered. He then told her he was headed to our house to kill everyone. Fiona was frightened and wanted us all to be safe, and for that I am deeply grateful to her."

I stood there on Mary's porch trying to feel afraid or shocked by what my father had just told me. The only fear inside me was for my sons and my parents. My dad clearly possessed enough fear for my life, even if I didn't.

I approached Mary's front door and knocked. Mary opened the door with her warm welcoming smile.

"Well, hello, what brings you here today?" she asked. Just seeing Mary's kind face in front of me instilled a feeling everything would be fine. I quickly introduced her to my dad and then explained our plight.

"I'm filing for divorce and my husband has threatened to kill us. We need a place for the boys and I to stay for just a few hours until my dad can figure out if the threat is real and come up with a plan to keep us safe."

Without any hesitation Mary said, "Of course you and the boys can stay here."

"My husband doesn't know where you live, nor does he even know much about you, Mary. I wouldn't put your life at risk."

"They'll be safe here, Frank," Mary said, looking at my father.

Mary Romo was probably one of the kindest women I had ever met. Her daughter Lucy and I had been friends for about five years, and for the first two years she had lived with her mother. We carpooled to college, so I picked her up from Mary's house quite often. I had grown quite fond of Mary, so even after Lucy moved out, there were a couple of times I had stopped by for a short visit.

Once my dad and mom left, Mary fixed us something to eat and found some activities for the boys to do. Then her and I sat and visited. She kept the conversation on positive things and her warm, caring way made the time pass quickly. Her home was as warm as her heart. Family pictures abounded on the walls. The furniture was soft and very comfortable. My sons had never been here before, but they appeared to feel right at home.

At around four-thirty in the afternoon, there was a knock on the door. "Laurie, take the boys and stand in the hallway out of sight. I will answer the door," Mary said.

I heard her open the door. "Oh good! It's you, Frank," she said. The boys and I came out of the hallway to greet him.

"It's all clear. I can take you home."

"That's good news. I'll take the boys in the other room so you two can talk a minute," Mary said.

Once the boys weren't in the room, Dad began to tell me what had transpired.

"Well, I spoke to Fiona a second time. She told me that after she called to warn us, she also called the police. The police found James walking down Valley Blvd., about two miles away from our house. He was barefoot and carrying a pistol. As they approached him, he dropped the gun and began telling the police he didn't want to live anymore. They took him into custody because they determined he was a danger to himself and or others. They transported him to a mental health unit and placed him on a forty-eight-hour observation hold. So you and the boys are safe for the time being while he is locked up."

I rounded up the boys, hugged Mary, and thanked her for her incredibly kind act of letting us have safe harbor in her home. We then got in the car with my dad. The boys fell asleep on the way home.

The next day, Wednesday, August 7, my parents began to reach out to their friends for support, and their closest friends invited all of us for dinner the following day. I, on the other hand, wasn't reaching out to anyone. I had become desensitized about James and his threats. I did, however, feel more secure knowing he was locked up.

On Thursday, August 8, most of the day was quiet. We all were looking forward to having dinner with the Whitmores. Ben and Bonnie Whitmore were my parents' best friends. They spent a great deal of time together doing various activities, such as camping, playing cards every week, and traveling together. Ben was a very large man, with not an ounce of fat on his body. He was six feet, three inches tall and weighed two hundred seventy-five pounds. He had made a career in the Marine Corps, serving twenty-plus years which included three tours in Vietnam during the Vietnam War. He was a gentle giant and a hero to all of us who knew him, and especially to me as he appeared to adore me and would do anything to ensure I was happy and safe. That fact became clear on that very warm August night at their home.

We were just finishing eating dinner when Ben noticed James standing in the middle of their front yard and signaled to my dad.

"Laurie, call the police and stay inside the house," Dad said as he darted through the door and into the front yard. Simultaneously, Ben slipped out the back door. My mother and Bonnie took the boys into the den so they couldn't see what was going on. I stood still like a statue in the Whitmore living room, listening.

"Frank, please let me see my wife and boys! I'm beggin' ya!! I just wanna talk to them for a minute," James pleaded.

"James, now is not a good time. I'm sure in a few days when things calm down, you'll get to see them," Dad said.

"I just want to see my wife!" he said as he tried to push my dad out of the way to get to the front door. It was at that moment when I realized where Ben had stationed himself. He was hiding in the bushes at the side of the house and when James tried to get past Dad, he stepped out right in front of him. "Stay put!" Ben yelled, looking directly down at the top of James's head. It startled James so much he abruptly stopped. I could see them both from where I was standing. James looked up at Ben and didn't move. Suddenly, there were three Fontana City police officers standing behind James on the front lawn. "Fontana PD. James Hawkins, can I speak to you for a moment?" said the officer standing directly behind him.

James turned slowly and said, "I just wanna see my kids."

The second officer stood behind the first one. He appeared to be in support of the one speaking to James, while the third one approached my dad and said," Sir, can you please step over here onto the porch and tell me who you are and what is happening here."

I was listening to everything. I was relieved the police were there. "My name is Frank Kelly. I am the father-in-law to James. He was arrested this week. On Tuesday, he threatened to kill my daughter, their sons, and my wife and me. My daughter has hired a divorce attorney. We're just waiting for a visitation agreement so he can see his sons. My daughter wants nothing to do with him."

As the third officer walked down the porch steps, the other two asked James to move off the Whitmore property and onto the sidewalk. I couldn't hear what they were saying, but after a few minutes, James walked away down the street to where he had parked his car. The three officers huddled together to talk briefly. Then the one who had talked to my dad approached him and said, "James has left for now. We have asked him to stay away, but if he returns, just give us a call. I get the feeling he won't return tonight, but you never know."

After the officers left, we all seemed to breathe a sigh of

relief and my dad suggested that we call it a night and return home. I thanked Ben and Bonnie for their love and support and gave Ben an especially tight hug. Unfortunately, James was not finished chasing me.

James stayed away the next day, but on Saturday evening he showed up on my parents' porch. Dad answered the door and acknowledged James's request to speak to me. He closed the door and turned around. I was standing right behind him with an answer before he could speak.

"No is my answer. Dr. Johnson recommends I not speak to him. I . . . can't. I'm not ready yet." I was trembling inside. My body was reacting even though my heart was numb. There was no guilt or feeling of obligation present in me like in the past when dealing with James. All of that was gone, wiped clean, erased.

"Don't worry, sweetheart. Go on in the den with your mom and the boys. I'll deal with him," Dad said.

"Thanks, Dad," I said as I wiped a lone tear from my cheek. I stepped back into the middle of the living room and stood still for a moment. I watched my dad carefully open the front door slightly and slip through the narrow opening onto the porch with James. I continued to stand there just in case Dad needed someone to call the police.

I heard him say, "James, I'm sorry to tell you she doesn't want to talk to you yet."

"Oh Frank! Why? I need to see her. It'll make me feel so much better just to see her," James pleaded. His voice sounded like that of a child who truly doesn't understand why they are in trouble.

"James, you all have been through a lot this week."

"Frank, I got divorce papers yesterday afternoon. I can't believe she already wants a divorce. Can you please talk to her and change her mind?"

"I'm sorry to tell you this. But there's one thing I know about my daughter. Whenever I have seen her make a decision about something serious, she's never changed her mind. You can talk to her until you're blue in the face, but she doesn't budge. I'm afraid this is one of those situations."

I heard James sobbing. "Please try!"

"Son, I'm so sorry. I'll talk to her, but I would be very surprised if she changes her mind about the divorce." I remained in the same spot in the living room, even though Dad had told me to go into the den. Once again, I could hear James sobbing. My dad was so kind, I imagined he was patting James on the shoulder to console him.

"James, I know life has taken a bad turn for you. Things will get better. You just can't see how right now. It might be better for you if you accept Laurie's decision and move on with your life. I have hope you will be happy again," I heard Dad say while James continued to sob. My body had ceased trembling, but my mind could muster no sympathy for the sobs of this broken man I used to call my husband.

"Okay, you really need to leave and see if you can get some rest, son. It will get better," Dad said. I could hear no reply from James, just more sobbing. Dad came through the door and seemed surprised I was still standing in the living room. He shut the door quickly and turned off the porch light.

"Why didn't you go into the den like I asked?" Dad whispered.

"I wanted to listen to see if I needed to call the police," I whispered back. The sobbing began to get quieter, and we heard a car door and an engine start.

"I think he's leaving," I said.

"Yes. Good," Dad said.

"Thanks, Dad, for telling him what you told him. I'm not

going to change my mind. I'm going through with the divorce," I said.

"I know you are. There is no doubt in my mind," Dad said. I was relieved James left, but I knew this wasn't going to be his last attempt to take back control.

Chapter 35:

The Fear Factor

On Sunday, August 11, there was no attempt by James or any of his family to contact me. It was an eerie silence, and I knew deep inside there was more to come.

On Monday, August 12, I met with my divorce attorney for the second time, and we discussed the details of the divorce, such as custody of our sons, and the division of property.

"Mr. Roberts, I want sole custody of our sons. I'm willing to negotiate anything else, such as who gets the house and items inside it. But I will not negotiate about custody. That criminal does not deserve any rights to our sons."

"Due to the nature of the crime, he has been charged with I'm pretty confident I can win sole custody for you. You will probably have to grant him visitation since he is their father."

"I would like to limit the visitation if we can."

"I understand how you feel, and we can certainly work to limit it, especially if he is convicted."

He gave me more paperwork to fill out to prepare for our first court appearance. The appointment went longer than I anticipated.

After I left the attorney's office I hurried and drove straight back to my parents' house. Dad met me at the door. He had a worried look on his face again because I had been gone longer than he expected. He gave me all the fatherly warnings about going places by myself, and I assured him I was being careful.

The vehicle I took for my use was a 1984 Chevy Sprint. James and I purchased this car together just nine months before we separated. My reasoning for taking the newer vehicle was based on what I thought was logic. I was confident I would have an income and be able to pay the $324 monthly payment. James's financial future was up in the air, especially if he was convicted and went to prison. The vehicle I left James was a 1978 Ford Truck we owned. We held the title and there was no payment on this vehicle. But my mind wasn't operating in the selfish, vengeful mode of his mind.

I had anticipated James might try to damage the Sprint, so I parked it in the driveway near the front porch. This way I would be able to hear if someone made any noise near it. That evening at about eleven o'clock I heard a noise and opened the front door to witness the Sprint driving away. I ran to the phone to call the police. Once I was connected and explained the situation to the dispatcher, I was appalled to discover James had pre-warned authorities he was going to take possession of the car. The dispatcher explained that because his name was on the registration, he had the right to confiscate the vehicle. I hung up the phone feeling like someone had just knocked me down. This feeling didn't last long. I quickly decided I would turn this small defeat into an opportunity. I was finished being the victim and grabbed the reins and told myself I really didn't want to drive a car we owned together. I was ready to go out and purchase my own vehicle in my own name.

The next morning, I was determined to go car-shopping.

Dad was at work. Mom agreed to watch the boys while I ran some errands using her car.

The fresh air filled my lungs as I walked outside that morning. I was beginning to feel alive again. This was the first time in my life I was going car-shopping completely by myself. I wasn't sure I had enough credit to purchase a vehicle in my name alone, but I was going to try, and the fact I could even attempt such a task was invigorating.

I wanted to be a sensible car shopper so I decided I would look for a used car. I was pretty sure I wouldn't qualify for a brand-new car. I stopped at several dealerships until I landed at one where I saw a vaguely familiar face. He was standing on the steps of the showroom. I walked up to him and said, "Excuse me, by any chance is your name Marshall?"

"It is. Do I know you?" he asked.

"My name is Laurie, and I was friends with Cheryl Presley. You and I only met once at a party. You were dating her."

Through our conversation, I discovered he and Cheryl married and then divorced only a few years later. I also discovered Marshall was the general manager of the car dealership. I shared with him my story about my separation from James and why I was left without a vehicle.

"Well, I can certainly help you. I'm sure we can get you in a vehicle today. One in just your name."

The next thing I knew I was reading over a contract to purchase a 1979 Pontiac Firebird all on my own. I trusted Marshall, but still read over the contract carefully as I wanted to prove to the world I was a competent, independent woman.

I drove my mother's car home and waited for my father to get home from work. I told my mother what I had accomplished, and she appeared to be very proud of me. When my father arrived home, I told him about the purchase and requested a ride to pick the car up. He appeared to be a little nervous for fear I had been swindled. I showed him the contract and told him all about Marshall. As I spoke, I could feel my face smiling a genuine smile.

When he finished reading the contract, he looked at me and said, "I'm proud of you."

"I'm proud of me too," I said. Mom, Dad, and I joined together in a group giggle.

Driving around in a car I purchased on my own gave me hope for my life in the future. This purchase had given me a slight boost of confidence. My emotional state was improving, and the numb feeling was disappearing. Strength was replacing years of being afraid. Fear was no longer an integral factor in my life.

Chapter 36:

The Spell Was Yet to Be Broken

"Hi Laurie. How are you doing?" Carrie asked.

"I'm hanging in there. How are you? I miss you," I said.

"Well, we saw James last night."

"Oh, okay."

"He needed our help."

"Oh. Help with what?"

"He asked us to help him search the room where he stored his photography equipment. He told us he wanted to find pictures showing he was innocent. Do you think he is innocent?"

"I don't think so."

"He said you would say that. I'm pretty angry at you."

"You are? Why?"

"Well . . . James, without Mitch's knowledge, handed me a letter telling me things you'd told him about me and my affair. In the letter he threatened to tell Mitch if I remained friends with you."

"Wow. I'm so sorry."

"Well, that's not all. He also told me about you and Mitch . . . you're a bitch. I don't want to ever talk to you again."

Then all I heard was a dial tone.

I was hurt but moving on without Mitch and Carrie in my life meant I was shedding a layer of my relationship with James.

"Mom. Look at those plums! They look delicious. Should I grab a few?" I asked. Dad was watching the boys and a visit to the grocery store with my mom was a pleasant break. I needed it after my conversation with Carrie the day before. The smell of the fresh produce surrounded my nostrils. I closed my eyes for a second to imagine I was in a grove of plum trees.

"Sweetheart, I forgot to get a bag of sugar when we were in that aisle. Can you please go pick up one for me?" Mom asked.

"Sure!" I said as I walked away from her and down the aisle where the sugar was located. I bent down to grab the sugar bag on the bottom shelf, when I heard someone walk up behind me.

"Laurie," the person said. I rose up and turned around. Suddenly, my eyes were filled with a wet substance. I wiped my eyes with my hands and realized standing in front of me was our neighbor, Mrs. Ono.

"How could you do such a horrible thing to such a nice man!" she shouted.

Mrs. Ono was a very short, usually very nice, Filipino woman, who had just spit in my face. Even though she was about five inches shorter than me, her spit reached right up to my eyes. Her youngest son, Will, who was twenty-two years old at the time, was with her and he looked shocked. Without another word, she shuffled on down the sugar aisle.

"I'm so sorry," Will said.

"What on earth did James tell her I did?" I asked.

"I'm not sure. She shouldn't have spit on you."

"I'm fine, Will. It's not your fault."

"I saw the police cars at your house. They don't come and arrest you for no reason. I can see why you might have left him."

"Thanks, Will," I said as I traveled down the aisle back toward my mom.

Evidently, a part of me was still numb, as I didn't cry or get angry at what had just happened. When I brought the sugar to my mom, I asked her for a tissue, giving her the excuse that something was in my eye. I didn't think it was necessary to upset her, so I kept the incident to myself. I vowed to myself I was going to stay strong against the lies James was obviously spreading. I tried to look forward to a future without this monster.

Chapter 37:

The Aftermath

It was as if my legs were glued to the seat of my mom's car. She got out of the car. I rolled the window down and called out to her.

"Mom, here's the house key. I need to sit here for a moment."

"Okay, dear. We'll go in and get started. Take all of the time you need."

There I sat, frozen, staring at the house on Shadow Street. It looked larger than ever before and overwhelmed me. I looked down at my hands. There was the wedding ring, still on my finger. I grabbed it, pulled it off and put it inside my purse in a zipper pocket. I raised my head up and surveyed the neighborhood. No one was in my view. I didn't want to see any of them. This house, this neighborhood represented years of pain and torture for me. We planned this activity on a day when James was scheduled to be in court for his arraignment to ensure he wouldn't show up unexpectedly.

Finally, I found the courage to step out of the car and head for the front door.

I could hear Bonnie's voice calling out, "Put everything in

the boys' room in boxes!"

As I stepped closer to the house, I noticed my feet were dragging as if something was weighing them down. As I stepped through the threshold, my skin became warm and tingly. The warm feeling turned to a burning sensation quickly and my feet stopped my body from moving any further. My mom looked at me and asked, "Are you okay?"

"My skin feels funny."

She walked over to me, looked at my arms, pulled up my shirt a little and said, "Oh my goodness! You're covered with hives, my dear." My mother and Bonnie sat me down in a chair and gave me a drink of water.

The burning feeling turned into itching, and I started scratching my arms, my face, my legs, and my stomach. My mother grabbed some calamine lotion from the medicine cabinet and rubbed it on the areas where I was itching. As soon as I stopped scratching, Bonnie began to ask me questions.

"What furniture do you want to take? I can call Ben and have him bring our truck to pick up what you want. Have you arranged for a storage unit? If so, I can have Ben take what furniture you want directly there."

"I did arrange for a storage unit already. I want to take the boys' bunk beds for sure. Also . . . the couch and refrigerator? What do you think?"

"Yes, those items are essential. Remember, take what you need to set up a new home for you and the boys."

I sat, while everyone worked. I was unable to move for a few more minutes. Then, my brother came up to me and asked, "What do you want out of your bedroom, Sis?"

My feet became free from their bondage, and I stood straight up and said to him, "I know what I don't want. That bed!"

"No problem. We won't take the bed. It'll be all right,"

Tommy said in his usual loving manner.

I took a deep breath and followed him into the bedroom, helping him pack my clothes. With Bonnie's guidance all the kitchen appliances were packed, except for the stove. We also packed half of the dinnerware and half of the silverware. Bonnie and I agreed we should leave items for James.

Bonnie Whitmore was a very strong woman as she had raised her two children virtually alone, while Ben was overseas fighting in the Vietnam War. She advised me regarding the care and welfare of my children. Approximately a week after the encounter with James at her home, she advised me to go to the home I had shared with James and retrieve everything I needed to start a new life with my children. So she gathered a crew to accomplish this task.

Members of the crew included my mother, brother, some of his friends, Bonnie, Bonnie's daughter Valerie, Belinda, and Lucy.

By late morning, the crew had packed up everything the boys and I needed to start our lives over. I was the last one to leave the premises. I shut the door behind me and thanked God for allowing this exit to go without any interference from James or the neighbors.

Recovering from any trauma is difficult, especially when it is imposed upon you by a person who has vowed to love and protect you.

Fiona called later that day and spoke to Dad. She told him James showed up at the house after his arraignment. When he realized I had been there and retrieved items from the house, he went into a rage, smashing the bathroom sink with a hammer, breaking all the mirrors, turning over all the furniture left behind. He called Fiona on the phone crying. She feared he might commit suicide, so she hurried to the house. When she arrived, she discovered the damage and found him in the middle of the living room floor screaming and sobbing.

The next day at my appointment with Dr. Johnson, I described to him my emotional and physical reaction upon returning to the house on Shadow Street.

"Well, young lady. You're quite the interesting case. I believe you had a case of hysterical hives induced from the stress of returning to the scene of the crime."

"Really? I just thought I encountered something I was allergic to."

"I've read about this type of hives but have not personally known anyone who had them. From your description of how you felt just before the onset of the hives, as well as the timing of when you broke out, I'm pretty sure my diagnosis is correct."

"Wow. I guess this makes me your star patient."

We both chuckled. It was so good to laugh instead of cry.

Chapter 38:

Picking Up the Pieces Along the Way

"I hate you!" Michael screamed.

I ran to the den to see what was going on. As I reached the doorway, I saw my small-framed mother sitting on top of Michael's behind.

"Mom, what happened?"

"Honey, I'm sorry, but this was the only way I could get him to stop throwing things at me. I didn't want to spank him," she said, while my five-year-old son's legs and feet were thrashing below her.

"Mom, you can get up now. I will take it from here."

She nodded and pulled herself upward and off Michael. As soon as he was freed, he ran to me.

"Why were you throwing things at Grandma?" I asked.

"I was mad."

"Mad at Grandma? What did she do to make you mad?"

"I wasn't mad at Grandma. I was just mad."

"Mad at what?"

"I dunno. Just mad," he said with his sweet little voice.

I hugged him and said, "You need to tell your grandma you

are sorry. Then I need you to sit in this chair for five minutes and think about what you did."

At this point I was beginning to shinny up the slippery pole toward emotional improvement, but what I failed to recognize was that my children were there right alongside me. They overheard conversations, especially Michael, and I know it was causing confusion. They knew their father had been arrested, but I was so wrapped up in my own emotions, I took no notice of their inner struggles. Their behavior, at times, was erratic and was a reaction to what was going on around them.

September had arrived. I was getting ready to head back to work and college classes, and the boys were going to go back to school. My mother approached me later in the afternoon after Michael's throwing episode.

"Sweetheart, I think you need to spend some one-on-one time with Michael. You need to do it now, especially before school starts back up."

"Okay, Mom. I will definitely plan to do something with just him and I. You look worried. Is it about what he did this afternoon?"

"I believe it is related to his angry behavior. Earlier, he asked me questions about his dad. He wanted to know why he was arrested. I told him people get arrested when they do something bad and break the law. He threw a small, short tantrum, saying he wanted to know what his dad did. I told him it was something he needed to talk to you about. Then about an hour later is when he started throwing things at me."

"I didn't realize he was thinking about that. If you don't mind watching John, I will take Michael to the park so we can talk alone."

I trusted my mother's opinion and heard the urgency in her voice and agreed this had to be discussed with Michael today. My mind pondered nervously to figure out how to tell a five-year-old his father had molested one of his friends in the neighborhood.

"Michael, Mommy needs you to come with her for a little trip in the car to the park. Just you and I."

I took my sweet Michael by the hand, and we walked together to the car. Both of us sat quietly on the short drive to the park. When we arrived, he asked to play on the playground equipment, and I agreed he could for ten minutes and then we needed to talk. The warm breeze touched my face and transported me back to when I was a child. How lucky I was to have lived a carefree childhood with no divorce, no severe emotional trauma thrust upon me. My children did not have it so lucky. Yet, while watching him play on the jungle gym, he looked like he didn't have a care in the world.

"Michael, time to come talk to me," I called out.

"Okay, Mommy. Here I come!" he yelled as he ran up to me, jumped in my lap and gave me a hug and told me he loved me.

Those beautiful blue eyes looked up at me, making me more nervous about bringing this subject up. "I heard from your grandma you have some questions about your dad?"

"Yeah. I wanna know what bad thing he did. Why did the policemen take him away?" I paused for a moment. He stared intently at me waiting for an answer. I wanted to make sure I could explain James's crime in a way that a five-year-old could understand.

"Well, do you remember Sally?"

"Yes. She came over to our house and played. She's my friend."

"Well, your dad touched her in her bathing suit area . . . and adults are not supposed to do that to children. It's against the law, and it's why he was arrested."

Michael immediately sighed with relief and said, "Mommy, I thought he chopped someone up and killed them!" He hugged me tight. Shame was written all over my face. I had no idea these thoughts had been torturing his little mind.

As my divorce court dates came closer, an organization called Society's League Against Molesters, or SLAM, contacted my attorney, and asked him to have me call them.

"Do you know anything about this organization?" I asked Mr. Roberts.

"Yes, I do. Two friends of mine are members. It was founded in 1982 by a grandmother, Patti Linebaugh, whose two-and-a-half-year-old granddaughter was brutally raped and murdered. In just the three years it has existed, SLAM has already forced the addition of mandatory sentencing to California's molester law and eliminated automatic hospital treatment for many convicted offenders. One of their missions is to support victims of child molesters. The members of SLAM, as well as myself, feel you and your children fall in this category. They want to support you any way they can."

An organization willing to support me? I was anxious to make the call to discover what their support would entail. I called the number and a woman answered, "Hello, this is Jane Cantor speaking. How can I help you?"

I explained who I was, and she responded with knowledge about my case. She explained she was the president of the local chapter of SLAM and that they would be sending some of their members to sit in the courtroom during the divorce proceedings to show their support for me. I was extremely grateful for this support, but SLAM had more work to do with this case.

"We will also be attending Mr. Hawkins's trial and sentencing to ensure justice is served. The judges in these cases know who we are and hopefully our presence is applying enough friendly pressure to ensure these types of offenses are dealt with in a serious enough manner to ensure some sort of justice for the victims."

"Thanks again. I'm so thankful your organization exists. I can really use the support," I said.

"Also, I wanted to talk to you about Mr. Hawkins's visitation with your sons. He hasn't had any visitation with them yet, correct?"

"No, not yet."

"Well, we can make arrangements for supervised visitation before your first court date. This would show the court you are being cooperative."

"Oh . . . I guess. If you think it would be good for my case."

"Great. I will contact your attorney, with your permission, and ask him to compose a temporary order for supervised visitation with SLAM as the group named to arrange such visitation. Jay will then contact you to get your signature."

"I absolutely give you permission to contact Jay. Maybe James will stop bothering me if he gets some visitation with his sons."

"He might. The judge will definitely look at it as a good move on your part."

The temporary order was granted, and visitations were arranged for Saturdays from ten in the morning until noon at the San Bernardino YMCA. As the first Saturday approached, I began to feel numb again. I was not looking forward to seeing James in person. I told the boys the day before that they were going to have a visit with their dad, and they both seemed excited. That morning we all got up early, and I made the boys pancakes. I had no appetite. We arrived in the parking lot of the YMCA ten minutes early. The boys jumped out quickly, while I slowly wrangled my legs out of the car. My whole body had gained a sense of extreme heaviness. As I walked through the door, I could see James sitting in the lobby behind the sign-in table manned by members of SLAM. I held onto the boys' hands tightly and told them to stay with me. As soon as they saw James, they yelled out to him and waved. The volunteer smiled at me and explained the procedure. Without looking at James, I could feel his mad, glaring stare piercing my skin, while I signed the boys' names on the sheet. I looked up briefly when I finished and confirmed my suspicion. There he was, staring at me as if to convey the message I was to blame for this whole mess. His look changed quickly when the volunteer called his name, took the boys by the hand, and began to walk down the hall with him following behind. I could hear her announce he and the boys would visit together in room number one.

A second volunteer sitting at the table said to me, "Don't worry, we have volunteers sitting in every room to supervise the visit."

After I left, I decided to do a little shopping while the boys had their visit to try to alleviate some of my stress and make the time go by a little faster. My thoughts quickly went to brainstorming how I would react to James when I saw him again. I convinced myself I wasn't going to be afraid of him. "When he looks at me, I will just smile and look past him," I told myself. This was some of the advice Dr. Johnson gave me. He also told me to believe in myself and be happy I was no longer with James. He could no longer control me.

When the visitation ended, the boys ran to me. James walked out to the parking lot behind me. I quickly put the boys into the car. Before I could get in, he was right behind me and said, "I see ya got a car, Laurie."

"Yes, I did," I said with conviction.

"I also see ya still pile papers in the back seat."

"I've gotta go now. Bye," I said, and jumped in the car and drove off. I faced my fear of him head on and immediately discovered the heavy feeling trapping my body had disappeared. I visualized his emotional grip on me weakening.

My attorney met with me several more times prior to the court proceedings regarding property, as well as custody. I agreed to all of James's requests, part of which was to pay me $5,000 for my interest in the house on Shadow Street. He agreed to me obtaining full physical custody of the boys with visitation arrangements for him. He requested visits every other weekend, overnight, unsupervised. I had lost all trust in James when it came to children, even our own. Emotionally, I was holding a tight grip on our children and was having trouble compromising at all.

Our first court appearance resolved all the property issues. All that was left to decide were the details of his visitation, and on this we were unable to agree. As a result, the judge ordered us to visit a court-appointed family counselor to resolve our disagreement. I wasn't sure we could find any middle ground with a counselor, but I agreed to attend the sessions. As I sat there in the courtroom, I tried to make myself appear confident and self-assured. So far my attorney had prepared me, and everything was going according to the plan we had discussed. Then James's attorney stood up and made a request.

"Your honor, my client is requesting changes regarding the current visitations. We are requesting changes in the temporary visitation order. We're asking for my client's sister Fiona Hawkins Reed to replace the organization SLAM as the supervising agent, and her home in Fontana be the location rather than the San Bernardino YMCA. In addition, we are requesting the time change from ten o'clock to noon, to ten o'clock to six o'clock on the second and fourth Saturdays each month."

My attorney whispered to me, "I think we should agree. At least the visits are still supervised and not overnight."

"I'm not happy about it, but if you say we should agree, then I will," I whispered back.

"Attorney Roberts, can you and your client agree to this change? If not, I need solid evidence supporting your disagreement," the judge said.

"My client and I are in agreement with the changes, Your Honor," my attorney said.

I wasn't happy about the change, but my logical mind understood that James couldn't be forced to visit his sons at the YMCA forever. Besides, the boys loved their Aunt Fiona, and at this point, she was the only person in the Hawkins family I trusted.

I left the courtroom feeling slightly pushed around, but began to think of the safety of my boys instead of feeling sorry for myself. It is generally a good thing for children to have visitation with a parent. I just wasn't sure in this case because the parent in question had committed a crime against a child. I asked myself these questions: "If it weren't for James incriminating himself by submitting a roll of film to get developed, would he have ever been caught? Did he want to be caught, or did he think he couldn't be caught?" This doubt haunted me. As my mind searched for the answer, I began to wonder if my sons had been sexually abused by him.

At home in the evening, after the first court appearance, I had a conversation with my mom regarding my worries concerning my sons. She suggested I make an appointment with their pediatrician and ask him to check to see if there was any evidence of sexual abuse. I called the next morning and explained the situation to the clerk at the appointment desk. She scheduled an appointment for the next day. After the exam was over, Dr. Clark, the pediatrician, called me into his office alone to reveal his findings.

"Laurie, they both checked out well. I don't see any visible signs of sexual abuse. They are both strong, healthy boys. I only found one mark on John. He has a red ring around the top part of his penis. Have you noticed it? If you have, how long has it been there?" he asked.

"I had noticed it a few months ago, but it doesn't seem to bother him. I thought maybe it was some sort of skin irritation."

He agreed with me and then reassured me that in his professional opinion the boys had not been sexually abused. His words were a relief. I still possessed some worry regarding my sons being around James, and always worried the ring around John's penis was something James did to him, especially when it disappeared a few months later and never returned.

I was trying to rebuild my life, as well as the life of my children. I was becoming extremely overprotective and difficult to reason with when it came to my sons. It was this dominant part of me who entered the court-appointed counseling session the week after our first court appearance.

The counseling session started off on the wrong foot emotionally for me just because I had to sit in a small room facing James. I tried to look past him at a picture on the wall to maintain my composure. The counselor assigned to our case was a man, Ron Purdy. It wasn't his fault he was a man, but it made me susceptible to feelings of vulnerability, and at this point created a boiling pot of anger inside me bubbling to escape.

He started the session by lecturing both of us regarding the reason we had been sent there by the court.

"Evidently, the judge in your case has determined you two cannot agree on a visitation schedule regarding your sons. Both of you need to put your emotions aside and focus on what is best for your children. You were sent here so I can help mediate your disagreement and help you come to an agreement. This can only be accomplished if both of you are willing to compromise. James, I would like you to speak first about what you want regarding the visitation schedule. Laurie, please refrain from speaking out at all while James is speaking. James, I ask you to do the same when it is Laurie's turn to speak."

The charming personality of James emerged as he stated, "I believe since we've agreed she got full custody, I should be able to see them every other weekend for the whole time, 'specially 'fore I go to prison as well's after I get out. I should get ta have them overnight on Friday and Saturday so we can do some fun stuff together. After all, she'll get ta see them every day while I'm locked up."

"All right, James. I think you are making a reasonable request. Laurie, now it is your turn to tell us what you want regarding the visitation schedule."

"My desire is to protect my children from this man, as much as I can. I don't believe they are safe overnight with him. I know I can't require supervision forever, but overnight is out of the question. He is not to be trusted with children."

The next words Mr. Purdy spoke infuriated me. "Well, please correct me if I'm wrong, but his crime involved a female, not a male, correct?"

I replied in a loud, strong voice, "Really? You honestly believe my sons are safe with him just because they are boys? He has a mental problem. And he's a criminal."

"Please calm down. I can see you feel very strongly about the situation."

He looked over at James and said, "James, it looks like she isn't willing to negotiate about the overnight stays."

"She's crazy."

"Nevertheless, we need to recognize her strong feelings. I don't think I'm going to be able to convince her today to change her mind. Thank you both for coming. This concludes our session. I'll send my report to the judge."

As I left the counseling session that day, I felt like my emotions were breaking into pieces again. I was really angry. Mr. Ron Purdy had no idea what I had been through up to this point. If he had known, he might have treated the situation differently. Maybe it was my fault for not telling him more? It was so hard to talk freely in the small room, with James sitting right in front of me. I needed to start doing better.

School began the week after our counseling session. The boys were excited to return to school, and I was excited to start a long-term substitute teaching assignment, in a special education class at Fontana High School. On the second day of school, the school secretary buzzed me on the intercom and told me there was a flower delivery for me, and they were sending someone down to my classroom to bring it to me. A few minutes later, the messenger came in with a large bouquet of flowers. The students in the classroom all chanted, "Ooooo!"

I read the card. The note read, "Please come back to me, I need you so much. I love you with all my heart. Love, James." I tossed the note into the trash. The next day at about the same time, another bouquet arrived with the same message. Three days in a row, the same time, the same bouquet. On the morning of the fourth day, I arrived at work early and stopped in to see the school secretary and told her I was getting a divorce, and my husband sending me flowers wasn't going to change my mind. I asked her to refuse any future deliveries and she agreed.

Two weeks later my classes at the university began. The flower deliveries had stopped, but now at night, after classes, my friend Lucy and I began to see James lurking in the parking lot. We always carpooled to the university, so I was never alone. One of those nights he had his German Shepherd with him.

"Look over there, James is about two rows away from us. He has his dog with him. Isn't his dog trained to attack?" Lucy asked.

"Yes."

"Okay, we're walking to the security station," Lucy said.

We turned around and walked toward the small building at the entrance of the parking lot. When we went inside, Lucy approached the person sitting inside and explained that my crazy soon-to-be ex-husband was stalking us in the parking lot and he had an attack-trained dog with him. We were told to wait while they called for an escort. James must have watched us enter the security station, because when the security officer walked us to Lucy's car, there was no sign of him.

Our second time in court really did not help me gain any self-confidence. What it did do was help me to find my ability to begin to fight back.

The report Mr. Purdy submitted to the judge, with regards to me and my attitude, was not particularly flattering, I am sure. This judge, whose name I will never forget, was Judge Dixon. Judge Dixon appeared to be very gruff and had a very stern voice. As court got underway, he immediately stated, "I have read the mediation report and have come to a decision. But I will listen to either party if they would like to make a statement."

Like a jack-in-the-box, I popped right up and said, "Your honor, I just want you to understand my position and why I feel so strongly."

He looked me straight in the eye and stated, "Don't you think you have done enough to this man?"

"I haven't done anything to this man! He did it all to himself," I blurted out.

Judge Dixon then pounded his gavel and said, "Young lady, sit down and be quiet before I charge you with contempt of court. Does the defendant want to make a statement?"

"No, Your Honor," said the opposing attorney.

Judge Dixon went on to say, "My ruling is for the defendant regarding the visitation schedule. He is to have every other weekend starting at six o'clock Friday evening until Sunday evening at six o'clock. Petitioner is awarded sole physical custody of the minor children, John and Michael Hawkins."

I left the courtroom feeling defeated, even though I had been granted sole physical custody of my sons. I didn't want to see James as he walked out of the courthouse, so I went into the women's restroom. Inside the restroom, to my surprise, I found four women discussing Judge Dixon and his negative treatment of them in the courtroom. One was crying.

"That bastard hates women and has no respect for them," one woman exclaimed.

The woman crying said through her sobbing, "I tried to explain to him about the lies my husband was telling him and he told me he believed some of it was true and I needed to work on being a better mother."

As I left the courthouse that day, I told myself to focus on the positive. I now officially had sole physical custody of my two sons.

Realizing I was now a single parent brought on the realization that these two amazing boys were now totally my responsibility. Thank God I had very supportive parents who had room for us to live with them. My goal was to make life as normal as possible. John was attending the same school since he was enrolled in a district-wide program. I only had to contact the transportation to change addresses. Michael, on the other hand, had to change schools. Cypress Elementary was within walking distance from my parents' home, and I had time in the morning to walk or drive him to school. In the afternoon, my mother's plan was to walk to the school and escort Michael home. The day after

I was awarded sole custody, I received a phone call from my mom, while I was finishing up at work. "Honey, please come quick. Michael wasn't there where he was supposed to be. I can't find him!"

I kept my voice calm. I didn't want her to know, but I was in a total panic believing James could have picked him up. His promise to take our sons and hide them away from me swirled around in my mind. Was this his plan all along? Did he just pretend he agreed with me having sole custody?

When I arrived at the school, my mom had already spoken to the school security person. She told us she was going to search for Michael. After a few minutes, I was crying, but now it was my mom staying calm reassuring me he would be found. The school security woman drove her car around and, after what seemed like an eternity, she came back with Michael in her car. He became confused and walked out the wrong gate and in the wrong direction. I held him tightly, telling him I loved him, and so thankful my fear had not come to fruition. The myths James had fed me for years were beginning to unravel, and I was beginning to glue my broken emotional pieces back in place, and this time with a much stronger glue.

Chapter 39:

Reality Strikes Again

I stood watching through the window, waiting for their arrival. The smells in this home surrounded me like a warm blanket. This would be the first time in three years I set eyes on my sister. Amanda had moved to Oregon in 1981 with her husband, Jake. She was not a person who called on the phone or wrote letters very often. If she called, it was usually to convey important information. In late September, she called. I answered the phone.

"Hey, Sis. This is Amanda. I've left that bastard Jake. I have a new boyfriend and . . . I'm pregnant. And, well, I probably need to talk to Mom and Dad. I have even more news. Zach, my boyfriend, and I are moving to California."

"That is great news. Here's Mom." Mom was standing next to me anxious to take the phone from my hand. I walked away and informed my dad about who was on the phone. When I returned, I overheard Mom say, "Of course, dear, you can stay here until you get settled. I will ask your father, but we'll make it work. You know Laurie and the boys are staying here. She's getting a divorce too."

Mom handed Dad the phone and he sounded happy.

"Amanda, it will be so good to have all of you kids living close to us. We'll support you any way we can. You and Zach can stay in our camper."

Zach and Amanda's journey to California was not an easy one. They were driving a 1963 Chevy Truck, and it broke down several times before their arrival. My parents wired them funds to make the necessary repairs. They finally arrived after twelve days on the road.

Zach was a very tall, muscular, good-looking man. He had red hair and a matching mustache. His Irish appearance fit right into the Kelly family. At our first meeting he was very friendly and affectionate and everyone in our family seemed to like him. Unfortunately, because I was an emotional wreck, I wasn't as trusting as everyone else, and time would reveal his true character.

One evening my mother and I were standing at the dining room window. "Look, I can see something light up in the darkness inside our camper," Mom said. The camper and truck were parked in the driveway, right in front of the house. Amanda and Zachary had already retired for the night.

"It looks like Amanda or Zach are lighting up a cigarette or something," I said, knowing full well they were smoking marijuana.

"That doesn't look like cigarettes . . . oh no, please don't tell me they are smoking dope. She's pregnant . . . oh no."

She immediately yelled for Dad. He calmed her down, convincing her they were adults and at least for the time being all their children and grandchildren were living nearby.

"Yeah, I guess it's better to count our blessings," Mom said.

When Zach and Amanda were participating in our daily family activities, they were loving and kind to one another. They truly looked in love and excited about the arrival of their child. My sister bragged about Zach all the time, but both had been quiet about the reason for their move to California. One afternoon, while she and I were sitting alone, she said, "Zach is such a skilled carpenter. He has built many boats. There was a demand for him up in Oregon . . . but we weren't being treated well by law enforcement up there. We needed to have a fresh start."

"What do you mean you needed a fresh start?"

"Well, someone gave a false report to the local sheriff up there. They said Zach had broken into their home and stolen money. They arrested him. I found out who really did it, but they wouldn't believe me. Zach got sentenced to a month in jail. After he served his sentence, we decided to move down here, before someone filed another false report."

"How did you and Zach meet?"

"Well, Jake was a horrible alcoholic. When he was drunk, he yelled at me and pushed me around. Zach and Jake were friends, so he came over to our house almost every day. He saw how mean Jake was to me. One day Jake passed out cold on the couch. That's when Zach told me he didn't like the way Jake was treating me. So I started crying. I told him I didn't want to be with Jake anymore. And that's when Zach told me he loved me."

"Is that when you left Jake?"

"For sure. Zach helped me pack my things, while Jake was lying there on the couch stone-cold drunk."

"Weren't you afraid Jake would wake up?"

"Nah. When he got like that, he always slept for at least four or five hours. A bomb could go off and he wouldn't wake up."

"When did Jake realize you left him?"

"Oh, I think he figured it out the next day when I didn't come home. He called around to some of our friends. I'm sure one of them told him. I never went back to that place. I moved in with Zach and have been with him ever since. He's the love of my life, for sure."

I was truly happy for her, but still there was something, some feeling, warning me not to trust Zach. I shrugged this feeling off, just believing I might be a little jealous Amanda had found a wonderful man to be with, unlike me.

It was a Friday, and I left the classroom as soon as the students did, which was unusual. The boys were scheduled to go with James that evening for his visitation, and I wanted a little extra time with them by being there when they arrived home from school. As I approached the house, I noticed my mom was not there, but Zach and Amanda were. The door was unlocked so I went in. I heard a muffled scream coming from the kitchen. I rushed in and what I saw horrified me. Zach had my pregnant sister by the throat, with one hand pressing her against the refrigerator. He let go immediately when he realized I was there. He threw an angry look at me and walked away into another room without saying a word.

"Oh, Amanda! Are you okay?" I asked.

"Yeah, I'm fine. Ya know I've a mouth. I shouldn't have talked to Zach the way I did. He's never done that before. I really made him mad. Please promise you won't tell Mom and Dad."

"No matter what you said, Amanda, you don't deserve to be choked like that."

"He didn't hurt me, honest."

"Okay, I promise. But you know what he did to you is not right. If he does this again, I will have to tell someone or get you some help. I can't watch you be abused."

"Oh, he doesn't abuse me. He isn't anything like Jake and certainly not like James. I think Zach is just overwhelmed with all of us in one place."

"I guess that may explain his behavior."

"Of course it does. For sure."

About two weeks later, Zach and Amanda found an apartment to rent near my brother and moved out of my parents' house. I kept my promise to my sister to keep her secret. The reality was, I carried a tremendous amount of guilt about betraying my friend Carrie and didn't want to do the same to my own sister. I kept hearing Dr. Johnson's voice saying, "You can feel guilt, but don't make decisions based upon the guilt." Unfortunately, this was one occasion I didn't follow his advice. Reality came to strike me fifteen years later when Zach beat my sister to death.

Chapter 40:

Moving Forward

My position above gave me a bird's eye view of the man standing below some sort of car port awning. He was standing next to a copper-colored car. I could only see the top of his head. He had short brown hair and was wearing a tan jacket. As I viewed him from above, I was acutely aware I was enveloped by warmth and love. Who was this man? Where was I standing? These were the questions I posed to myself when I awakened from this new reoccurring dream.

Even in my deepest moments of despair, I had a sense there was more in the future for me and my sons. These positive thoughts kept me moving forward. I had finished my bachelor's degree and was working as a substitute teacher, so I was confident I possessed the ability to support my children and myself. As a plan for future security, I had begun attending post-graduate classes required to begin student teaching.

When you fall off the horse, get right back on and ride again. This was the philosophy I grasped hold of in connection with dating. So when Lucy, who was single at the time, suggested we go get a drink after class, I thought it was a good idea. Even my mother thought I needed to break loose and have some time for enjoyment, and she trusted Lucy to make sure I remained safe. We started going to a local steakhouse, Rayburn's, that had a bar attached. Lucy deemed it was a safe place because her cousin was part of the security team there. Starting in early October, we began to visit *Rayburn's Steakhouse*, sometimes twice a week after classes.

I was extremely nervous, and both Lucy and I were worried about James following us, so we took extra steps to ensure he didn't. We would drive away in our separate cars and travel to her apartment. We would stay there for a few minutes waiting and watching to make sure James didn't follow us. Next, we would leave in Lucy's car and head for Rayburn's, taking side streets.

Once we arrived, I danced with as many men as I could in the short amount of time we were there. I wasn't interested in bonding with any of them. I just wanted to have fun. I did meet one man for coffee the next day, but there was no spark, and we didn't meet again.

Valerie invited me in mid-October to go with her to a nightclub on a Saturday night and then have a sleepover at her parents' home. James had visitation with the boys on that weekend, and my mother once again was enthusiastic about me having some fun. James had, as far as we knew, stopped stalking me. As a result, I was comfortable driving by myself to meet Valerie at the nightclub. She suggested we drive separately, just in case she found a fellow she wanted to go home with that evening.

I arrived at the nightclub parking lot shortly after Valerie. She had on high heels and lots of makeup. She had pulled her long blond hair up into a ponytail and it swayed back and forth in rhythm with her behind in the black short miniskirt she was wearing. I, on the other hand, was dressed like a schoolmarm.

I was wearing a skirt whose length hung just below my knees, with no makeup, and flat dress shoes. I am sure the contrast was striking, but we didn't care. As we walked into the nightclub, the lights were flashing, the music blaring Madonna's hit song "Like a Virgin." Valerie ordered us a drink and then told me she was going to circulate the room and would check back with me in a little while. I stood sipping on my drink when a good-looking man approached me. He was dressed as conservatively as I was. He asked to buy me a drink and then we introduced ourselves. He told me his name was Gary Peterson. We tried to have a conversation, but the music was so loud my voice was getting hoarse trying to speak above the noise for him to hear me.

"I have a room at the motel just down the road from here. Would you like to go there so we can talk?" he asked.

I surprised myself by saying, "That sounds good to me, but I need to let my friend know I am leaving." I quickly found Valerie. She wasn't as protective as Lucy.

"You found a guy already? Good for you. He looks nice. Have fun. I'll see you back at my mom's house."

Upon arriving at the motel, he walked over to my side of the car and opened my door. He extended his hand. I accepted it as he pulled me toward him and gave me a very passionate kiss. It was at that very moment I knew he wanted more than conversation. I don't know exactly why, but I walked with him to his room anyway. His eyes were kind, I told myself, and his embrace was caring. We sat on the bed, and he leaned gently against my body as he kissed me. Suddenly, I burst into tears.

He pulled back and said, "Are you okay? Did I do something to hurt you?"

"It isn't you . . . it's me. I haven't been . . . with anyone since I separated from my husband. I don't mean to cry. But I can't stop myself. I don't think I can . . . you know . . . be with you . . . I'm not ready."

"I can see you aren't ready. I'm okay just sitting here and talking to you."

"Gary, I was in a very abusive relationship. He was abusive in many ways, but especially when it came to sex. He forced me . . . to do . . . things with other men . . . against my will," I said through my tears.

"Well, I'm not that kind of guy. I'm not like that. I had a girlfriend once who had been raped, so I understand. When we first met, we would just cuddle and talk. I never forced her to have sex with me. And I'll not force you. I'm okay with just talking and cuddling."

From that point on Gary began to listen to my story about my life with James and my ensuing divorce. We continued to chat until about two in the morning, when I told him I needed to leave. He gave me his phone number and told me if I needed to talk more, I could call him. I learned through our conversations he was a mural painter and was here in the area painting murals for a chain of hardware stores. I also learned Gary was a kind man who cared about women, a trait James never possessed.

When I arrived at the Whitmore residence, Valerie was already there. Bonnie Whitmore was standing in the doorway with her arms crossed, with an angry look on her face. As I approached her, she said, "Where in the hell were you? It's almost three in the morning. Valerie has been here for over half an hour."

"I'm so sorry, Bonnie. I didn't mean to worry you. I lost track of time. I was with a really nice guy named Gary. We just talked and cuddled in his motel room. He was really super nice."

"Do you know how lucky you are? Not all men would have just talked in their motel room. How could you be so careless? Especially after what you have been through?"

"I know. I took a chance. I guess I was lucky. I'm sorry."

"Well, I'm not going to tell your mother. She worries a lot about you."

"I know."

"Thank God you're okay." Valerie looked at me and winked. I went to sleep that night with a restored faith in men. I was hopeful the man in my dreams was out there waiting for me.

Chapter 41:

Dreams Do Come True

The half-naked man dressed in the Baby New Year costume was visible out of the corner of my eye. I did not want to dance with him, so I looked around to plan an escape route. I turned my head and there, right in front of me, was the solution. His smile lit up the room and his eyes were focused right on me. His short dark-brown hair accentuated his beautiful blue eyes. I walked toward this handsome, kind-eyed man wearing a polo shirt and light-brown slacks, and said, "Would you like to dance?"

"Yes, of course. I was just going to ask you, but you beat me to it!" he said with a smile. Despite all the chaos surrounding me in my life, I continued to forge ahead with going to Rayburn's with Lucy. This night was October 31, Halloween, and my broken heart had just stumbled upon the glue to mend it.

We quickly began dancing and introduced ourselves. His name was Liam.

"Well, I'm in the Air Force, stationed at Norton, and my friend and I just finished a two-week-long exercise training, and this was our first opportunity to leave base, so we came here," he said.

When he put his arms around me as we danced our first slow dance, it was as if someone opened an umbrella of protection over us. Somehow, I knew he was the one I had been waiting for. We spent the evening talking about our likes, dislikes, teenage antics, and for the first time in a long time, I really laughed. It appeared we thoroughly enjoyed one another's company.

Lucy Romo was a very devoted friend, who I considered to be part of my family. She had promised my mother she would watch out for me and was determined to do just that. Her long, flowing, silken jet-black hair surrounded her beautiful compassionate face as she gave me the look, transmitting the message to be careful about what information I gave to this stranger. I knew she was being protective, but I couldn't sever this connection. After my one encounter with Gary, he never called. I called him once and a woman answered who, when I asked, identified herself as his wife. This time felt different.

The next morning, Liam called me and asked if I wanted to meet him at Rayburn's that evening. Without hesitation I said "Yes." I told my sister about this date, and she was excited to help me get ready.

"Sis, if you want, I can style your hair, and I have a blouse you can borrow. It's for sure really fancy, but comfortable. And . . . I will put makeup on you."

"Okay. Thanks. I'll take all the help I can get," I replied as we both giggled.

We had arranged to meet at seven-thirty that evening, but due to my nervousness and eagerness, I arrived a half hour early. I sat at the bar where I was able to view the door and see him when he arrived. I hadn't shared with Liam about my impending divorce, and I didn't know any details about his prior love life. I did know he was from Buffalo, New York, had two sisters, and two brothers. Also, he was currently serving a four-year tour in the Air Force.

When he arrived, he rushed through the door looking all around until he spotted me. When our eyes met, he smiled and walked right up and kissed me. His gentle kiss was overwhelmingly wonderful, and I believe it was at that moment he completely melted my heart.

"You look so beautiful!"

"Thank you, Liam. My sister helped me look this way."

"Well, you were beautiful to begin with, but she did a nice job. Hey, I told you a lot about me last night. Now I would like to hear more about you."

We danced a few dances, but most of the time we sat and talked. I told him about John and Michael. I finally got up the courage to tell him about James.

"I'm . . . in the middle of a very nasty divorce. My soon-to-be ex-husband was very abusive to me," I said.

"Oh, what'd he do to you?" Liam asked.

"He hit me and . . . sexually abused me by forcing me . . . to have sex with other men," I said, nervously waiting to hear his response.

"What a bastard. Did he hurt your boys too?"

"He hit John once and left welts. I stepped in front of both boys any time he looked like he was going to hit them. Usually, most of the time, he'd hit me instead or punch a wall."

"He sounds like a real loser. How did you hook up with such a person?"

"We met in high school."

"Oh, you were really young. My sister had a baby when she was only fifteen, but the guy turned out to be a good one."

The longer we spoke, the more comfortable I became. He seemed to be truly interested and sympathetic to my plight with

James. I expressed to him my shame about giving into James's demands and my fears. All I saw was very caring eyes and looks of concern for me.

There were so many shocking parts of my life I revealed on that first date. Toward the end of the evening, there was only one major fact I had not disclosed. I decided to just blurt it out.

"When James was arrested, I left and didn't look back."

"Oh, what was he arrested for?"

"He molested a neighbor girl."

"Get out. Really? This guy is really bad news."

"Yes, he is. I'm just so happy to be free of him."

I studied his face carefully to see if I was scaring him away and quickly changed the subject.

"What's your last name, Liam?"

"Oh, it's O'Brian."

"My maiden name is Kelly. We were both born with Irish names."

"Is your family Catholic too?"

"No. We're Protestant."

"Well, I guess we're just a pair of rebels," he said as he winked at me.

"Yeah, I guess we are," I said through my nervous giggles.

At the conclusion of the date, we walked to his car and sat in the front seat talking, kissing, and hugging. He was a smaller man than James, but when he put his arms around me, I was enveloped in a zone of warmth and security. These were the arms of a protective, gentle soul.

As he walked me to my car, he asked if he could see me again the next day, and added his desire for us to go to a place where we could take the boys so he could meet them. I happily agreed and chose for us all to go to the San Diego Zoo.

~

Relationships are often tricky, especially with someone like me who was carrying extensive baggage. So far, Liam had accepted all of me with open arms. But I had not revealed the full extent of John's disabilities yet.

The boys took to Liam immediately and he appeared to enjoy their company. As we wandered through the zoo, John's autistic behaviors became apparent. At one point I asked Liam, "Is John's behavior bothering you at all?"

"Should it?"

His answer was so refreshing to me. I wrapped my arms around his neck and looked into his eyes and said, "No."

I found out later Liam's aunt had three disabled children and he helped her take care of them, so he had an affection for John deeper than I realized.

At the end of the day as we walked out into the parking lot, Liam and I held hands and gave each other a short kiss. Michael reacted immediately with a scream and began crying. I started to comfort him, but Liam asked if he could take over. I agreed. What I witnessed next filled my heart with joy and confirmed my intuition: Liam was the man I had been waiting for to come into my life.

Liam swooped Michael up into his arms, hugged him and said, "I like your mommy a lot, and that's why I kissed her. I know I'm not your daddy, but I would love it if you would let me see you, your mommy and John every day." Michael immediately stopped crying and gave Liam a great big hug.

Liam did indeed live up to his promise to Michael and came every day to see us. My family was amazed I already had a boyfriend a little less than three months after I separated from James.

When my mother told Tommy, he said, "What? What do you mean she has a boyfriend? Already? Wow! She went from being abused and traumatized to entering a new relationship in sixty seconds." My whole family was happy for me, but cautiously optimistic.

November came and soon it was Michael's birthday, which was on the same day as his father's, November 16. Liam and Michael had been talking about his birthday since they met. I was fortunate his birthday fell on my weekend, so a small party was planned at the local pizza parlor and some of Michael's classmates and our family attended. Michael wanted Liam to sit next to him. I watched happily as Michael whispered in Liam's ear constantly and giggled every time he did. I hadn't heard his sweet giggle since that dreaded day in August. Liam bought a remote-controlled black sports car for Michael, and when we arrived back home, he said to me as he was holding it, "Mommy, this is my favorite gift in the whole wide world."

There was no phone call from James on Michael's birthday. When his visitation weekend arrived, I expected to hear the words "happy birthday" coming from James right away when he came to pick up the boys. Yet, once again, I was anticipating a normal response and once again that isn't what happened. James got out of his car with an angry look on his face. He opened the back car door and gruffly barked at the boys to get in without one word regarding Michael's birthday. Next he said to me, "I can't believe you didn't call, or do anything for my birthday." My response was immediate and natural. "Why would I?"

December came and Liam and I grew closer. Liam was living in the dormitory on the Air Force Base, and I was still living with my parents, so our private time together was limited. I decided to look for a place to live. I found a townhome for rent, and it was only about two miles from my parents' home. It was two levels, with three bedrooms, and appeared to be large enough to house me and my two sons. I quickly put a deposit down.

My family was nervous concerning the rapid pace the relationship between Liam and me was proceeding at. None of us had met any of his family, but I had talked to his mom and dad on the phone. Regardless, I knew he was the one I wanted to spend the rest of my life with and saw no reason to slow down.

James, I believe, could also sense Liam and I were falling in love. Michael talked about people he liked, and I am sure he had mentioned Liam to James. When Michael returned to me after one of his weekend visitations, he was angry and visibly upset. I tried talking to him to get to the bottom of his anger, but it was Liam who was able to figure it out.

"Hey, buddy. Come and sit with me. Let's have a talk," Liam said to Michael.

"I'm mad. I don't want to sit near you," Michael said standing there with his arms crossed.

"You're mad at me?"

"Well, I'm supposed to be mad at you."

"Why?"

"My daddy says I am supposed to be mad at you."

"Oh. I know you're a very good boy and always do what Mommy and Daddy ask you to do. I love you and if you're supposed to be mad at me, then that's what you need to be."

"But I don't want to be mad at you. Daddy says you sent him away so you could have Mommy."

"Do you believe that, Michael?"

"No. So . . . I don't have to be mad at you, right?"

"Right."

I watched as Michael ran and jumped into Liam's lap and gave him a big hug. They had already developed a father-son relationship.

James was angry at everything and everyone. His trial was set to begin in January, and I'm sure he realized the evidence against him was strong. Now he was using his five-year-old son to try to continue to damage my life.

John was not able to communicate his feelings to us and every weekend he spent with James, he came back an emotional wreck. It would take several days of careful effort by me, Liam, and my entire family to reinstate John's emotional security, only to have it stripped again the next time he visited James.

After the boys and I moved into the townhome, Liam continued to come over every day. After only a week, I asked Liam to move in with us and he happily agreed. "Living on the Air Force Base is nothing compared to living in a home with the people you love," he told me.

Liam scrambled to get ready on the first weekday morning after he moved in. I had a few more minutes before I needed to get ready to leave, so I was still upstairs in my nightgown when he came to kiss me goodbye. Instinctively, I went to the upstairs window to watch as he walked to his car. As I looked out, my heart and mind embraced what my soul already knew. There it was, the scene from my dream. The top of his head was the only part of him visible to me as he got into his copper-colored Monte Carlo.

Christmas came and the four of us celebrated as a family. The boys visited James on Christmas Day, so Liam and I had Christmas dinner with my parents, Amanda, Zach, and Tommy. There was no worry or tension about Liam's behavior. His witty sense of humor made everyone laugh. My dad asked Liam many questions about his family, and they talked about life back east. My mom didn't like the idea we were living in sin, but really liked Liam. I made a comment about how hard it was to make the bed in the apartment. Her response was, "I don't want to know anything about your bed! I only want to talk about Liam. I really like him. I just don't know if it is right for you two to live together without being married."

"Mom, first, I can't get married yet because I'm not divorced. Second, I'll never marry someone ever again without having lived the day-to-day life with them first. I don't want to get trapped with another James-type of man."

"Okay, sweetheart. I understand. I just don't want to talk about your bed, okay?"

My head was gently nestled in his chest as we sat on the couch watching television. It was Monday, January 6, 1986. I had completed my first day of student teaching and was exhausted. As we sat cuddling, a commercial showing a bride and groom came on the television. Liam turned his head and looked at me and said, "You know, that looks like something we should do."

I rose up immediately and said, "Really? Are ya asking me to marry you?"

"Of course I am, sweetheart. I love you so much and want to spend the rest of my life with you and those wonderful sons of yours."

I was so excited, but there was one more hurdle to freedom from James; the final divorce decree was yet to come.

Chapter 42:

Riding the Continuum: The Final Decree First

Sunshine peeked out at me through the clouds above as if to wink at me as Liam and I walked up my parents' driveway to tell them we were engaged. Michael and John were skipping behind, giggling.

We knocked on their door. As my mother opened it, Michael burst through, yelling, "Grandma, Grandpa! Liam is gonna be my daddy!"

"Well, congratulations! Are you two sure about this?" my mom asked.

Liam and I looked at each other, and I said, "Absolutely!"

Liam walked over to my dad and said, "Sir, I want to ask you if I can have your daughter's hand in marriage. And yes, I'm absolutely sure this is what I want."

Dad shook Liam's hand and welcomed him to the family.

As happy as I was about planning our wedding, there was still a dark cloud hanging over us: James and my impending divorce. There was one more court date set, and it was scheduled for March 17, 1986.

In mid-February, Mr. Roberts called. "Laurie, this is Jay calling. I wanted to let you know James had been convicted of the crime Lewd and Lascivious Acts with a Minor Child – California Penal Code 288PC. He will be sentenced on February 27 and then incarcerated shortly thereafter. I feel it is important to add a copy of James's criminal conviction to the final divorce court paperwork. So . . . how do you feel about taking a field trip to the San Bernardino County Courthouse to pick it up for me? It will help me and save you some money."

"I can do that, Jay."

"Great! Just tell them you are picking it up for my office. They will probably call me to confirm."

As I approached the clerk at the desk in the San Bernardino County Courthouse, I said,

"I'm here to pick up a copy of the criminal record for James Hawkins."

The clerk was professional but stern. She questioned why I was sent to pick up the records. She told me they usually only release this type of record to attorneys and that she would have to call Jay Roberts to verify he sent me. I sat nervously in one of the three small, yellow, plastic chairs pushed up against the wall in between the entrance and exit of this office, while she left to go make the phone call. I watched as people came in and out, all with serious looks on their faces. My mind was filled with worry. I kept thinking that if she denied my request, then it might delay the divorce, and Liam and I would have to wait to get married. After a few minutes she returned.

"I talked to your attorney and my supervisor, and I'll release the records to you. However, you're not to open the sealed envelope. Take it straight to Jay Roberts's office." As she handed me the envelope, she finally smiled at me and said, "Good luck,

Ms. Hawkins."

My last meeting with Jay Roberts was very short. "All I need to do now is file all of the documents necessary for court. All you need to do is to show up on the assigned date, March 17. This will be your final court date, Laurie. This will be it. The judge will assign a final decree date. And . . . James was sentenced to one year in the California Correctional Institution in Tehachapi. I thought you should know. Also, you're not obligated to provide him with any visitation while he is prison." I thanked him and got up to leave.

"Before you leave . . . I have one more thing to tell you about. You might not be happy with me after I tell you."

This tall, professionally dressed man dropped his head and said, "Well, I was evidently slow on procuring your rights to James's retirement funds from General Dynamics. As a result, he has already withdrawn all the funds. I didn't get to it in time. I'm so sorry. I was more focused on the other aspects of the case. He was savvier than I gave him credit for."

"Nothing surprises me anymore when it comes to James. I wasn't depending on the money."

I left his office happy to know the end of this marriage was in full view straight ahead, and I would have a year of respite from him while he served what I believed to be a very short sentence for his hideous crime against Sally.

James reunited with Linda sometime in January during his trial. At pickups and drop-offs, he appeared to be anxious to share with me stories about their life together. I, on the other hand, was anxious to not stop and have any conversations with him.

"Hey, I bought a minivan for Linda. She'll need it while I do my time. I like ta take care of my women," James said at one of the drop-offs after his conviction. I just smiled and hugged the boys and went into my parents' house (our new designated drop-off and pickup place) as quickly as I could. Also, Michael often burst out with stories regarding all the cool stuff his "Old Dad," as he called James, was buying.

I was getting new unwelcome information every week leading up to the final decree. I became aware he had opened new credit card accounts in both of our names because I began to get the bills. One of the bills I received listed many items of women's lingerie. I called the credit card companies and complained and asked them to take my name off them. They informed me they were more than willing to honor my request once I sent them a copy of the final divorce decree, which I didn't have yet.

Despite all this chaos, Liam and I continued to make plans for our wedding. I was excited about marrying him but was not at all interested in planning a big wedding. Liam had never been to Las Vegas and was hoping to go there on a honeymoon trip, so I suggested we get married there. He agreed and the planning began. I was split into two halves: one was filled with joy and hope for the future, and the other was filled with pain from the past and fear of what might spill into my life and spoil my plans for the future.

With the final court date being set for March 17, Liam and I set our wedding date for April 5. We were hopeful the judge would grant the final date of dissolution sometime between March 17 and April 5.

March 17, 1986, finally arrived. Since my lawyer wasn't attending this court session, my mother volunteered to go with me. As we arrived at the San Bernardino Court House parking lot, I noticed three large prison transport buses sitting at one end of it with their engines running. I asked myself, "Is this what James will encounter when he comes to start his prison term? Will he even feel any remorse on the long drive to Tehachapi?

Will his year of prison create any amount of suffering comparable to Sally's?" I had no answers to these questions. My thoughts were interrupted by my mom's voice. "Laurie, there is an empty parking spot. Let's try to get to the courtroom quickly," she said nervously. Mom knew Mr. Roberts had informed me that James was invited to attend court on this day, so she was a little nervous about running into him in the courtroom. I just wanted it over with.

When my mother and I entered the courtroom, we both noticed the absence of people there. We looked on the morning docket and saw only four cases were being heard. The bailiff was an older man and he smiled at us as we looked for a seat. We weren't seated very long when the judge entered the courtroom. Unlike the other judges who had presided over my divorce case, this one came in smiling and looked happy. My case was the last one on the short morning docket. All three of the cases before me went rather quickly. One was postponed, and the other two cases were quickly presented and resolved. Next it was time for my case, and James was not there.

I was so nervous I couldn't keep my legs still. My blue skirt rippled like the waves in the ocean. My mother kept putting her hand on my knee and patting it to help me stay calm. The bailiff announced my case. The judge took notice that I was the only one present, asking, "Are you the petitioner in the Hawkins vs. Hawkins case?"

"Yes, Your Honor."

He then read over the agreement silently and stated, "All of the paperwork submitted looks in order. Therefore, I see no reason not to approve the dissolution of this marriage." He then pounded his gavel. I must have had a puzzled look on my face, because the judge looked directly at me and asked,

"Do you have any questions?"

"Ah, yes. What day will my divorce be final?"

"My dear, it is final on this day, March 17."

What happened next surprised me. The bailiff approached me and announced the judge had requested my presence at the bench. I immediately got up to comply with his request. The judge looked at me and smiled and said, "Congratulations, young lady. May I shake your hand?"

I nodded my head and he then got up from his seat and walked down and shook my hand. No one else was left in the courtroom but, me, my mother, the judge, and the bailiff. As he was shaking my hand, he softly said, "Mr. Hawkins will not be bothering you for a while. He is boarding the bus as we speak to travel to the prison to serve his sentence."

For a brief moment, I forgot where I was and spontaneously hugged the judge. He laughed, and said, "Normally we wouldn't allow that, but today, under the circumstances, we will."

As I turned around, the bailiff was standing right behind me. It startled me a little, until he reached out his hand to shake mine and said, "Congratulations! Good riddance."

This was the first time in all the divorce hearings I walked out happy.

Chapter 43:

Riding the Continuum: Love and Marriage

He smelled so good. His arm wrapped around my body like a loving shield. My heart was full of joy as the limo pulled up to the Little White Chapel in Las Vegas. He gently put my hand in his and helped me out. John, Michael, and my parents ran up to greet us. I had picked out a colorful pink-flowered dress, and Liam was in a well-fitted brown suit. It was April 5, 1986, and we were minutes away from becoming husband and wife.

Everything was falling into place. I had completed my student teaching and signed a contract with the Fontana Unified School District to teach first grade. The university had waived my second quarter of student teaching, and I was now going to bring home a teacher's salary. Marriage to a wonderful man and permanent employment translated to stability for the boys and me.

Liam and I walked hand in hand to the entrance of the chapel and were informed there was an hour's delay. "I can wait an hour more to marry you, Liam. I have waited my whole life for you. What is one more hour?" I said as Liam gently squeezed my hand.

As we waited, my dad spoke to Liam about all the responsibilities he was taking on. He was younger than me and had never been married, so my dad was nervous.

"Liam, you understand you're taking on a ready-made family, right?" my dad said.

"Yes, sir. I am well aware of it."

"You do understand this family has even greater responsibilities. John is a child with lots of problems, and my daughter is carrying a mountain of emotional distress from her previous marriage."

"Dad! Are ya trying to chase him away?" I interjected.

"No, my dear. I just want to make sure Liam understands what he is taking on."

"I'm going into this relationship with my eyes wide open, sir. My aunt lived with us, and she had three children diagnosed with muscular dystrophy. I helped her care for them. I also watched her husband bail on his family. I'll never do what he did."

I sat there quietly, witnessing Liam's strength under pressure from my protective dad.

"One last thing, Liam. What made you two want to get married now?"

"Well, given the circumstances of her previous marriage, I think it's important for her emotional security, as well as the boys', for us to get married now."

"Well, you're probably right, son."

"And besides, I'm madly in love with your daughter, and she knew you two didn't approve of our living together without being married."

The wait to get married finally ended. Amanda and Tommy were our witnesses, and Valerie, with her new husband, made the trip to join our celebration. The ceremony was officiated by a minister, and I will never forget the gleam in Liam's eyes the moment he said, "I do." As I repeated my vows, I looked over at my mother's face and saw tears flowing down. On this occasion it was a good sight, as I knew in my heart they were happy tears.

After the ceremony, we all enjoyed a family meal together, and then Liam and I went off on our own to enjoy our honeymoon.

As soon as the hotel room door closed, Liam embraced me in a passionate kiss. He whispered in my ear, "You're so pretty, my love. I'm the luckiest man in the world to be able to call you my wife." He gently picked me up and laid me on the bed while continuing to kiss me. He whisked my dress over my head and removed his shirt and resumed his loving kiss. His warm, tender hands aroused every part of my body. He began kissing my chest and as he did, he removed my bra and focused his kisses on my breasts. His movement was gradual, deliberate, but soothing. When he reached my panties, he looked up at me and smiled.

"I love you," he said as he slowly removed them. My body shivered with excitement. I watched him as he removed the rest of his clothing. He then began gently massaging my vaginal area as he proceeded to place his penis inside. He worked diligently to make sure I was enjoying this experience. This was our first sexual experience as husband and wife, but all our encounters before this night were always as gentle and caring. "He really cares about me," I thought to myself. I recalled the first time he and I had had sex. I had broken down and cried, telling him, "So this is what real love making feels like."

After we both climaxed, we lay on the bed and cuddled for about an hour. We talked, laughed, and kissed the entire time. This was a real marriage with a real man, mate, and partner.

We spent the rest of the evening and the next three days thoroughly enjoying one another's company. This was true marital bliss with a husband who truly loved me for me.

At the end of our Las Vegas honeymoon, we returned home, where I was to begin my career as a teacher and the wife of Liam O'Brian. My name was now Laurie O'Brian. Shedding the Hawkins name was cathartic for me—part of purging my past life.

James, too, was beginning his new life—as a convicted felon serving his first of several sentences in a California prison.

Chapter 44:

My Mind's Inquiry

"No! Stop!" I yelled. I was running as fast as I could but wasn't getting anywhere. I kept ending up back in the house on Shadow Street. Suddenly there he was. I used my fingernails to claw him. He grabbed me by the neck. I screamed. I was being shaken. "Wake up, sweetheart. Wake up. You're dreaming," Liam said. I opened my eyes to see a scratch on his arm.

"Did I do that?"

"Yeah. But I'll live. I'm just worried about you. It sounded like you were having a nightmare."

"I was. James was chasing me and no matter how fast I ran, he still caught me."

"You're with me now, and I'll never let him hurt you or the boys again."

Those words calmed me down immediately after each nightmare. After years of living in fear, I was finally safe.

Feelings of hopelessness and defeat creep into my soul when I drift back into the time I spent with James Hawkins. I am comforted by the belief I was being guided and directed toward a path laid for me. Is there such a thing as a coincidence? I believe I may have evidence to the contrary. For example, was it a coincidence I found Dr. Johnson's business card in my pocket at the exact moment I needed to find someone to help me? There was no internet in 1985, and searching for a specific type of service could have taken a few minutes, hours, or even days, due to my state of mind at the time.

Beyond coincidence, there is the warning I received from Anna Hawkins. Critics might say I imagined her presence in my dreams. My mother always told me I had a gift, one that connected me to the spiritual world. Throughout my life, beginning when I was a child, I had foretelling dreams.

Life is definitely a journey, and we as humans tend to try to forge the path the way that we want it to go. Unfortunately, we are not in charge. James continued his attempts to interrupt our lives throughout the years. Divorcing him was a milestone, breaking the severe abuse, but because we had two children together, he had an avenue through which he continued to try to disrupt our lives. As a family, we stood strong against his insanity. Once the boys became adults, they acquired the ability to see through his lies and deceptions, but up to that point, he did everything possible to inject misery as often as he could. The story of James and his unbelievable endeavors didn't suddenly end, but continued for more than thirty years beyond the ones chronicled in this book.

A Note From the Author

I would really appreciate it if you could leave a review of this book at your point of purchase. Reviews not only give me feedback, from which I can learn and grow, but also help others to know if this is a book they'd like to read.

Please keep in touch:
Follow @finuld_laurie on Twitter
Like Laurie Finucane on Facebook

Acknowledgments

I want to thank all my family and friends who have supported me through this whole process. A special thank-you to Ken, Sean, Ryan, Hilaire, Laura, Jane, Eileen, Traci and Dawn.

One great big thank-you goes to Tahlia Newland of Escarpment Publishing for her expertise and guidance.

Book Club Questions

1. What scene would you point out as the pivotal moment in the narrative? How did it make you feel?

2. What scene resonated with you most on a personal level? Why? How did it make you feel?

3. What surprised you most about the book? Why?

4. What was your favorite chapter and why?

5. Have any of your personal views changed because of this book? If so, how?

6. How honest do you think the author was?

7. What aspects of the story could you most relate to?

8. Why do you think the author chose to write their memoir?

CPSIA information can be obtained
at www.ICGtesting.com
Printed in the USA
LVHW040320030822
725066LV00001B/40